GROWTH ALTERNATIVE OF THE JAPANESE ECONOMY

Structure and Simulations of Dynamic Econometric Model with Input-Output System (DEMIOS)

ECONOMETRICS IN THE INFORMATION AGE: THEORY AND PRACTICE OF MEASUREMENT

ISSN: 2010-1236

Series Editors: Lawrence Klein & Kanta Marwah

This series of publication focuses on frontier econometric methods and applications with special reference to the analysis of modern economic and social problems and phenomena. Development of global financial markets, use of longitudinal data to study household consumption behavior and health-care management, evaluation of policy effectiveness, macro-econometric modeling and big-data analysis are important topics that fit well in this series. Research that blends new statistical techniques with conventional and large economic data will be given priority.

Published

Vol. 7 *Growth Alternatives of the Japanese Economy: Structure and Simulations of Dynamic Econometric Model with Input-Output System (DEMIOS)*
by Shuntaro Shishido & Osamu Nakamura

Vol. 6 *Klein's Last Quarterly Econometric Model of the United States: Wharton Quarterly Econometric Model: Mark 10*
by Lawrence R Klein
edited by Shinichi Ichimura, Soshichi Kinoshita & Mitsuo Yamada

Vol. 5 *Econometric Modeling of Japan and Asia-Pacific Economies*
edited by Soshichi Kinoshita

Vol. 4 *Macroeconometric Modeling of Japan*
edited by Shinichi Ichimura & Lawrence R Klein

Vol. 3 *Econometric Modeling of China*
edited by Lawrence R Klein & Shinichi Ichimura

Vol. 2 *Interregional Input-Output Analysis of the Chinese Economy*
edited by Shinichi Ichimura & Hui-Jiong Wang

Vol. 1 *Selected Papers of Lawrence R Klein: Theoretical Reflections and Econometric Applications*
edited by Kanta Marwah

Econometrics in the Information Age:
Theory and Practice of Measurement – Vol. 7

Series Editors: Lawrence Klein & Kanta Marwah

GROWTH ALTERNATIVE OF THE JAPANESE ECONOMY

Structure and Simulations of Dynamic Econometric Model with Input-Output System (DEMIOS)

Shuntaro Shishido
The International University of Japan, Japan

Osamu Nakamura
The International University of Japan, Japan

World Scientific

NEW JERSEY • LONDON • SINGAPORE • BEIJING • SHANGHAI • HONG KONG • TAIPEI • CHENNAI

Published by

World Scientific Publishing Co. Pte. Ltd.

5 Toh Tuck Link, Singapore 596224

USA office: 27 Warren Street, Suite 401-402, Hackensack, NJ 07601

UK office: 57 Shelton Street, Covent Garden, London WC2H 9HE

Library of Congress Cataloging-in-Publication Data
Names: Shishido, Shuntaro 1924– author. | Nakamura, Osamu, 1957– author.
Title: Growth alternatives of the Japanese economy : structure and simulations of dynamic econometric model with input-output system (demios) / by Shuntaro Shishido (The International University of Japan, Japan) and Osamu Nakamura (The International University of Japan, Japan).
Description: New Jersey : World Scientific, [2019] | Series: Econometrics in the information age: theory and practice of measurement ; Volume 7 | Includes bibliographical references and index.
Identifiers: LCCN 2018056451 | ISBN 9789813278219 (hc : alk. paper)
Subjects: LCSH: Economic development--Mathematical models. | Input-output analysis--Japan. | Japan--Economic conditions--20th century. | Japan--Economic conditions--21st century.
Classification: LCC HD75.5 .S535 2019 | DDC 339.2/30952--dc23
LC record available at https://lccn.loc.gov/2018056451

British Library Cataloguing-in-Publication Data
A catalogue record for this book is available from the British Library.

For any available supplementary material, please visit
https://www.worldscientific.com/worldscibooks/10.1142/11210#t=suppl

Desk Editors: Herbert Moses/Sylvia Koh

Typeset by Stallion Press
Email: enquiries@stallionpress.com

Foreword

This book presents the basic structure of an econometric model called DEMIOS and its forecast and analyses of Growth Alternatives of the Japanese Economy up to 2020. DEMIOS is an abbreviation of Dynamic Econometric Model with Input–Output System, which Professor Shuntaro Shishido and his group have explored over 30 years mainly for the purposes of searching the optimum economic policies to develop the Japanese economy further. From the very beginning, they designed the model as a Keynes–Leontief Model in the sense of integrating Keynesian macroeconometric model with Leontief's Input–Output (I–O) System. They fondly called it KLM.

Modeling of a rapidly growing national economy like Japan requires to deal with the changing composition of various industries, the changes in their technologies, and the changes in the behavior patterns of households, corporations and governments. Hence, it is natural that most reputable econometric models in the US or Japan have disaggregated not only macroeconomic variables but also used the Leontief I–O system for the industrial sectors. An example may be found *in Klein's Last Quarterly Econometric Model of the US Economy*, just published by World Scientific, 2018.

Professor Shishido really belonged to the oldest generation of I–O experts in Japan. He and I were among a handful group of economists, around 1955, who produced the first Japanese I–O table for Year 1951. Indeed, when he organized a research project for DEMIOS, he did so as a joint project with a group of US economists including Professor L. R. Klein and F. G. Adams. Initially the model started with 64 sectors but now has 81 sectors, due to the needs to handle industrial adjustment required by advancement of IT (information technology) in the 1990s and later. As it is called the Third Industrial Revolution, its impact on industrial activities may be very drastic, and our life style, including household behavior or working stile, may change. An increase in sectors from 64 to 81 in the early 2000s made it easier to cope with these changes but may not be enough.

Another additional feature of DEMIOS is that it includes a Demography Block. One of extremely serious problems in the world now is the population problem caused by a steady decline in fertility rate in almost all developed economies and an increase of population in certain under-developed areas on the globe. That has caused many worry-some situations in human misery, abnormal migration and complex political instability. The issues in Japan may be comparative small, but their model deals with our population problems more carefully than any other models I know of. The Japanese population has already started to decline. How could Japan maintain its growth with declining population and supply of labor force? Or shouldn't we allow significantly more immigrants from abroad?

Perhaps this demographic problem and the IT revolution are the two vital issues that Japan is facing now and during some decades to come. I know that some government offices are tackling with these issues in cooperation with some micro-econometricians. I know also that some foreign economists have already published their research findings like: F. G. Adams, Y. Kumasaka, L. R. Klein and A. Shinozaki, *Accelerating Japan's Economic Growth-Resolving Japan's Growth Controversy*, Routledge, 2011. I hope that some Japanese economists will take up these issues again soon.

During the past few years I have urged Professor Shishido several times to publish this DEMIOS and its applications in its entirety, because as I told him, the audience at international conferences or readers of professional journals or a chapter in some books are limited to those who happen to be there. But your own book is different. Someday, somewhere, some young boy or girl or scholar will find it and read it. Believe me, your book is worth reading for any econometrician, because I find some new ideas and attempts which I myself do not find elsewhere yet. He promised me to take my advice. How disappointing it was when I heard that he suddenly passed away on November 22, 2016. How happy I am now to see his younger colleague Professor Osamu Nakamura has taken it up as the co-author to complete the remaining works by writing and editing the whole manuscripts.

Thus, it is my great pleasure and honor to write a foreword to this book and introduce Professor Shishido's last life work to the world.

With the two authors I sincerely pray that the DEMIOS research work will contribute to policy analyses for economic and business activities through modeling and forecasting of the Japanese economy for many years to come.

Shinichi Ichimura
August 1, 2018

About the Authors

Osamu Nakamura is a Professor at the International University of Japan (IUJ). He received his PhD from Soka University. He was a Faculty of the Applied Economic Research Institute, Department of Economics, Soka University and is now a Faculty of the Graduate School of International Relations, International University of Japan (IUJ).

Shuntaro Shishido was a Professor Emeritus of the Tsukuba University and the International University of Japan (IUJ). He received his bachelor's degree from The University of Tokyo. He worked at the Ministry of International Trade and Industry and was a part of the Economic Planning Agency. He was a Professor and the Vice President of the Tsukuba University. He was the President of the International University of Japan and the Economic Research Institute for North-east Asia (ERINA).

Acknowledgments

The authors are indebted and grateful to many professors and colleagues, in particular, to Professor Shinichi Ichimura who supported our studies and recommended us to publish this book as an editor of the Klein's econometric series of World Scientific; and to Professor Motohiro Kurokawa, Mr. Akira Kawakami and Mr. Kiyoshi Tamashiro who have worked together with us in the DEMIOS Project during more than 30 years. Without their support and cooperation, we could not complete this book. In addition, we also appreciate Ms. Silvia Koh, our in-house editor of World Scientific for her excellent work to this book project.

Contents

Foreword v

About the Authors ix

Acknowledgments xi

List of Figures xvii

List of Tables xix

Chapter 1. Introduction **1**

1.1. Dynamics of the Japanese Economy 1
1.2. The Objectives of DEMIOS: A KLM as Policy Tools . . . 3
1.3. Organization of the Book 4

Chapter 2. General Feature of DEMIOS **7**

2.1. Basic Structure of the Model: DEMIOS 7
2.2. Sectoral Classification and Database Development 10
2.2.1. Sectoral classification 10
2.2.2. Database development 10
2.3. Modeling and Forecasting of DEMIOS 12
Appendix 15

Chapter 3. Input–Output Model Block **21**

3.1. Production and Factor Demands Sub-block 21
3.1.1. Production 21
3.1.2. Factor demands 22
3.2. Prices and Factor Costs Sub-block 24
3.3. I–O Sub-block and VRAS Algorithm 27

3.4. Final Demand Sub-block: Disaggregation of Final Demand 29
Appendix: Regression Results for Sectoral M, IP, LW, W, PX and E 36

Chapter 4. Macroeconomic Model Block 67

4.1. Macro Model Block in DEMIOS: Linkage Between Macro and Sectoral Variables 67
4.2. Macroeconomic Block: Structure of the Model and Regression Results 68
4.2.1. Real expenditure sub-block 68
4.2.1.1. Real household final consumption expenditure 68
4.2.1.2. Real housing investment 70
4.2.1.3. Real private inventory changes 70
4.2.1.4. Real government consumption 71
4.2.1.5. Real non-housing investment, real exports of goods and services and real imports of goods and services 72
4.2.2. Nominal expenditure sub-block 72
4.2.3. Prices and wage rates sub-block 74
4.2.4. Production and labor force sub-block 77
4.2.5. Income distribution sub-block 81
4.2.6. Money and finance sub-block 85
4.2.7. Government finance sub-block 86
4.2.8. Foreign variables and BOP sub-block 89

Chapter 5. Cohort-Type Demographic and Labor Force Block 91

5.1. Simplified Demographic Model 91
5.2. Cohort-type Demographic and Labor Supply Model 93
5.2.1. Population variables 94
5.2.1.1. The number of birth (NPB) 95
5.2.1.2. The number of deaths 97
5.2.1.3. The number of population by age group . . . 99
5.2.2. Labor supply in the cohort-type demographic and labor supply model 103

Chapter 6. Scenario Projections by DEMIOS 107

6.1. National Resilience Plan and its Effects on the Japanese Economy 107
6.1.1. Introduction 107

6.1.2. Assumption of two scenario simulations 108
6.1.3. Simulation results: The effects on the Japanese economy 108
6.1.4. Conclusion 113
6.2. Growth Alternatives in Abenomics by DEMIOS 113
6.2.1. Assumptions of future scenario simulation 114
6.2.2. Three growth scenario projections, FY2014–2020 . . 115
6.2.3. Simulation results: Major macroeconomic variables and sectoral variables 115
6.2.4. Conclusion 121
6.3. Analysis of Huge Earthquake Damages of East Japan: Huge Damage and Reconstruction — An Example of Leontief Cross 122
6.3.1. Nation-wide reconstruction program up to 2020 and its impacts on regional economies 125
6.3.2. Regional sub-model 129
Appendix 131

Chapter 7. Concluding Remarks **167**

7.1. Summary and Policy Recommendation 167
7.2. Further Study in the Future 171

Bibliography 173

Index 175

List of Figures

1.1 The Japanese sectoral economies (ISIC, value added), 1970–2010. 2
2.1 Flowchart of DEMIOS. 8
3.1 Flowchart of sectoral prices and factor costs and TFP in VRAS. 29
4.1 Exchange rate (EXR), purchasing power parity (PPP), and interest rate parity (IRP). 77
4.2 Estimated GDP gap, 1990–2010 (%). 79
6.1 The effects of government investment increases on real GDP, its components and nominal GDP, FY2016–2020. 109
6.2 Real GDP in the baseline and three scenario projection, FY2014–2020 (in billions of yen). 116

List of Tables

1.1	Share of manufacturing sector output in total value added for major countries, 1970–2010 (in %)	3
2.1	Sectoral classification of DEMIOS (81 sectors).	11
2.2	DEMIOS sectoral classification and the I–O table codes.	13
A2.1	Basic sector classification, I–O table (517 rows × 405 columns): Classification code and sector name.	15
3.1	Breakdown of aggregate consumption into 12 items.	30
3.2	Regression results of real household consumption expenditure on a 12-category basis by the Rotterdam School Model.	32
A3.1	Major sectoral import regression results.	36
A3.2	Regression results of sectoral business investment.	39
A3.3	Regression results of wage and salaried employees by sector.	46
A3.4	Regression results of sectoral wage rates.	51
A3.5	Regression results of sectoral output price (PX).	57
A3.6	Regression results of real exports by sector: Major manufacturing sectors.	64
4.1	Regression results of major endogenous variables in the real expenditure sub-block.	69
4.2	Regression result of nominal government consumption.	74
4.3	Regression result of nominal wage rates.	76
4.4	Regression results of major endogenous variables in the production and labor force sub-block.	78
4.5	Regression results of major variables in the income distribution sub-block.	84
4.6	Regression results of the money and finance sub-block.	87
4.7	Regression results of personal income tax and corporation tax revenue.	89
5.1	Regression results of major demographic variables.	94

5.2 Fertility rates regression results by age group, 25–29, 30–34 and 35–39. 96
5.3 Death rates of babies aged zero and of the population aged 10–14 for male and female. 98
5.4 Regression results of average life expectancy for male and female. 99
5.5 Regression results of male and female population aged zero. 100
5.6 Regression results of male and female population aged 1–4. 101
5.7 Regression results of male and female population aged 5–9 and population aged 75–79. 102
5.8 Regression results of male and female population aged over 80. 103
5.9 Regression results of labor force population by age group and by gender. 105
6.1 Real government investment for two scenario projections, FY2015–2020 (in trillions of yen). 108
6.2 The baseline projection, FY2015–2020. 110
6.3 National resilience plan, FY2015–2020. 111
6.4 The dynamic Keynes multiplier by DEMIOS, FY2016–2020. 113
6.5 Scenario 1: Growth scenario. 117
6.6 Scenario 2: Growth plus leisure expansion scenario. . . . 118
6.7 Scenario 3: Growth plus consumption tax hikes. 120
6.8 Direct damage ratio: Four prefectures in Tohoku. 123
6.9 The effects of the East Japan disaster on Tohoku four prefectures — Aggregate damage ratio (= 1− damage ratio). 124
6.10 The baseline forecast, FY2011–2020. 126
6.11 Growth scenario forecast, FY2011–2020. 127
6.12 Growth alternatives by the regional sub-model, FY2010–2020: Ratio in 2020/2010. 130
A6.1 Sectoral output (X) in the baseline projection for national resilience plan, FY2014–2020. 131
A6.2 Sectoral wage and salaried employees (LW) in the baseline projection, FY2014–2020. 135
A6.3 Sectoral output (X) in the national resilience plan, FY2014–2020. 138
A6.4 Sectoral wage and salaried employees (LW) in the national resilience plan, FY2014–2020. 142
A6.5 Sectoral output (X) in Abenomics scenario 1, FY2014–2020. 145

A6.6 Sectoral wage and salaried employees (LW) in Abenomics scenario 1, FY2014–2020. 149
A6.7 Sectoral output (X) in Abenomics scenario 2, FY2014–2020. 152
A6.8 Sectoral wage and salaried employees (LW) in Abenomics scenario 2, FY2014–2020. 156
A6.9 Sectoral output (X) in Abenomics scenario 3, FY2014–2020. 160
A6.10 Sectoral wage and salaried employees (LW) in Abenomics scenario 3, FY2014–2020. 163

Chapter 1

Introduction

1.1. Dynamics of the Japanese Economy

As is widely known, the Japanese economy after World War II achieved a high economic growth from the ashes. The growth rates of real GDP recorded more than 10% annually on average in both the 1950s and the 1960s. Particularly, the high growth in the 1960s was very special as it was announced in advance as the *Income Doubling Plan* by the Ikeda Cabinet[1] and the government deliberately pursued the long-term policy to materialize it. Most economists and journalists doubted its success, but indeed real GDP quadrupled after the decade.

In addition, even after the high growth era, Japan maintained its strong growth performance around 4–5% on average despite the oil crises in the 1970s, whereas most other advanced countries suffered from stagflation. However, it coped with the oil crises and accompanying hyperinflation, however, by the positive investment behaviors and R&D of private companies and public sectors. Thus, the resulting technological progress and structural changes in manufacturing industry made it possible for Japan to save energy and become one of the top advanced economies in the postwar world. (See Vogel, 1979).

On the other hand, the strengthened supply side with positive investments and technical progress produced the trade imbalance (surplus) with the rest of the world, especially the US. As the result, the Japan–US trade

---

[1]One of authors, S. Shishido, participated in the government's preparation of Income Doubling Plan as a planning officer of General Policy Bureau (Saburo Okita as Chief) of the Economic Planning Agency under PM Hayato Ikeda. Then, the government officials estimating econometric models and forecasting alternative scenarios for this plan were equipped only with Tiger calculators. Prof. L. R. Klein, visiting Osaka University then dropped in EPA, told that the Japanese economy could not achieve the goal of the Plan by materializing 7.2% growth rate in the 1960s.

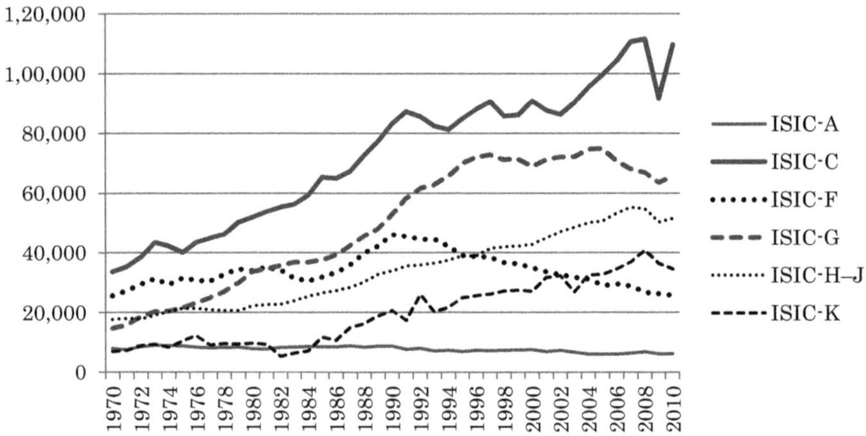

Fig. 1.1. The Japanese sectoral economies (ISIC, value added), 1970–2010.

Note: ISIC-A: agriculture, forestry and fishing; ISIC-C: manufacturing; ISIC-F: construction; ISIC-G: wholesale, retail trade and hotels; ISIC-H–J: transport, storage and communication; ISIC-K: finance and insurance activities.

Source: Developed by the Authors based on UN National Accounts Statistics (SNA), ISIC version 4.

friction intensified so that Japan was obliged to accept the appreciation of yen against US dollar under the pressure of the US government in September 1985. It was called *Plaza Accord*. Even thereafter, however, the Japanese economy kept its positive investment to strengthen the supply side and diversify the industrial composition toward products with higher value added. Thus, despite the burst of asset bubble in 1991, it has maintained its economic dynamism of manufacturing industries owing to IT revolution, etc. despite the lasting deflation, as shown in Fig. 1.1. Figure 1.1 shows that the Japanese sectoral composition has maintained some distinctive features except for agriculture, forestry and fishery sector (ISIC-A) and construction sector (ISIC-F). Particularly, manufacturing sector (ISIC-C) and wholesale, retail trade and hotels sector (ISIC-G) have maintained their vital activities, despite the lasting deflation since the mid-90s except for 2008–2009 of the world financial crisis.

International comparison of Table 1.1 shows that the Japanese economy has been constantly led by the manufacturing sector. Its share in total value added was around 18–19% in the 1970s and the 1980s and slightly increased to 19–20% in the 2000s. On the other hand, it decreased in US, UK, France and Germany, except for South Korea, during the past

Table 1.1. Share of manufacturing sector output in total value added for major countries, 1970–2010 (in %).

	1970	1975	1980	1985	1990	1995	2000	2005	2010
Japan	19.4	18.3	18.0	19.3	19.7	18.7	19.1	19.9	21.8
US	13.6	13.2	13.4	12.3	11.7	12.5	13.2	13.1	13.0
UK	19.4	18.4	18.8	16.6	16.7	15.2	14.0	11.9	11.0
France	14.7	14.4	14.0	13.3	12.8	12.7	13.1	13.3	12.5
Germany	30.2	27.3	26.6	26.1	25.0	21.5	21.7	22.3	22.2
South Korea	8.7	13.5	16.6	18.6	21.2	21.6	26.0	28.3	31.4

Note: Developed by the Authors based on the UN SNA.

four decades. Particularly, in UK and Germany the decline was very sharp; in UK from 18–19% in the 1970s to 11–12% in the 2000s, and in Germany from 30% in the 1970s to around 22% in the 2000s.

The Japanese economy maintained, however, its share at relatively high level over 20%, despite the steadily appreciating yen and while vigorously exporting FDI to the rest of the world. In view of economic dynamics and the structural changes in Japanese manufacturing industries, it is very important for us to utilize a Keynes–Leontief model (KLM) for future forecasts and policy scenario simulations especially for the analyses of Japanese economy.

1.2. The Objectives of DEMIOS: A KLM as Policy Tools

The KLM-type[2] model aims at attaining three advantages. The first is to make macroeconomic policy including fiscal-monetary policy and sectoral indicative planning policy more easily manageable. Particularly, the latter is essential for strategic sectors such as energy sectors, export promotion or import substitution sectors, or infrastructure sectors. The sectoral forecast can encourage the business investment by indicating requirement for their output, fixed capital, employment, etc. thereby helping them reduce information cost. The second advantage is the price

[2]Prof. L. R. Klein, when he participated in the ERINA (Economic Research Institute of North-East Asia) conference at Niigata city in 2000, emphasized the importance of establishing database, including SNA and I–O tables for policy analyses. He emphasized also the importance of developing a KLM not only for national economy but also for regional economies. ERINA has developed a Niigata Prefecture KLM under the direction of Shishido, who was Director of ERINA and employed it for regional economic development policies (Shishido *et al.*, 2005).

effects especially at the time of the flouting exchange rate system in the global economy. Since international environments cause the economic impact nowadays and tend to be increasingly important, the KLM can serve to provide the vital information on price changes to be caused.

The price analysis can be extended to damage analysis such as casualties caused by earthquakes as discussed later in Chapter 6. Input–Output (I–O) matrix for price repercussion has another use for positive effect of infra-structure or similar type of capital on capacity utilization and energy saving. These issues are also discussed in the context of price and capacity analysis. The third advantage is the better information on the fiscal budget *revenue*. Because of the disaggregation of productive goods, the various distributed income, such as corporate income, wage income, unincorporated income, etc. can be estimated and give more accurate estimation of total tax revenues by type. This advantage of KLM-type model can offer more accurate and detailed forecasts of fiscal revenues, which used to be roughly obtained by short-term macro models.

As we shall discuss later, the fiscal position of general government, including central and local governments, has worsened, and social security system is suffering from serious debt burdens. Therefore, the KLM can be used as a strategic tool for dealing with such serious issues in Japan.

In Chapter 6, various types of policy simulation are presented. Before discussing various policy scenarios, impacts of different policy *multipliers* are presented, such as those of public investment, government consumption, tax reductions, discount rate of the Bank of Japan, etc. Particularly, noteworthy is an impact of public investment accommodated by the Bank of Japan which contributes to the strengthening of Japan's infrastructure and GDP as well as the reduction of government debt through an automatic increase in tax revenues. It has killed two birds with one stone. As *ex post* historical simulation during 1990–2005, it is stressed that the effect of excessive contractionary economic policy, such as drastic cut of public investment gave downward pressures on the Japanese economy, resulting in chronic shortage in tax revenues and increase in fiscal debts and serious underutilization of productive capacity.

1.3. Organization of the Book

Chapter 2 discusses general feature of DEMIOS, focusing on the basic structure of the model, sectoral classification and database development.

Chapter 3 explains the input–output block and explains its four sub-blocks: (1) the production and factor demands sub-block; (2) the prices and factor costs sub-block; (3) the input–output sub-block with the VRAS algorism; and (4) the final demand sub-block. Chapter 4 discusses the macroeconomic model block to analyze the structure of the eight sub-blocks: (1) the real expenditure sub-block; (2) the nominal expenditure sub-block; (3) the prices and wage rate sub-block; (4) the production and labor force sub-block; (5) the money and finance sub-block; (6) the government finance sub-block; (7) the income distribution sub-block; and (8) the external and balance of payment (BOP) sub-block.

Chapter 5 introduces the demographic and labor force block with cohort-type data, focusing on the simplified demographic sub-model which is employed for the mid-term scenario projections. On the other hand, the cohort type of demographic and labor force sub-model is utilized for the long-term projections. Chapter 6 presents three scenario projections: (1) the growth alternatives in Abenomics; (2) the national resilience plan; and (3) the analysis of huge earthquake damages of East Japan.

Finally, Chapter 7 concludes each chapter with (1) summary of each chapter; (2) policy recommendations based on the studies and analyses; and (3) our discussions on the further studies required.

Chapter 2

General Feature of DEMIOS

2.1. Basic Structure of the Model: DEMIOS

DEMIOS is a multi-sectoral econometric model, integrating Keynesian-type macroeconometric model with Leontief-type input–output (I–O) model. In the present system, DEMIOS consists of three model blocks: (i) the I–O block, (ii) the macroeconomic block and (iii) the demographic and labor force block. The total number of endogenous and exogenous variables exceeds 3,500. They are forecasted up to the year 2030 at this moment.[1]

Demand-side variables are mainly influenced by Keynesian theory and supply side consists of production variables of Leontief type based on technical conditions. The world trade, fiscal and monetary policy factors tend to affect the demand side of the economy, while the changes in technology and relative prices tend to influence supply-side variables such as sectoral output, employment, investment, etc., which again tend to feedback to macroeconomic variables of demand side.

Other causal impacts are demographic variables, which are related to population changes such as birth and death rates, migration rate, affecting labor force, employment, household behavior such as consumption, and social transfers of governments.

Figure 2.1 shows all the above important variables as a flowchart. This chart depicts symbolically the socioeconomic relations of DEMIOS and can be used for medium term policy simulations on the Japanese economy. The I–O block contains four sub-blocks: (1) the production

[1]For econometric modeling and forecasting, the DEMIOS project is now employing Eviews-9. In the initial stage of DEMIOS development, the Project utilized TROLL system. In the 1990s for the NIRA-LINK Project, the Project employed SIMNEW which was a Project LINK system for scenario simulations, during around 10 years.

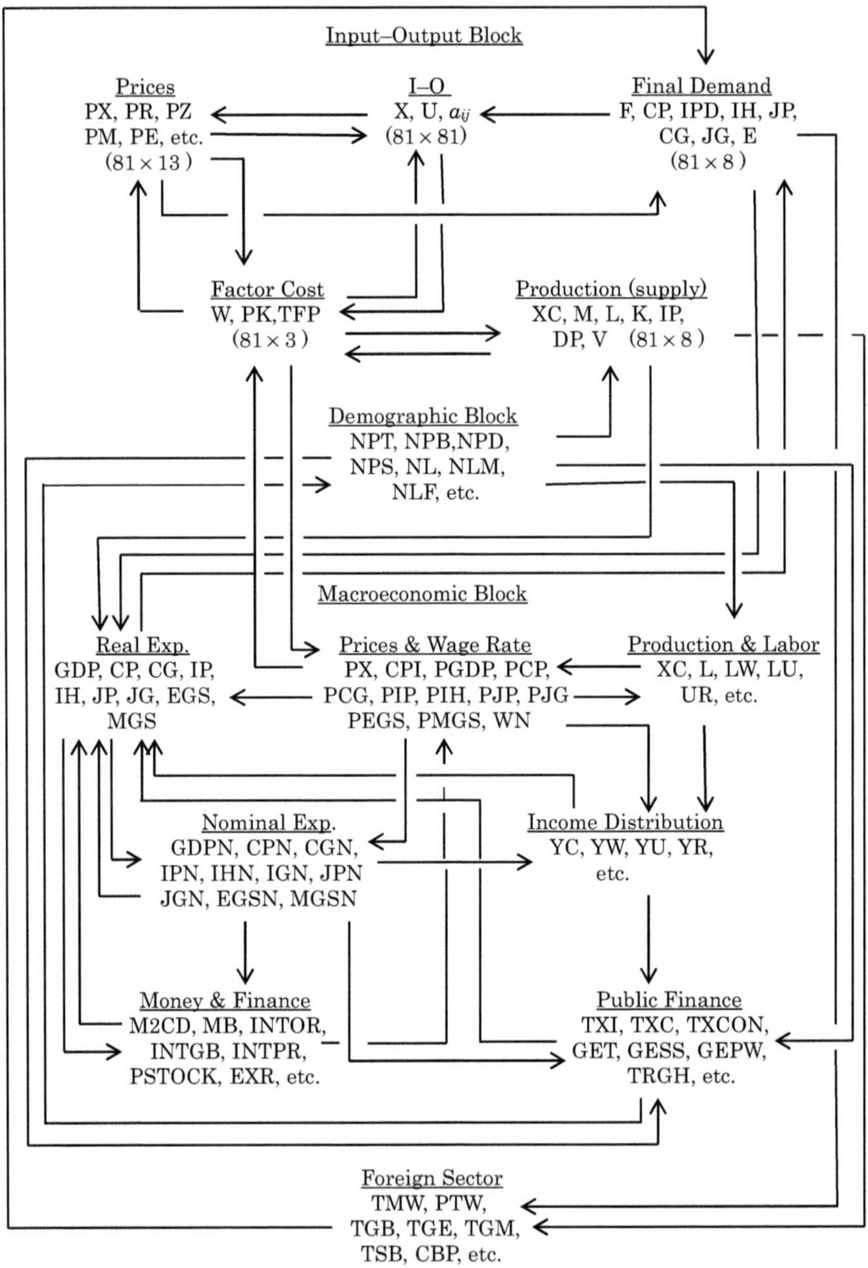

Fig. 2.1. Flowchart of DEMIOS.

sub-block; (2) the prices and factor cost sub-block; (3) the I–O sub-block; and (4) the final demands sub-block. The macroeconomic block includes eight sub-blocks: (1) the real expenditure sub-block; (2) the nominal expenditure sub-block; (3) the prices and wage rates sub-block; (4) the production sub-block; (5) the income distribution sub-block; (6) the money and finance sub-block; (7) the government finance sub-block; and (8) exchange rate and balance of payment (BOP) sub-block.

Fig. 2.1. (*Continued*)

Note: List of Variables: **Input–output block** — X: production; F: final demand; U: intermediate demand; a_{ij}: input coefficient; PX: output prices; PR: total input prices; PZ: input prices; PM: import price; PE: export price; CP: private consumption; IPD: business investment demand; IH: housing investment; JP: private inventory changes; CG: government consumption; JG: government inventory changes; E: exports; W: wage rates; PK: capital cost; TFP: total factor productivity; XC: capacity output; M: imports; L: labor demand; K: capital stock; IP: business investment; DP: depreciation of capital; V: value added. **Demographic block** — NPT: total population; NPB: the number of birth; NPD: the number of death; NPS: the number of net migrants; NL: the number of labor; NLM: the number of male labor; NLF: the number of female labor. **Macroeconomic block** — GDP: real GDP; CP: real private consumption; CG: real government consumption; IP: real non-housing investment; IH: real housing investment; JP: real private inventory changes; JG: real government inventory changes; EGS: real exports of goods and services; MGS: real imports of goods and services; PX: output price; CPI: consumer price index; PGDP: implicit deflator of GDP; PCP: implicit deflator of CP; PCG: implicit deflator of CG; PIP: implicit deflator of IP; PIH: implicit deflator of IH; PJP: implicit deflator of JP; PJG: implicit deflator of JG; PEGS: implicit deflator of EGS; PMGS: implicit deflator of MGS; WN: nominal wage rates; XC: capacity GDP; L: labor demand; LW: wage and salaried employees; LU: incorporated enterprises worker; UR: rate of unemployment; GDPN: nominal GDP; CPN: nominal private consumption; CGN: nominal government consumption; IPN: nominal non-housing investment; IHN: nominal housing investment; IGN: nominal government investment; JPN: nominal private inventory changes; JGN: nominal government inventory changes; EGSN: nominal exports of goods and services; MGSN: nominal imports of goods and services; YC: corporation income; YW: wage and salaried income; YU: unincorporated enterprises income; YR: property income; M2CD: money stock (M2 + CD); MB: base money; INTOR: official discount rate; INTGB: government bond yield (10-year); INTPR: prime rate; PSTOCK: stock prices (TOPIX); EXR: exchange rate; TXI: income tax revenue; TXC: corporate tax revenue; TXCON: consumption tax revenue; TRG: total tax revenue (general account); TMW: real world trade; PTW: deflator of TWM; TGB: trade balance; TGE: export of goods in BOP; TGM: import of goods in BOP; TSB: service balance; CBP: current balance of payment.

The demographic and labor force block contains two sub-blocks: (1) The cohort-type demographic sub-block and (2) The cohort-type labor force sub-block. These three model blocks and their sub-blocs are discussed in Chapters 3, 4 and 5 in more detail.

2.2. Sectoral Classification and Database Development

2.2.1. *Sectoral classification*

In the original version, DEMIOS development was initiated under a 64-sectoral classification system in 1985. However, during the course of Japan–US collaboration, as stated earlier, some important sectors are chosen to disaggregate further, especially machinery, information and service sectors.

In the present system of DEMIOS with 81 sectors, there are 13 primary sectors, 39 manufacturing sectors, 4 construction sectors, 24 service sectors and one unallocated sector, as shown in Table 2.1. In comparison with the previous version, DEMIOS with 64 sectors, the general machinery sector is disaggregated to the office machinery sector and the other general machinery sector, and the electric machinery sector is disaggregated to the industrial electric machinery sector and the consumer electric machinery sector. In addition, the communications and information services sector is also disaggregated to the communications sector and information processing services sector. Their disaggregation is heavily dependent on advancement of IT and its diffusion in the society.

2.2.2. *Database development*

The database of DEMIOS covers the annual time series from 1974 to 2004 for sectoral variables in the I–O block and from 1970 to 2010 for macroeconomic and demographic variables in the macroeconomic block and the demographic block. In addition, for important equations, they are extended up to 2014. The essential information for DEMIOS is statistical data, covering National Accounts Statistics (SNA), input–output tables and related statistical series which are available on an annual basis.

The National Accounts Statistics series are available on an annual basis. The input–output (I–O) tables developed by the central government are available on every five year, but the Ministry of Economy, Trade and Industry publishes tentative I–O tables on an annual basis, since the benchmark I–O tables have usually been published four or five years

Table 2.1. Sectoral classification of DEMIOS (81 sectors).

01 General crops	42 Office machinery
02 Industrial crops	43 Other general machinery
03 Livestock for foods	44 Industrial electrical machinery
04 Livestock for fiber	45 Consumer electrical machinery
05 Agriculture services	46 Precision machinery
06 Forestry	47 Automobiles
07 Fishery	48 Railway vehicle
08 Coal mining	49 Shipbuilding
09 Crude petroleum	50 Aircraft
10 Natural gas	51 Other transport equipment
11 Iron mining	52 Miscellaneous manufacturing
12 Non-metal mining	53 Housing construction
13 Other mining	54 Industrial construction
14 Meat and dairy products	55 Public construction
15 Manufactured sea foods	56 Other construction
16 Grain products	57 Electric power
17 Other foods	58 Gas
18 Beverages	59 Water and sanitary service
19 Feedstuff	60 Waste disposal
20 Tobacco	61 Wholesale and retail trade
21 Natural and chemical textiles	62 Automobile mechanical repair
22 Other textiles	63 Hotel and restaurant
23 Wearing apparel	64 Railways
24 Leather and leather products	65 Trucks and buses
25 Wood and wood products	66 Water transportation
26 Furniture	67 Air transport
27 Pulp and paper	68 Other transportation
28 Printing and publishing	69 Communications
29 Coal product	70 Finance and insurance
30 Petroleum products	71 Real estate
31 Basic and intermediate chemicals	72 Information processing services
32 Fats, oils and final chemicals	73 Other corporation services
33 Rubber products	74 Research and development
34 Plastic products	75 Public services
35 Cement	76 Education
36 Other ceramics	77 Medical insurance
37 Iron products	78 Other public services
38 Rolling, casting and forgings	79 Other services for individuals
39 Aluminum (including secondary)	80 Office supplies
40 Other non-ferrous products	81 Unallocated
41 Metal products	82 Total

later. The relations between 81 sectors in DEMIOS and I–O table basic classification are accounted, as shown in Table 2.2.

Sectoral employment, investment, capital stock, producer prices, wage rate are made available by the DEMIOS project, on the basis of 81 DEMIOS classification system. The project also estimated annual I–O tables on a constant and current price basis, providing the basis for RAS multipliers as discuss later in Chapter 3.

The producer price and output series on an annual basis for 81 sectors are most important and all these data were developed by the project. Regarding fixed capital stock, fixed investment, and depreciation for both private and public corporate sectors and general government on an 81-sector basis the data estimation works were carried out by a research group of University of Tsukuba and International University of Japan. In particular, compiling the I–O tables on an 81-sector basis was very important works based on the original I–O tables. The relation between the DEMIOS classification and the I–O table codes is shown in Table 2.2 and the basic sector classification I–O table in 2000 is also shown in Table A2.1.

Fiscal data of general government are all taken from the National Accounts and the Ministry of Finance, while monetary and financial data are all taken from annual statistical series of the Bank of Japan (BOJ). Foreign trade and balance of payments are taken from the database of the Ministry of Finance and BOJ.

2.3. Modeling and Forecasting of DEMIOS

In modeling and forecasting of DEMIOS, the project has taken account of the fundamental issues raised by the Cowles Commission. In particular, the endogeneity issue, including omitted variables, measurement error and simultaneity, is our major concern in modeling and forecasting of DEMIOS with more than 3,500 variables. In addition, owing to the contribution of Granger to econometrics (see Engle and Granger, 1987), the project has considered the cointegrating relationships and the superconsistency in simultaneously determined structural equation models.

Therefore, in modeling, unit root tests, cointegrating relationships tests, etc., are performed to eliminate spurious estimators. Furthermore, in forecasting with scenario projections, the project has utilized a block-recursive-type method by the Gauss–Seidel method with 0.1% convergent criteria and the model is solved by block within a small loop

Table 2.2. DEMIOS sectoral classification and the I–O table codes.

DEMIOS sector (81 sectors)	Sectoral code in I–O table*
01 General crops	0111-01–0115-09
02 Industrial crops	0116-01–0116-09
03 Livestock for foods	0121-01–0121-05
04 Livestock for fiber	0121-09
05 Agriculture services	0131-01–0131-02
06 Forestry	0211-01–0123-01
07 Fishery	0311-01–0312-02
08 Coal mining	0711-01
09 Crude petroleum	0721-01
10 Natural gas	0721-02
11 Iron mining	0611-01
12 Non-metal mining	0621-01–0622-02
13 Other mining	0629-09
14 Meat and dairy products	1111-01–1112-03
15 Manufactured sea foods	1113-01–1113-09
16 Grain products	1114-01–1114-02
17 Other foods	1115-01–1119-09
18 Beverages	1121-01–1129-03
19 Feedstuff	1131-01–1131-02
20 Tobacco	1141-01
21 Natural and chemical textiles	1511-01–1514-01
22 Other textiles	1519-01–1519-09
23 Wearing apparel	1521-01–1529-09
24 Leather and leather products	2411-01–2412-02
25 Wood and wood products	1611-01–1619-09
26 Furniture	1711-01–1711-03
27 Pulp and paper	1811-01–1829-09
28 Printing and publishing	1911-0
29 Coal products	2121-01–2121-02
30 Petroleum products	2111-01
31 Basic and intermediate chemicals	2011-01–2031-02
32 Fats, oils and final chemicals	2032-01–2079-09
33 Rubber products	2311-01–2319-09
34 Plastic products	2211-01
35 Cement	2521-01–2523-03
36 Other ceramics	2531-01–2599-09
37 Iron products	2611-01–2611-04
38 Rolling, casting and forgings	2621-01–2649-09
39 Aluminum (including secondary)	2711-03
40 Other non-ferrous products	2711-01–2722-09 (exc. 2711-03)
41 Metal products	2811-01–2899-09
42 Office machinery	3111-01–3112-01

(*Continued*)

Table 2.2. (*Continued*)

DEMIOS sector (81sectors)	Sectoral code in I–O table*
43 Other general machinery	3011-01–3031-09
44 Industrial electrical machinery	3211-01–3241-09
45 Consumer electrical machinery	3251-01–3421-09
46 Precision machinery	3711-01–3719-03
47 Automobiles	3511-01–3541-03
48 Railway vehicle	3621-01–3621-10
49 Shipbuilding	3611-01–3611-10
50 Aircraft	3622-01–3622-10
51 Other transport equipment	3629-01–3629-09
52 Miscellaneous manufacturing	3911-01–3921-01
53 Housing construction	4111-01–4111-02
54 Industrial construction	4112-01–4111-02
55 Public construction	4131-01–4131-03
56 Other construction	4132-01–4132-09
57 Electric power	5111-01–5111-04
58 Gas	5121-01–5122-01
59 Water and sanitary service	5211-01–5211-03
60 Waste disposal	5212-01–5212-02
61 Wholesale and retail trade	6111-01–6112-02
62 Automobile mechanical repair	8514-10–8515-10
63 Hotel and restaurant	8612-01–8613-01
64 Railways	7111-01–7112-02
65 Trucks and buses	7121-01–7132-01
66 Water transportation	7141-01–7143-01
67 Air transport	7151-01
68 Other transportation	7171-01–7189-09
69 Communications	7311-01–7321-03
70 Finance and insurance	6211-01–6212-02
71 Real estate	6411-01–6422-02
72 Information processing services	7331-01–7351-03
73 Other corporation services	8511-01–8519-09
74 Research and development	8221-01–8222-01
75 Public services	8111-01–8112-01
76 Education	8211-01–8213-04
77 Medical insurance	8311-01–8314-02
78 Other public services	8411-01–8411-02
79 Other services for individuals	8611-01–8619-09 (exc. 8612-01)
80 Office supplies	8900-00
81 Unallocated	9000-00

Source: Basic sector classification I–O (520 × 407) code in 2000, the Ministry of Internal Affairs and Communications.

and large loop. For solving the model, endogenous variables are solved by block in the small loop through seven blocks as follows.

(1) the I–O sub-block in the input–output model block,
(2) the prices and wage rates sub-block in the input–output model block,
(3) the final demand sub-block in the input–output model block,
(4) the real expenditure sub-block and the external and BOP sub-block in the macro model block,
(5) the nominal expenditure sub-block, the prices and wage rates block and the income distribution sub-block in the macro model block,
(6) the production and labor force sub-block, the money and finance sub-block and the government finance sub-block in the macro model block, and
(7) the demographic sub-block and the labor force sub-block in the demographic and labor force block.

After solving endogenous variables by block in the small loop, the whole model is solved within the large loop.

For testing the performance of the model, the Goldberger tests, including the partial test, the total test and the final test are conducted as a traditional test in econometric modeling and forecasting, as well.

Appendix

Table A2.1. Basic sector classification, I–O table (517 rows × 405 columns): Classification code and sector name.

0111-01	Rice
0111-02	Wheat, barley and the like
0112-01	Potatoes and sweet potatoes
0112-02	Pulses
0113-01	Vegetables (outdoor)
0113-02	Vegetables (under facilities)
0114-01	Fruits
0115-01	Sugar crops
0115-02	Crops for beverages
0115-09	Other edible crops
0116-01	Crops for feed and forage
0116-02	Seeds and seedlings
0116-03	Flowers and plants
0116-09	Other inedible crops
0121-01	Dairy cattle farming
0121-02	Hen eggs
0121-03	Fowls and broilers
0121-04	Hogs
0121-05	Beef cattle
0121-09	Other livestock
0131-01	Veterinary service
0131-02	Agricultural services (except veterinary service)
0211-01	Silviculture
0212-01	Logs
0213-01	Special forest products (inc. hunting)
0311-01	Coastal fisheries
0311-02	Offshore fisheries
0311-03	Distant water fisheries
0311-04	Marine culture

(*Continued*)

Table A2.1. (*Continued*)

0312-01	Inland water fisheries
0312-02	Inland water culture
0611-01	Metallic ores
0621-01	Materials for ceramics
0622-01	Gravel and quarrying
0622-02	Crushed stones
0629-09	Other non-metallic ores
0711-01	Coal mining
0721-01	Crude petroleum
0721-02	Natural gas
1111-01	Slaughtering and meat processing
1112-01	Processed meat products
1112-02	Bottled or canned meat products
1112-03	Dairy farm products
1113-01	Frozen fish and shellfish
1113-02	Salted, dried or smoked seafood
1113-03	Bottled or canned seafood
1113-04	Fish paste
1113-09	Other processed seafood
1114-01	Grain milling
1114-02	Flour and other grain milled products
1115-01	Noodles
1115-02	Bread
1115-03	Confectionery
1116-01	Bottled or canned vegetables and fruits
1116-02	Preserved agricultural foodstuffs (other than bottled or canned)
1117-01	Sugar
1117-02	Starch
1117-03	Dextrose, syrup and isomerized sugar
1117-04	Vegetable oils and meal
1117-05	Animal oils and fats
1117-06	Condiments and seasonings
1119-01	Prepared frozen foods
1119-02	Retort foods
1119-03	Dishes, sushi and lunch boxes
1119-04	School lunch (public)**
1119-05	School lunch (private)*
1119-09	Other foods
1121-01	Refined sake
1121-02	Beer
1121-03	Whiskey and brandy
1121-09	Other liquors
1129-01	Tea and roasted coffee
1129-02	Soft drinks
1129-03	Manufactured ice
1131-01	Feeds
1131-02	Organic fertilizers, n.e.c.
1141-01	Tobacco
1511-01	Fiber yarns
1512-01	Cotton and staple fiber fabrics (inc. fabrics of synthetic spun fibers)
1512-02	Silk and artificial silk fabrics (inc. fabrics of synthetic filament fibers)
1512-03	Woolen fabrics, hemp fabrics and other fabrics
1513-01	Knitting fabrics
1514-01	Yarn and fabric dyeing and finishing (processing on commission only)
1519-01	Ropes and nets
1519-02	Carpets and floor mats
1519-03	Fabricated textiles for medical use
1519-09	Other fabricated textile products
1521-01	Woven fabric apparel
1521-02	Knitted apparel
1522-09	Other wearing apparel and clothing accessories
1529-01	Bedding
1529-09	Other readymade textile products
1611-01	Timber
1611-02	Plywood
1611-03	Wooden chips
1619-09	Other wooden products
1711-01	Wooden furniture and fixtures
1711-02	Wooden fixtures
1711-03	Metallic furniture and fixture
1811-01	Pulp
1812-01	Paper
1812-02	Paperboard
1813-01	Corrugated cardboard
1813-02	Coated paper and building (construction) paper
1821-01	Corrugated card board boxes
1821-09	Other paper containers
1829-01	Paper textile for medical use
1829-09	Other pulp, paper and processed products
1911-01	Newspapers
1911-02	Printing, plate making and book binding
1911-03	Publishing

(*Continued*)

Table A2.1. (*Continued*)

2011-01	Chemical fertilizer
2021-01	Industrial soda chemicals
2029-01	Inorganic pigment
2029-02	Compressed gas and liquefied gas
2029-03	Salt
2029-09	Other industrial inorganic chemicals
2031-01	Petrochemical basic products
2031-02	Petrochemical aromatic products (except synthetic resin)
2032-01	Aliphatic intermediates
2032-02	Cyclic intermediates
2033-01	Synthetic rubber
2039-01	Methane derivatives
2039-02	Oil and fat industrial chemicals
2039-03	Plasticizers
2039-04	Synthetic dyes
2039-09	Other industrial organic chemicals
2041-01	Thermo-setting resins
2041-02	Thermoplastics resins
2041-03	High function resins
2041-09	Other resins
2051-01	Rayon and acetate
2051-02	Synthetic fibers
2061-01	Medicaments
2071-01	Soap, synthetic detergents and surface active agents
2071-02	Cosmetics, toilet preparations and dentifrices
2072-01	Paint and varnishes
2072-02	Printing ink
2073-01	Photographic sensitive materials
2074-01	Agricultural chemicals
2079-01	Gelatin and adhesives
2079-09	Other final chemical products
2111-01	Petroleum refinery products (inc. greases)
2121-01	Coal products
2121-02	Paving materials
2211-01	Plastic products
2311-01	Tires and inner tubes
2319-01	Rubber footwear
2319-02	Plastic footwear
2319-09	Other rubber products
2411-01	Leather footwear
2412-01	Leather and fur skins
2412-02	Miscellaneous leather products
2511-01	Sheet glass and safety glass
2512-01	Glass fiber and glass fiber products, n.e.c.
2519-09	Other glass products
2521-01	Cement
2522-01	Ready mixed concrete
2523-01	Cement products
2531-01	Pottery, china and earthenware
2599-01	Clay refractories
2599-02	Other structural clay products
2599-03	Carbon and graphite products
2599-04	Abrasive
2599-09	Miscellaneous ceramic, stone and clay products
2611-01	Pig iron
2611-02	Ferro alloys
2611-03	Crude steel (converters)
2611-04	Crude steel (electric furnaces)
2621-01	Hot rolled steel
2622-01	Steel pipes and tubes
2623-01	Cold-finished steel
2623-02	Coated steel
2631-01	Cast and forged steel
2631-02	Cast iron pipes and tubes
2631-03	Cast and forged materials (iron)
2649-01	Iron and steel shearing and slitting
2649-09	Other iron or steel products
2711-01	Copper
2711-02	Lead and zinc (inc. regenerated lead)
2711-03	Aluminum (inc. regenerated aluminum)
2711-09	Other non-ferrous metals
2721-01	Electric wires and cables
2721-02	Optical fiber cables
2722-01	Rolled and drawn copper and copper alloys
2722-02	Rolled and drawn aluminum
2722-03	Non-ferrous metal castings and forgings
2722-04	Nuclear fuels
2722-09	Other non-ferrous metal products
2811-01	Metal products for construction
2812-01	Metal products for architecture
2891-01	Gas and oil appliances and heating and cooking apparatus
2899-01	Bolts, nuts, rivets and springs

(*Continued*)

Table A2.1. (*Continued*)

2899-02	Metal containers, fabricated plate and sheet metal
2899-03	Plumber's supplies, powder metallurgy products and tools
2899-09	Other metal products
3011-01	Boilers
3011-02	Turbines
3011-03	Engines
3012-01	Conveyors
3013-01	Refrigerators and air conditioning apparatus
3019-01	Pumps and compressors
3019-02	Machinists' precision tools
3019-09	Other general industrial machinery and equipment
3021-01	Machinery and equipment for construction and mining
3022-01	Chemical machinery
3023-01	Industrial robots
3024-01	Metal machine tools
3024-02	Metal processing machinery
3029-01	Machinery for agricultural use
3029-02	Textile machinery
3029-03	Food processing machinery
3029-04	Semiconductor making equipment
3029-09	Other special machinery for industrial use
3031-01	Metal molds
3031-02	Bearings
3031-09	Other general machines and parts
3111-01	Copy machine
3111-09	Other office machines
3112-01	Machinery for service industry
3211-01	Electric audio equipment
3211-02	Radio and television sets
3211-03	Video recording and playback equipment
3212-01	Household air-conditioners
3212-02	Household electric appliances (except air-conditioners)
3311-01	Personal Computers
3311-02	Electronic computing equipment (except personal computers)
3311-03	Electronic computing equipment (accessory equipment)
3321-01	Wired communication equipment
3321-02	Cellular phones
3321-03	Radio communication equipment (except cellular phones)
3321-09	Other communication equipment
3331-01	Applied electronic equipment
3332-01	Electric measuring instruments
3341-01	Semiconductor devices
3341-02	Integrated circuits
3359-01	Electron tubes
3359-02	Liquid crystal element
3359-03	Magnetic tapes and discs
3359-09	Other electronic components
3411-01	Rotating electrical equipment
3411-02	Relay switches and switchboards
3411-03	Transformers and reactors
3411-09	Other industrial heavy electrical equipment
3421-01	Electric lighting fixtures and apparatus
3421-02	Batteries
3421-03	Electric bulbs
3421-04	Wiring devices and supplies
3421-05	Electrical equipment for internal combustion engines
3421-09	Other electrical devices and parts
3511-01	Passenger motor cars
3521-01	Trucks, buses and other cars
3531-01	Two-wheel motor vehicles
3541-01	Motor vehicle bodies
3541-02	Internal combustion engines for motor vehicles and parts
3541-03	Motor vehicle parts and accessories
3611-01	Steel ships
3611-02	Ships (except steel ships)
3611-03	Internal combustion engines for vessels
3611-10	Repair of ships
3621-01	Rolling stock
3621-10	Repair of rolling stock
3622-01	Aircrafts
3622-10	Repair of aircrafts
3629-01	Bicycles
3629-09	Other transport equipment
3711-01	Camera
3711-09	Other photographic and optical instruments
3712-01	Watches and clocks
3719-01	Professional and scientific instruments

(*Continued*)

Table A2.1. (*Continued*)

3719-02	Analytical instruments, testing machine, measuring instruments
3719-03	Medical instruments
3911-01	Toys and games
3911-02	Sporting and athletic goods
3919-01	Musical instruments
3919-02	Audio and video records, other information recording media
3919-03	Stationery
3919-04	Jewelry and adornments
3919-05	"Tatami" (straw matting) and straw products
3919-06	Ordnance
3919-09	Miscellaneous manufacturing products
3921-01	Reuse and recycling
4111-01	Residential construction (wooden)
4111-02	Residential construction (non-wooden)
4112-01	Non-residential construction (wooden)
4112-02	Non-residential construction (non-wooden)
4121-01	Repair of construction
4131-01	Public construction of roads
4131-02	Public construction of rivers, drainages and others
4131-03	Agricultural public construction
4132-01	Railway construction
4132-02	Electric power facilities construction
4132-03	Telecommunication facilities construction
4132-09	Other civil engineering and construction
5111-01	Electricity (nuclear power)
5111-02	Electricity (thermal power)
5111-03	Electricity (water power, etc.)
5111-04	Private power generation
5121-01	Gas supply
5122-01	Steam and hot water supply
5211-01	Water supply
5211-02	Industrial water supply
5211-03	Sewage disposal**
5212-01	Waste management service (public)**
5212-02	Waste management services (private)
6111-01	Wholesale trade
6112-01	Retail trade
6211-01	Financial service
6212-01	Life insurance
6212-02	Non-life insurance
6411-01	Real estate agencies and managers
6411-02	Real estate rental service
6421-01	House rent
6422-01	House rent (imputed house rent)
7111-01	Railway transport by JR (passenger)
7112-01	Railway transport (freight)
7121-01	Bus transport service
7121-02	Hired car and taxi transport
7122-01	Road freight transport
7131-01	Self-transport by private cars (passengers)
7132-01	Self-transport by private cars (freight)
7141-01	Ocean transport
7142-01	Coastal and inland water transport
7143-01	Harbor transport service
7151-01	Air transport
7161-01	Freight forwarding
7171-01	Storage facility service
7181-01	Packing service
7189-01	Facility service for road transport
7189-02	Port and water traffic control**
7189-03	Services relating to water transport
7189-04	Airport and air traffic control (public)**
7189-05	Airport and air traffic control (industrial)
7189-06	Services relating to air transport
7189-09	Travel agency and other services relating to transport
7311-01	Postal service
7312-01	Fixed telecommunication
7312-02	Mobile telecommunication
7312-03	Other telecommunication
7319-09	Other services relating to communication
7321-01	Public broadcasting
7321-02	Private broadcasting
7321-03	Cable broadcasting
8111-01	Public administration (central)**
8112-01	Public administration (local)**
8211-01	School education (public)**
8211-02	School education (private)*
8213-01	Social education (public)**
8213-02	Social education (private, non-profit)*

(*Continued*)

Table A2.1. (*Continued*)

8213-03	Other educational and training institutions (public)**
8213-04	Other educational and training institutions (profit-making)
8221-01	Research institutes for natural science (pubic)**
8221-02	Research institutes for cultural and social science (public)**
8221-03	Research institutes for natural sciences (private, non-profit)*
8221-04	Research institutes for cultural and social science (private, non-profit)*
8221-05	Research institutes for natural sciences (profit-making)
8221-06	Research institutes for cultural and social science (profit-making)
8222-01	Research and development (intra-enterprise)
8311-01	Medical service (public)
8311-02	Medical service (non-profit foundations, etc.)
8311-03	Medical service (medical corporations, etc.)
8312-01	Health and hygiene (public)**
8312-02	Health and hygiene (profit-making)
8313-01	Social insurance (public)**
8313-02	Social insurance (private-non-profit)*
8313-03	Social welfare (public)**
8313-04	Social welfare (private, non-profit)*
8314-01	Nursing care (In-home)
8314-02	Nursing care (In-facility)
8411-01	Private non-profit institutions serving enterprises
8411-02	Private non-profit institutions serving households, n.e.c.*
8511-01	Advertising services
8512-01	Information services
8512-02	News syndicates and private detective agencies
8513-01	Goods rental and leasing (except car rental)
8514-01	Car rental and leasing
8515-10	Repair of motor vehicles
8516-10	Repair of machine
8519-01	Building maintenance services
8519-02	Judicial, financial and accounting services
8519-03	Civil engineering and construction services
8519-04	Worker dispatching services
8519-09	Other business services
8611-01	Motion picture and video production, and distribution
8611-02	Movie theaters
8611-03	Theater and entertainment facilities
8611-04	Amusement and recreation facilities
8611-05	Stadiums and companies of bicycle, horse, motorcar and motorboat races
8611-06	Sport facility service, public gardens and amusement parks
8611-07	Theatrical companies
8611-09	Other amusement and recreation services
8612-01	General eating and drinking places (except coffee shops)
8612-02	Coffee shops
8612-03	Eating and drinking places for pleasures
8613-01	Hotel and other lodging places
8619-01	Cleaning, laundry and dyeing services
8619-02	Barber shops
8619-03	Beauty shops
8619-04	Public baths
8619-05	Photographic studios
8619-06	Ceremonial occasions
8619-07	Miscellaneous repairs, n.e.c.
8619-08	Places for private lessons
8619-09	Other personal services
8900-00	Office supplies
9000-00	Activities not elsewhere classified
9099-00	Total of intermediate sectors

Note: Meanings of the symbols are as follows: **: Producers of government service activity; *: Producers of private non-profit service for households.

Source: The Ministry of Internal Affairs and Communications.

Chapter 3

Input–Output Model Block

3.1. Production and Factor Demands Sub-block

3.1.1. *Production*

The production side is derived as a dual price–cost relationship and theoretically the following system is formulated based on the conventional Leontief input–output (I–O) technique.

$$D_i = U_i + F_i + E_i,$$

$$X_i = D_i - M_i,$$

$$M_i = f((+)D_i, (-)Pm_i/Px_i),$$

$$Ur_i = \sum_i a_{ij} \cdot X_j,$$

where U_i is the sectoral intermediate demand, a_{ij} the input coefficient, X_i the sectoral output, D_i the sectoral total demand, F_i the sectoral final demand, E_i the sectoral exports, M_i the sectoral imports, Pm_i the sectoral import price (PM_i), Px_i the sectoral output price (PX_i) and Ur_i the sectoral intermediate input, respectively.

Therefore, based on the above equations, sectoral total input is derived within an identity and hence sectoral total factor productivity (TFP) is defined as the ratio of output to total input, as follows:

$$Z_j = Ur_j + w_j \cdot L_j + Pk_j \cdot K_j + Px_j A_j,$$

$$\tau_j = Z_j / X_j,$$

where Z_j is the sectoral total input, w_j the sectoral wage rates, L_j the sectoral labor, Pk_j the sectoral capital cost, K_j the sectoral capital stock, Px_j the sectoral output price, A_j the input coefficient matrix and τ_j the sectoral total factor productivity (TFP$_i$), respectively.

In the conventional Leontief I–O technique, the sectoral imports are accounted as one of the supply-side variables from the rest of the world and hence domestic production plus imports are equal to total demands, as follows:

$$X_i + M_i = U_i + F_i + E_i = D_i.$$

Therefore, it is very important to consider sectoral imports as endogenous variables in the I–O block. As noted above, the sectoral import functions also follow the modified Mundell–Fleming model with sectoral total demands as an income effect and relative prices of sectoral imports to sectoral output prices as a price effect, in which sectoral import prices in terms of US$ are converted to import prices in terms of yen by exchange rate, yen rate to US$. The sectoral imports are derived as the ratio of imports to total demands in the sectoral import functions. The regression results of major sectoral imports are shown in Table A3.1.

Furthermore, in DEMIOS sectoral capacity output is derived as a sectoral supply-side variable, taking account for capacity utilization rate of capital by sector and the ratio of total actual working hours to official working hours by sector, as follows:

$$\ln \mathrm{XC}_i = f((+)\ln(\mathrm{KP}_i \cdot \mathrm{CUR}_i), (+)\ln(L_i \cdot \mathrm{RTOH}_i), (+)\ \mathrm{TIME}),$$

where XC_i is the sectoral capacity output, KP_i the sectoral capital stock, CUR_i the sectoral capacity utilization rate of capital, L_i the sectoral number of employees, RTOH_i the ratio of total actual working hours to official working hours by sector and Time the time trend, respectively.

In the old version of DEMIOS with 64 sectors, sectoral capacity output (XC_i) was fully integrated in the I–O block, in which the sectoral capacity outputs were estimated by considering full capacity utilization of capital by sector and the maximum ratio of total actual working hours to official working hours by sector and influenced to the output prices.[1]

3.1.2. *Factor demands*

Even in the Leontief general equilibrium system, the dynamic path of supply–demand relationships is important, especially for the mid-term and

[1]In the current version of DEMIOS with 81 sectors, however, the development of sectoral capacity outputs is now under way for database and regression analysis. Some major sectoral capacity outputs have been developed which are integrated in the model, but other sectors ones are in the process of development.

long-term analyses. Therefore, factor demands, including sectoral capital stock and sectoral labor demand, are also endogenously determined in the I–O block.

Sectoral capital stock is derived from an identity with business investment as an inflow and depreciation of capital as an outflow. Sectoral business investment function basically follows the Jorgenson-type investment function with sectoral output with a positive sign condition (+), one-year lagged capital stock as a stock adjustment with a negative sign condition (−), sectoral relative output price to sectoral total input price, government bond yield (10-year) with a negative sign condition (−) and accumulated government investment as a proxy of the social infrastructure with a positive sign condition (+). Sectoral depreciation of capital is determined by sectoral output with a positive sign condition (+), sectoral capital stock with a positive or negative sign which depends on the sectoral economies and government bond yield (10-year) with a negative sign condition (−). The general specification of these three equations is as follows:

$$\mathrm{KP}_i = \mathrm{KP}_i(-1) + \mathrm{IP}_i - \mathrm{DP}_i,$$

$$\mathrm{IP}_i = f((+)X_i, (-)\mathrm{KP}_i(-1), (-)\mathrm{PX}_i/\mathrm{PZ}_i, (-)\mathrm{INTGB}, (+)\textstyle\sum \mathrm{IG}(-n)),$$

$$\mathrm{DP}_i = f((+)X_i, (+/-)\mathrm{KP}_i(-1), (-)\mathrm{INTGB}),$$

where KP_i is the sectoral capital stock, IP_i the sectoral business investment, DP_i the sectoral input price, INTGB the government bond yield (10-year) and IG the government investment, respectively.

In these factors of production, sectoral business investment is the most critical as a dual effect of investment, affecting both the demand side and the supply side of the economy. Unlike conventional specification of the model for business investment, one of the features of the present model is government investment influences with a two- or three-year time lag to several private sectors such as agriculture, basic manufacturing sectors, public utilities, etc. The regression results of all sectors' business investments are listed in Table A3.2.

The sectoral number of employees as a labor demand is also very important not only for the supply side but also for the demand side by way of income distribution. In the model, the total number of employees by sector consists of wage and salaried employees and workers in unincorporated companies by sector. Accordingly, sectoral wage and salaried employees and sectoral unincorporated company's workers are determined in this sub-block. The general specification of the models for these sectoral variables is as follows:

$$L_i = \mathrm{LW}_i + \mathrm{LU}_i,$$
$$\mathrm{LW}_i = f((+)X_i, (-)W_i/\mathrm{PX}_i, (+)\mathrm{LW}_i(-1)),$$
$$\mathrm{LU}_i = f((+)X_i, (-)W_i/\mathrm{PX}_i, (+)\mathrm{LU}_i(-1)),$$

where L_i is the number of employed by sector, LW_i the sectoral wage and salaried employees, X_i the sectoral output, LU_i the unincorporated enterprise workers by sector, W_i the nominal wage rates and PX_i the output price, respectively.

The sectoral wage and salaried employees are dependent on sectoral output with a positive sign condition (+), sectoral real age rates deflated by output price with a negative sign condition (−) and the Koyck type. In addition, the unincorporated enterprise workers by sector are also the same independent variables. In general, the number of unincorporated enterprise workers is very limited in total number of employed as a whole. Therefore, the number of wage and salaried employees is dominant in many sectors except for primary industry sectors. The regression results of all sectoral wage and salaried employees are listed in Table A3.3.

3.2. Prices and Factor Costs Sub-block

As discussed above, all of the supply and demand variables are cost–price sensitive in the I–O block. Accordingly, it is critical to determine costs and prices endogenously in the model.

Cost side: Unlike a conventional macroeconomic model, prices are uniquely determined in DEMIOS. Since they are mutually interdependent in I–O system and a feedback network between I–O block and macroeconomic block is also important, cost-push and demand-pull are complexly organized. The theoretical models are as follows:

$$Pz_i = Zn_i/Z_i,$$
$$Zn_i = Ur_i \cdot Pr_i + (W_i \cdot L_i + Pk_i \cdot Kp_i) + P_i \cdot V_i \cdot rt,$$
$$Ur_i = \sum_j a_{ij} X_i, \quad i \neq j, 1, 2, \ldots, 81,$$
$$P_i = (1 - \mu_i) Px_i + \mu_i Pm_i,$$

where Pz_i is the sectoral total input price, Zn_i the sectoral nominal total input, Ur_i the sectoral intermediate input, Pr_i the sectoral intermediate input price, W_i the sectoral wage rates, L_i the sectoral employment, Kp_i the sectoral capital stock, Pk_i the sectoral user cost of capital, rt the consumption tax rate P_i the sectoral average price with output price and import price, Px_i the output price, Pm_i the import price and μ_i the import dependency by sector, respectively.

The above equations are important, because the cost side of price formation is affected by not only costs of intermediate products such as row materials, fuels, etc. but also from primary input for wage rates, user cost of capital and consumption tax, etc. Accordingly, all cost side prices such as intermediate input price, wage rates, capital cost, etc. are determined endogenously in this sub-block.

In particular, in the present model, sectoral wage rates are linked with macro nominal wage rates through a feedback network between the I–O block and the macroeconomic block. In addition, sectoral wage rates influence some sectoral prices. Therefore, the sectoral wage rates are one of the key variables in this sub-block. The theoretical model specification of sectoral wage rates function is as follows:

$$\ln W_i = f\left((+)\ln(X_i/\mathrm{LW}_i)\Big/\left(\sum X_i\Big/\sum \mathrm{LW}_i\right),\ (+)\ln W\right),$$

where W_i is the sectoral wage rates, X_i the sectoral output, LW_i the sectoral wage and salaried employees and W the macro nominal wage rates, respectively.

According to the theoretical model, sectoral nominal wage rates are explained by relative sectoral output per employee to averaged sectoral output per employee with a positive sign condition (+) and the macro nominal wage rates which are determined in the macroeconomic block. As discussed above, from the macro nominal wage rates to the sectoral wage rates, one of the feedback relations is performed. In the actual economy, especially in Japan, private and public sectors wage rates changes are heavily dependent on the overall circumstances of wage rates changes in a society rather than individual companies' performances.

The regression results of sectoral wage rates are fairly good and the macro nominal wage rates are very significant in many sectors, as shown in Table A3.4.

Market side: Looking into market side, price functions of DEMIO covers both demand and cost conditions for related sectors as well as total economy. For example, in the case of output price, it is explained by several independent variables, which indicates not only overall market condition such as unemployment rate, import price of competitive products,but also cost conditions and technical progress of input factors such as related raw materials, wage rates, capital cost,consumption tax and exchange rate (¥/$).

In this sub-block, there are several price variables such as input price, output price, import price, etc., as well as factor costs. These sectoral prices are determined in the sub-block as follows:

$$Pz_i = Zn_i/Z_i,$$

$$Pm_i = Pm\$_i \cdot \mathrm{EXRI}/100,$$

$$Px_i = f((+)Zn_i/X_i, (+)D_i/X_i, (-)\mathrm{UR}, (+)Pm_i),$$

$$P_i = (1 - \mu_i)Px_i + \mu_i Pm_i,$$

where Pz_i is the price of total input, Zn_i the sectoral total nominal input, Z_i the sectoral total input, Pm_i the sectoral import price, $Pm\$_i$ the sectoral import price in terms of US$, EXRI the exchange rate (¥/$) index, Px_i the sectoral output price, D_i the sectoral demand for intermediate and final demands, X_i the sectoral output, UR the unemployment rate, P_i the sectoral average price with output price and import price and μ_i the sectoral import dependency, respectively.

Among these prices and factor costs, the output price is one the most important prices which is determined in a behavioral equation. As noted above, sectoral output price (Px_i) is dependent on the ratio of sectoral nominal total input to sectoral output (Z_i/X_i) with a positive sign condition (+), the ratio of sectoral total demand to sectoral output (D_i/X_i) with a positive sign condition (+), macro unemployment rate (UR) with a negative sign condition (−) and sectoral import prices (Pm_i) with a positive sign condition (+).

In the regression analysis, a log-linear function is employed and fairly good results are obtained. In particular, the first independent variable (Zn_i/X_i) and the last independent variable (Pm_i) are dominant as a level of significance, which means sectoral weighted average input price and import price and hence exchange rate are key variables for sectoral output prices. The regression results of all sectoral output prices are shown in Table A3.5.

3.3. I–O Sub-block and VRAS Algorithm

R. Stone proposed a new method for updating a_{ij} of base year for forecasting future a_{ij}, representing technical changes for all sectors. The formula is given by

$$a_{ij} = r_i \cdot a_{ij}^* \cdot s_i,$$

where a_{ij}^* is base year a_{ij}, a_{ij} target year a_{ij}, r_i substitution parameter, s_i efficiency parameter.

This formula has a merit to estimate technical changes in intermediate transactions from I–O table, but does not cover primary factors' input such as those for wages (labor services) and capital services. For more comprehensive analysis, RAS approach needs to cover these primary inputs by increasing the number of row, as shown below:

$$a_{kj} = (r_i + r_m) \cdot a_{kj}^* \cdot s_j, \quad k = 1, 2, 3, \ldots, n + m; \;\; j = 1, 2, 3, \ldots, n,$$

where a_{kj}^* is base year a_{kj}, a_{kj} target year a_{ij}, r_i substitution parameter, s_k efficiency parameter.

This method of extended RAS method, which is named "VRAS" with a rectangular matrix, has been adapted since the previous version. Both the r_k and s_j parameters are estimated annually as well as conventional RAS method and extrapolated annually up to 2020 for policy simulation. The VRAS algorism could be explained by matrix form, as follows:

$$a_{kj} = \begin{bmatrix} a_{11} & \cdots & a_{1n} \\ \vdots & \ddots & \vdots \\ a_{n1} & \cdots & a_{nn} \\ v_{11} & \cdots & v_{1n} \\ \vdots & \ddots & \vdots \\ v_{m1} & \cdots & v_{mn} \end{bmatrix},$$

$$k = 1, 2, 3, \ldots, n + m; \; j = 1, 2, 3, \ldots, n.$$

In addition, based on the above a_{kj}, the VRAS formula and parameters for inter-factor substitution parameter rand total savings (efficiency) parameters are specified as follows:

$$s_j = f(1/\tau_j),$$
$$r_k = f(P_k \ldots), \; k = 1, 2, \ldots, n+m,$$

where r_k is the sectoral substitution parameter, s_j the sectoral efficiency parameter, τ_j the sectoral total factor productivity and P_K the sectoral average price for output price, factor costs and import price, respectively.

Therefore, according to the VRAS algorism, the a_{kj} could be interpolated and extrapolated annually, based on the benchmark input coefficient a^*_{kj} as follows:

$$a_{kj} = (r_i + r_m) \cdot a^*_{kj} \cdot s_j \quad (k = 1, 2, 3, \ldots, n+m; \; j = 1, 2, 3, \ldots, n)$$

$$= (r_1, r_2, \ldots, r_k) \begin{bmatrix} a^*_{11} & \cdot & \cdot & \cdot & \cdot & a^*_{1n} \\ \cdot & \cdot & & & & \cdot \\ \cdot & & \cdot & & & \cdot \\ \cdot & & & \cdot & & \cdot \\ \cdot & & & & \cdot & \cdot \\ a^*_{n1} & \cdot & \cdot & \cdot & \cdot & a^*_{nn} \\ \cdot & & & \cdot & & \cdot \\ \cdot & & \cdot & & & \cdot \\ \cdot & & & & \cdot & \cdot \\ a^*_{k1} & \cdot & \cdot & \cdot & \cdot & a^*_{kn} \end{bmatrix} \begin{bmatrix} s_1 \\ s_2 \\ s_3 \\ \cdot \\ \cdot \\ s_n \\ \cdot \\ \cdot \\ \cdot \\ s_k \end{bmatrix}$$

$$= \begin{bmatrix} r_1 a_{11} s_1 & \cdots & r_1 a_{1n} s_n \\ \vdots & \ddots & \vdots \\ r_n a_1 s_1 & \cdots & r_n a_{nn} s_n \\ \vdots & \ddots & \vdots \\ r_k a_{k1} s_1 & \cdots & r_k a_{kn} s_n \end{bmatrix}$$
$$(k = 1, 2, \ldots, n+m)$$

$$= \begin{bmatrix} a_{11} & \cdots & a_{1n} \\ \vdots & \ddots & \vdots \\ a_{n1} & \cdots & a_{nn} \\ \vdots & \ddots & \vdots \\ a_{k1} & \cdots & a_{kn} \end{bmatrix}$$
$$(k = 1, 2, \ldots, n+m)$$

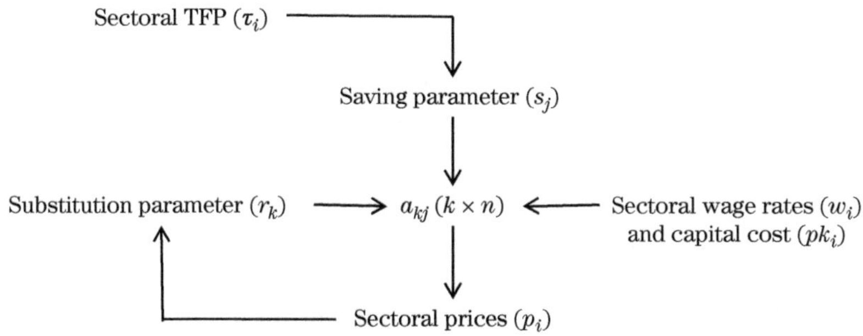

Fig. 3.1. Flowchart of sectoral prices and factor costs and TFP in VRAS.

In summary, the input coefficients derived from VRAS play very important roles in the I–O system. As shown in Fig. 3.1, the sectoral substitution parameter r_k and sectoral efficiency parameter s_j could be determined simultaneously when sectoral total factor productivity τ_j and value-added base prices such as sectoral wage rates and capital cost are given. In addition, it is noteworthy that sectoral prices such as input price, output price and hence average sectoral prices are also determined simultaneously in the system.

As easily understood in Fig. 3.1, cost down in a specific sector by technical progress results in not only declining of that sector prices but also increasing of intermediate demands of related sectors and decreasing of intermediate demands of competitive sectors through substituting effects. Furthermore, as a result, it causes declining of the consumer prices as well and hence positively influences to national economy, as a whole.

As discussed above, the VRAS algorism which implies a price determining mechanism is a general equilibrium-type dynamic forecasting system based on a sectoral technical progress. DEMIOS integrates the VRAS algorism and analyzes changes in not only sectoral technical progress, intermediate demand structure, prices and wage rates, etc. but also macroeconomic structure and dynamism (see Shishido *et al.*, 1991; Shishido and Nakamura, 1992a,b).

3.4. Final Demand Sub-block: Disaggregation of Final Demand

Final demand of DEMIS consists of eight categories: Household consumption, consumption of non-profit organization, housing investment, business investment, changes in inventories, government consumption, government investment and exports. Each category is broken down into 81 sectors by necessary adjustment of I–O table for the year 2000.

In the present version of DEMIOS, disaggregation of final demand components into 81 sectors is a little bit different among categories, but the way of disaggregating has a consistent rule for each category in integrating the I–O block with the macroeconomic block. As is well known in the Leontief economics, it is important how each final demand category is broken down and how the share of each sector in total and its changes are derived, as well as changes in input coefficient, because, their changes are related to the backward linkage and the effects and the changes in input coefficient are to the forward linkage and its effects on the sectoral and the macroeconomy.

Household consumption: Three steps are taken it: (1) aggregate consumption expenditure is first estimated by aggregate disposable income, age component, working hour, and interest rate; (2) 12 categories of consumption expenditure are estimated on the basis of relative prices and aggregate disposable income in real terms; (3) the 12 consumption categories are further broken down into 81 sector components. Price effects are again considered for relevant sectors on the 81 sector basis.

As for the breakdown of aggregate consumption into 12 consumption categories, the 12 categories are dependent on the objective base categories for household consumption. Therefore, these categories are different from the I–O sectoral base order, as shown in Table 3.1.

In the present model, based on the 12 household consumption categories and the I–O sectors, the linkage from macro household consumption

Table 3.1. Breakdown of aggregate consumption into 12 items.

01.	Foods and non-alcohol beverages
02.	Alcohol and tobacco
03.	Clothing and footwear
04.	Dwelling, electricity, gas and water supply
05.	Furniture, household appliances and services
06.	Insurance and medical services
07.	Transport
08.	Communication
09.	Amusement, leisure and culture
10.	Education
11.	Restaurant and hotel
12.	Others

to total of the 12-category base household consumption and to the 81-sectoral base household consumption is considered as follows:

$$\mathrm{CJT} = f((+)\mathrm{CH}),$$

$$\ln \mathrm{CJ}_j = f((-)\ln(\mathrm{PCJ}_j/\mathrm{PCJA}), (+)\mathrm{CJT}, (+)\ln \mathrm{CJ}_j(-1)),$$

$$j = 1, 2, \ldots 12,$$

$$\ln \mathrm{C}_i = f((-)\ln(\mathrm{PC}_i/\mathrm{PCJA}), (+)\mathrm{CJT}, (+)\ln \mathrm{C}_i(-1)),$$

$$i = 1, 2, \ldots, 81,$$

where CJT is the sum of household consumption within the 12 categories, CJ_j the household consumption on a 12-category basis, CP the macro household consumption expenditure, PCJ_j the implicit deflator of CJ_j, PCJA the average PCJ_j and C_i the household consumption on a 81-sectoral basis, respectively.

As discussed above, the three-step procedure completes the linkage from macro household consumption (CH) to the 12-category base household consumption (CJ_j) and to sectoral household consumption (C_i) by employing the Rotterdam School Model.[2] In the first step, the sum of the 12-category base household consumption is determined by macrohousehold consumption which is derived in the macroeconomic block. Next, the 12-category base household consumption is decided by the relative implicit deflator of the category base household consumption to average implicit deflator of the 12-category base household and the Koyck type by utilizing the Rotterdam School Model.

Finally, in the third step, sectoral household consumption is determined by the relative implicit deflator of the sectoral base household consumption to average implicit deflator of the 12-category base household and the Koyck type, as well as the 12-category base household consumption. (See Table 3.2 for the regression results of the 12-category base household consumption.)

[2]In this analysis, we utilize a simplified formula of the Rotterdam School Model approach, but the performance of the regression results is fairly strong as shown in Table 3.2. As for the Rotterdam School Model, see Barten (1964) and Theil (1965).

Table 3.2. Regression results of real household consumption expenditure on a 12-category basis by the Rotterdam School Model.

01. Foods and non-alcohol beverages

$$\ln CJ01 = 4.336 - 0.216 \ln PCJ01/PCJA + 0.184 \ln CJTL(-1) + 0.378 \ln CJ01(-1)$$

(3.486)*** (−1.113) (2.236)* (1.953)*

$$R^2ADJ = 0.974 \quad SD = 0.0583 \quad DW = 2.010$$

02. Alcohol and tobacco

$$\ln CJ02 = 0.257 - 0.562 \ln PCJ02/PCJA + 0.249 \ln CJTL + 0.629 \ln CJ02(-2)$$

(0.837) (−4.840)*** (4.837)*** (8.510)***

$$R^2ADJ = 0.973 \quad SD = 0.117 \quad DW = 1.698$$

03. Clothing and footwear

$$\ln CJ03 = 1.152 - 4.493 \ln PCJ03/PCJA + 0.802 \ln CJTL - 0.519 \ln UR(-1)$$

(0.308) (−6.056)*** (2.983)*** (−10.317)***

$$-0.358 \ln EXR(-1)$$

(−2.103)*

$$R^2ADJ = 0.912 \quad SD = 0.171 \quad DW = 0.685$$

04. Dwelling, electricity, gas and water supply

$$\ln CJ04 = -0.980 - 0.118 \ln PCJ04/PCJA + 0.220 \ln CJTL + 0.840 \ln CJ04(-1)$$

(−4.668)*** (−0.908) (3.436)*** (12.061)***

$$R^2ADJ = 0.999 \quad SD = 0.226 \quad DW = 1.174$$

05. Furniture, household appliances and services

$$\ln CJ05 = -1.708 - 0.122 \ln PCJ05/PCJA + 0.505 \ln CJTL - 0.087 \ln UR(-2)$$

(−0.095) (−0.573) (2.509)** (−1.728)

$$+0.525 \ln CJ05(-1)$$

(4.834)***

$$R^2ADJ = 0.986 \quad SD = 0.195 \quad DW = 1.945$$

06. Insurance and medical services

$$CJ06/CJTL = -0.0205 - 0.0578 \ PC06(-4)/PCAJ(-6) + 0.14269 \ CJTL/CJTL(-1)$$

(−0.595) (−2.232)* (5.499)***

$$-0.000489 \ ROUSP(-2) + 0.000129 \ EXR(-1)$$

(−9.652)*** (9.887)***

$$R^2ADJ = 0.913 \quad SD = 0.0043 \quad DW = 1.654$$

07. Transport

$$\ln CJ07 = -3.992 - 1.582 \ln PCJ07/PCJA + 1.141 \ln CJTL$$

(−3.149)*** (−3.069)*** (11.243)***

$$R^2ADJ = 0.955 \quad SD = 0.259 \quad DW = 0.380$$

08. Communication

$$CJ08 = -10939.270 - 17850.53 \ PCJ08(-4)/PCAVJ(-4) + 28810.31 \ PCJ07(-5)/PCAJ(-5)$$

(−0.712) (−6.009)*** (2.703)**

$$+0.0222 \ CJTL(-6) + 33.644 \ EXR(-1)$$

(1.152) (7.974)***

$$R^2ADJ = 0.981 \quad SD = 2694.010 \quad DW = 1.961$$

09. Amusement, leisure and culture

$$CJ09 = 45808.190 - 46356.470 \ PCJ09(-1)/PCAJ(-1) + 0.147 \ CJTL(-1)$$

(3.968)*** (−5.875)*** (14.114)***

$$-1749.783 \ UR$$

(−2.663)**

$$R^2ADJ = 0.973 \quad SD = 7979.929 \quad DW = 0.603$$

(*Continued*)

Table 3.2. (*Continued*)

10. Education

$$\ln CJ10 = \underset{(2.598)^{**}}{5.341} - \underset{(-1.222)}{0.217} \ln PCJ10/PCJA + \underset{(2.1573)^{*}}{0.330} \ln CJTL(-1) - \underset{(-5.578)^{***}}{0.111} \ln UR + \underset{(3.754)^{***}}{1.503} \ln(NP15/NPT)$$

$R^2ADJ = 0.968$ $SD = 0.054$ $DW = 1.202$

11. Restaurant and hotel

$$\ln CJ11 = \underset{(-4.558)^{***}}{-6.641} - \underset{(-3.820)^{***}}{1.357} \ln PCJ11/PCJA + \underset{(11.489)^{***}}{1.340} \ln CJTL + \underset{(2.979)^{***}}{0.000825} EXR$$

$R^2ADJ = 0.968$ $SD = 0.144$ $DW = 0.843$

12. Others

$$\ln CJ12 = \underset{(-9.229)^{***}}{-3.576} - \underset{(-13.101)^{***}}{2.240} \ln PCJ12/PCJA + \underset{(35.430)^{***}}{1.111} \ln CJTL$$

$R^2ADJ = 0.986$ $SD = 0.230$ $DW = 0.945$

Note: ***, ** and * present the level of significance at 1%, 5% and 10%, respectively.

Business investment: In the I–O block, there are two types of sectoral business invest including the one as a factor demand and another demand for the final demand. The former one is a business investment which has already discussed earlier in the production and factor demand sub-block, whereas the latter is one of the final demands in this final demand sub-block.

The sectoral business investment for the final demand is derived within a two-step procedure as follows:

$$IPDT = \sum_i IP_i,$$

$$IPD_i/IPDT = f((-)PIPD_I/PIPDT, (+)IPD_i(-1)/IPDT(-1)),$$

$$IP = f((+)IPDT),$$

where IPDT is the sum of the sectoral business investment demand for the final demand, IP_i the sectoral business investment as a production factor, IPD_i the sectoral business investment demand for the final demand, $PIPD_i$ the implicit deflator of sectoral business investment demand, PIPDT the average implicit deflator of business investment for the final demand and IP the macro real business (non-housing) investment, respectively.

In the case of business investment for the final demand, in the first step, total sectoral business investment for the final demand (IPDT) is derived from the sum of sectoral business investment (IP_i) in an identity. In the second step, sectoral business investment for the final demand is determined by relative prices of implicit deflator of business investment demand ($PIPD_i$) to average implicit deflator of business investment final demand (PIPDT) with a negative sign condition (−) and the Koyck type with a positive sign condition (+) in the share function.

Therefore, with respect to the feedback channel between the I–O block and the macroeconomic block, sectoral business investment is determined first, and the sum of the sectoral business investment determines the macro real business (non-housing) investment in DEMIOS.

Exports: Each sectoral export variable is directly estimated as a function of world imports and relative export prices after adjustment to exchange rate (¥/$), based on the modified Mandell–Fleming Model, as well as sectoral imports discussed in the production and factor demand sub-block of this chapter. Three factors play important roles: world import demand of relevant commodity, their relative prices and yen-US$ exchange rate, as follows:

$$E_i = f((+)TWM_i, (-)PE_i/EXR/PEW_i),$$

where TWM_i is the total world imports of relevant sector, PE_i the sectoral export price in terms of yen, PEW the world import price of relevant sector in terms of US$ and EXR the exchange rate (yen/US$), respectively.

The regression results are shown in Table A3.6 for major export sectors.

Housing investment, government consumption, government investment and inventory changes: Unlike the some final demand components as discussed above, calculation of sectoral final demand components such as housing investment, government consumption, government investment and inventory changes is derived as a fixed share on the 81-sector basis. In this model, these sectoral components are derived by the share matrix β_{ik}. It is a matrix which consists of eight column vectors, including (1) household consumption, (2) consumption of non-profit institution, (3) housing investment, (4) business investment, (5) government consumption, (6) government investment, (7) inventory changes and

(8) exports. For household consumption, business investment and exports, each β_{ik} is decided after deriving related sectoral final demand. However, for housing investment, government consumption, government investment and inventory changes, each sectoral final demand is derived from β_{ik} and the sum of the related sectoral final demand. The sum of the related sectoral final demand is derived by related macro-GDP components which are decide in the macroeconomic block, as follows:

$$\mathrm{IH}_{82} = f((+)\mathrm{IH}),$$

$$\mathrm{CG}_{82} = f((+)\mathrm{CG}),$$

$$\mathrm{IG}_{82} = f((+)\mathrm{IG}),$$

$$J_{82} = f((+)J),$$

$$\mathrm{IH}_i = \beta_{ik} \cdot \mathrm{IH}_{82},$$

$$\mathrm{CG}_i = \beta_{ik} \cdot \mathrm{CG}_{82},$$

$$\mathrm{IG}_i = \beta_{ik} \cdot \mathrm{IG}_{82},$$

$$J_i = \beta_{ik} \cdot \mathrm{J}_{82},$$

where IH_{82} is the sum of sectoral housing investment as the 81st sector, CG_{82} the sum of sectoral government consumption as the 81st sector, IG_{82} the sum of sectoral investment as the 81st sector, J_{82} the sum of sectoral inventory changes as the 82nd sector, IH the macro housing investment, CG the macro government consumption, IG the macro government investment, J the macro inventory changes, IH_i the sectoral housing investment final demand, CG_i the sectoral government consumption, IG_i the sectoral government investment and J_i the sectoral inventory changes, respectively.

As noted above, these four sectoral final demands are derived from the statistical relations between sum of the sectoral final demand and macro related variables and the share matrix. The future projections requires, therefore, to extrapolate the share matrix for these four variables, because the government consumption, government investment and their sectoral shares are important for the policy simulations as policy variables.

Appendix: Regression Results for Sectoral M, IP, LW, W, PX and E

Table A3.1. Major sectoral import regression results.

$$\mathrm{M01/D01} = \underset{(-0.38)}{-0.0103} - \underset{(-1.95)^{*}}{0.02075}\ \mathrm{PM01/PD01} + \underset{(8.77)^{***}}{6.37\mathrm{E}-05}\ \mathrm{CP82(-1)/NPT(-1)}$$
$$\underset{(-1.59)}{-0.0285}\ \mathrm{-D01/D01(-2)} + \underset{(2.06)^{*}}{0.000219}\ \mathrm{EXR}$$
$$R^2\mathrm{ADJ} = 0.931 \quad \mathrm{SD} = 0.0227 \quad \mathrm{DW} = 1.085$$

$$\mathrm{M03/D03} = \underset{(-2.07)^{*}}{-0.0581} - \underset{(-4.33)^{***}}{0.000966}\ \mathrm{PM03/PD03} + \underset{(3.14)^{***}}{0.00924}\mathrm{D03(-1)/D03(-2)}$$
$$\underset{(-1.46)}{-2.63 - \mathrm{E06}}\ \mathrm{EXR(-1)}\ \underset{(-1.96)^{*}}{-0.000988}\ \mathrm{DUM93}$$
$$R^2\mathrm{ADJ} = 0.529 \quad \mathrm{SD} = 0.00067 \quad \mathrm{DW} = 1.191$$

$$\mathrm{M07/D07} = \underset{(2.40)^{**}}{0.2294} - \underset{(-2.08)^{*}}{0.05179}\ \mathrm{PM07/PD07} + \underset{(4.06)^{***}}{0.000124}\ \mathrm{CP82/NPT}$$
$$\underset{(-3.81)^{***}}{-0.00072}\ \mathrm{EXR(-1)} - \underset{(-13.39)^{***}}{0.2264}\ \mathrm{DUM8805}$$
$$R^2\mathrm{ADJ} = 0.872 \quad \mathrm{SD} = 0.049 \quad \mathrm{DW} = 1.539$$

$$\mathrm{M08/D08} = \underset{(0.27)}{0.0479} - \underset{(-4.71)^{***}}{0.3008}\ \mathrm{PM08/PD08} + \underset{(7.80)^{***}}{0.2538}\ \mathrm{GDP/NPT}$$
$$\underset{(-4.48)^{***}}{-0.00131}\ \mathrm{EXR}\ \underset{(2.59)^{**}}{-0.2264}\ \mathrm{DUM0103}$$
$$R^2\mathrm{ADJ} = 0.959 \quad \mathrm{SD} = 0.156 \quad \mathrm{DW} = 1.495$$

$$\mathrm{M09/D09} = \underset{(4.64)^{***}}{2.3707} - \underset{(-2.43)^{**}}{1.2067}\ \mathrm{PM09(-4)/PD09(-4)} + \underset{(1.61)}{0.00179}\ \mathrm{GDP/NPT}$$
$$\underset{(-3.68)^{***}}{-0.2207}\ \mathrm{D09/D09(-1)} - \underset{(-3.94)^{***}}{0.0895}\ \mathrm{DUM0103} + \underset{(2.34)^{**}}{0.0516}\ \mathrm{DUM95}$$
$$R^2\mathrm{ADJ} = 0.611 \quad \mathrm{SD} = 0.045 \quad \mathrm{DW} = 2.273$$

$$\mathrm{M10/D10} = \underset{(4.86)^{***}}{1.3349} - \underset{(-1.76)}{0.2798}\ \mathrm{PM10/PD10} + \underset{(2.09)^{*}}{0.04865}\ \mathrm{GDP/NPT}$$
$$\underset{(-4.62)^{***}}{-0.3030}\ \mathrm{D10/D10(-1)} + \underset{(2.65)^{**}}{0.0778}\ \mathrm{DUM0103} + \underset{(0.84)}{0.0377}\ \mathrm{DUM97}$$
$$R^2\mathrm{ADJ} = 0.795 \quad \mathrm{SD} = 0.0937 \quad \mathrm{DW} = 1.507$$

$$\mathrm{M14/D14} = \underset{(3.59)^{***}}{0.3856} - \underset{(-10.17)^{***}}{0.1672}\ \mathrm{PM14/PD14} + \underset{(3.26)^{***}}{0.03503}\ \mathrm{GDP(-4)/NPT(-4)}$$
$$\underset{(-4.62)^{***}}{-0.1022}\ \mathrm{D14(-2)/D14(-3)} - \underset{(-2.11)^{*}}{0.10224}\ \mathrm{EXR}$$
$$R^2\mathrm{ADJ} = 0.922 \quad \mathrm{SD} = 0.0497 \quad \mathrm{DW} = 1.756$$

(*Continued*)

Table A3.1. (*Continued*)

$$M21/D21 = \underset{(-0.24)}{-0.02575} - \underset{(-0.89)}{0.0681}\ PM21(-2)/PD21(-2) + \underset{(4.81)^{***}}{0.000137}\ CP82/NPT$$
$$\underset{(-1.31)}{-0.0681}\ D21/D21(-1) + \underset{(9.11)^{***}}{0.1594}\ DUM0103$$
$$R^2ADJ = 0.929 \quad SD = 0.0969 \quad DW = 1.896$$

$$M23/D23 = \underset{(-0.14)}{-0.02796} - \underset{(-1.48)}{0.0681}\ PM23(-5)/PD21(-5) + \underset{(5.32)^{***}}{0.00022}\ CP82/NPT$$
$$+\underset{(7.58)^{***}}{0.2376}\ DUM0103$$
$$R^2ADJ = 0.904 \quad SD = 0.1494 \quad DW = 1.565$$

$$M24/D24 = \underset{(-1.99)^{*}}{-0.0112} - \underset{(-3.35)^{***}}{0.1372}\ PM24/PD24 + \underset{(18.69)^{***}}{0.000357}\ CP82/NPT$$
$$+\underset{(1.68)}{0.1121}\ D24/D24(-1) + \underset{(4.83)^{***}}{0.1180}\ DUM0103$$
$$R^2ADJ = 0.953 \quad SD = 0.1669 \quad DW = 1.315$$

$$M25/D25 = \underset{(-2.16)^{*}}{-0.1178} - \underset{(-2.46)^{**}}{0.0524}\ PM25(-1)/PD25(-1) + \underset{(14.75)^{***}}{0.000149}\ CP82/NPT$$
$$+\underset{(1.12)}{0.05252}\ D25/D25(-1) + \underset{(6.01)^{***}}{0.0561}\ DUM0103$$
$$R^2ADJ = 0.967 \quad SD = 0.0748 \quad DW = 1.470$$

$$M26/D26 = \underset{(1.76)}{0.09854} - \underset{(-3.50)^{**}}{0.03179}\ PM26/PD26 + \underset{(4.67)^{***}}{3.84 - E0.5}\ CP82/NPT$$
$$\underset{(-1.70)}{-0.08232}\ D26/D26(-1) + \underset{(7.76)^{***}}{0.0809}\ DUM0103$$
$$R^2ADJ = 0.918 \quad SD = 0.0471 \quad DW = 2.134$$

$$M33/D33 = \underset{(0.085)}{0.001498} - \underset{(-5.34)^{**}}{0.05844}\ PM33/PD33 + \underset{(12.77)^{***}}{0.00433}\ GDP/NPT$$
$$+\underset{(5.38)^{***}}{0.04105}\ DUM0104$$
$$R^2ADJ = 0.924 \quad SD = 0.0415 \quad DW = 0.924$$

$$M37/D37 = \underset{(2.73)^{**}}{-0.04840} - \underset{(-1.46)}{0.01136}\ PM37/PD37 + \underset{(11.59)^{***}}{0.01852}\ GDP/NPT$$
$$+\underset{(2.03)^{*}}{0.02642}\ IP/IP(-1) - \underset{(-2.575)^{**}}{0.00893}\ DUM0104$$
$$R^2ADJ = 0.849 \quad SD = 0.01305 \quad DW = 1.496$$

$$M38/D38 = \underset{(-2.98)^{***}}{-0.03012} - \underset{(-2.93)^{***}}{0.0131}\ PM38/PD38 + \underset{(12.20)^{***}}{0.01131}\ GDP/NPT$$
$$+\underset{(3.59)^{***}}{0.02643}\ IP/IP(-1) - \underset{(-1.65)}{0.02975}\ DUM0104$$
$$R^2ADJ = 0.886 \quad SD = 0.00801 \quad DW = 1.646$$

(*Continued*)

Table A3.1. (*Continued*)

$$M41/D41 = \underset{(-1.57)}{-0.0291} - \underset{(-2.54)^{**}}{0.01526}\ PM41/PD41 + \underset{(4.64)^{***}}{0.01275}\ GDP(-1)/NPT(-1)$$
$$+\underset{(0.88)}{0.00783}\ IP/IP(-1) + \underset{(8.77)^{***}}{0.018597}\ DUM0104 + \underset{(2.46)^{*}}{0.007812}\ DUM00$$
$$R^2ADJ = 0.924 \quad SD = 0.01073 \quad DW = 1.018$$

$$M47/D47 = \underset{(1.14)}{0.02845} - \underset{(-3.60)^{**}}{0.03180}\ PM47/PD47 + \underset{(2.49)^{**}}{0.01188}\ GDP/NPT$$
$$\underset{(-1.32)}{-5.64E-05}\ EXR(-2) + \underset{(2.56)^{**}}{0.00815}\ DUM0104 + \underset{(2.26)^{*}}{0.011+23}\ DUM96$$
$$R^2ADJ = 0.854 \quad SD = 0.01249 \quad DW = 0.957$$

Notes: (1) ***, ** and * present the level of significance at 1%, 5% and 10%, respectively.
(2) Sector classification: 01 General crops, 02 Industrial crops, 03 Livestock for foods, 04 Livestock for fiber, 05 Agriculture services, 06 Forestry, 07 Fishery, 08 Coal mining, 09 Crude petroleum, 10 Natural gas, 11 Iron mining, 12 Non-metal mining, 13 Other mining, 14 Meat and dairy products, 15 Manufactured sea foods, 16 Grain products, 17 Other foods, 18 Beverages, 19 Feedstuff, 20 Tobacco, 21 Natural and chemical textiles, 22 Other textiles, 23 Wearing apparel, 24 Leather and leather products, 25 Wood and wood products, 26 Furniture, 27 Pulp and paper, 28 Printing and publishing, 29 Coal product, 30 Petroleum product, 31 Basic and intermediate chemicals, 32 Fats, oils and final chemicals, 33 Rubber products, 34 Plastic products, 35 Cement, 36 Other ceramics, 37 Iron products, 38 Rolling, casting and forgings, 39 Aluminum (including secondary), 40 Other non-ferrous products, 41 Metal products, 42 Office machinery, 43 Other general machinery, 44 Industrial electrical machinery, 45 Consumer electrical machinery, 46 Precision machinery, 47 Automobile, 48 Railway vehicle, 49 Shipbuilding, 50 Aircraft, 51 Other transport equipment, 52 Miscellaneous manufacturing, 53 Housing construction, 54 Industrial construction, 55 Public construction, 56 Other construction, 57 Electric power, 58 Gas, 59 Water and sanitary service, 60 Waste disposal, 61 Wholesale and retail trade, 62 Automobile mechanical repair, 63 Hotel and restaurant, 64 Railways, 65 Trucks and buses, 66 Water transportation, 67 Air transport, 68 Other transportation, 69 Communications, 70 Finance and insurance, 71 Real estate, 72 Information processing services, 73 Other corporation services, 74 Research and development, 75 Public services, 76 Education, 77 Medical insurance, 78 Other public services, 79 Other services for individuals, 80 Office supplies, 81 Unallocated.

Table A3.2. Regression results of sectoral business investment.

$$IP01 = 526.520 + 4.30E-05\ X01(-1) - 0.00988\ KP01(-5) + 64.274\ PX01(-3)/PZ01(-3)$$
(1.753) (1.69) (−1.95)* (0.68)

$$+2.0814\ EXR(-2)$$
(5.09)***

$R^2ADJ = 0.8478$ SD = 204.02 DW = 0.840

$$IP02 = 50.014 + 1.65E05\ X02(-1) - 0.00599\ KP02(-5) + 14.708\ PX02(-4)/PZ02(-4)$$
(1.77) (1.20) (−3.29)*** (2.70)**

$$-1.7908\ INTGB(-2) + 0.1399\ EXR(-1) + 1.06E-05\ IGX5(-1)$$
(−1.44) (3.15)*** (3.04)***

$R^2ADJ = 0.755$ SD = 10.64 DW = 1.924

$$IP03 = 159.889 + 5.47E-05\ X03 - 0.00201\ KP03(-5) + 25.213\ PX03(-2)/PZ(-2)$$
(1.71) (2.14)* (−0.51) (0.83)

$$-5.091\ INTGB(-1) + 0.3369\ EXR(-3) + 2.49E05\ IGX5$$
(−1.79) (1.96)* (2.65)**

$R^2ADJ = 0.344$ SD = 24.38 DW = 1.460

$$IP04 = -3.506 + 0.000113\ X04 - 0.000598\ KP04(-1) + 13.741\ PX04(-2)/PZ04(-2)$$
(−0.43) (8.96)*** (−0.63) (2.11)*

$R^2ADJ = 0.870$ SD = 17.28 DW = 1.370

$$IP05 = 29.095 + 0.000134\ X05 + 0.00191\ KP05(-1) + 6.71E-06\ IGX5$$
(1.29) (3.48)*** (0.41) (1.37)

$R^2ADJ = 0.508$ SD = 17.81 DW = 0.986

$$IP06 = -12.884 + 8.86E-05\ X06(-1) - 0.0217\ (KP06(-6) + KP06(-7) + KP06(-8))$$
(−0.077) (0.92) (−1.39)

$$+26.058\ PX06(-2)/PZ06(-2) + IP06(-1)$$
(0.73) (3.28)***

$R^2ADJ = 0.380$ SD = 37.14 DW = 1.421

$$IP07 = 131.336 + 6.07E-05\ X07 - 0.0061\ KP07(-4) + 78.252 PX07/PZ07(-1) + 0.857\ P07(-1)$$
(−1.19) (2.40)** (−1.01) (1.00) (8.75)***

$R^2ADJ = 0.897$ SD = 117.74 DW = 2.661

$$IP08 = 0.704 + 7.72E-05\ X08 - 0.0089\ KP08(-2) + 2.999\ PX(-1)/PZ(-1)$$
(0.61) (10.51)*** (1.27) (3.11)***

$R^2ADJ = 0.920$ SD = 8.211 DW = 1.8234

$$IP09 = -0.44793 + 0.386\ X09(-1) + 0.00069\ KP09(-4) + 0.2834\ PX09(-2)/PZ09(-2)$$
(1.24) (6.73)*** (0.98) (2.39)**

$$-0.00804\ INTGB(-3)$$
(−1.93)

$R^2ADJ = 0.746$ SD = 0.434 DW = 1.786

$$IP10 = 4.273 + 4.78E-05\ X10 + 0.0112\ KP10(-1) - 0.635\ PX10(-1)/PZ10(-1)$$
(1.74) (1.58) (2.04)* (−3.02)***

$R^2ADJ = 0.325$ SD = 1.439 DW = 1.886

$$IP11 = -0.0036 + 7.30E-05\ X11 - 0.00285\ KP11(-2) - 0.0094\ PX11/PZ11$$
(−0.07) (6.59)*** (−0.23) (−0.27)

$$-0.0021\ INTGB(-3) + 0.00209\ PX11/PM11$$
(−0.48) (2.36)**

$R^2ADJ = 0.904$ SD = 0.146 DW = 1.008

(Continued)

Table A3.2. (*Continued*)

IP12 = 1.9947 + 0.000162 X12 − 0.00311 KP12(−2) − 0.02474 PX12(−6)/PX12(−6)
(1.55) (5.97)*** (−1.17) (−0.69)
R^2ADJ = 0.710 SD = 1.775 DW = 1.687

IP13 = 66.644 + 2.82E − 05 X13 + 0.0256 KP13(−3) − 18.269 PX13(−2)/PZ13(−2)
(1.43) (1.86) (1.57) (−0.83)
R^2ADJ = 0.128 SD = 18.767 DW = 1.573

IP14 = 604.266 + 1.44E − 05 X14 − 0.0451 KP14(−4) − 156.408 PX14(−1)/PZ14(−1)
(2.37)* (0.82) (−0.72) (−1.03)
−24.576 INTGB(−2) − 0.484 EXR(−4)
(−3.76)*** (−2.16)*
R^2ADJ = 0.885 SD = 84.093 DW = 1.961

IP15 = −88.905 + 2.54E − 05 X15(−1) + 0.00379 KP15(−4) + 115.387 PX15(−1)/PZ15(−1)
(−1.88) (2.76)** (0.14) (1.92)*
−6.182 INTGB(−3)
(−1.50)
R^2ADJ = 0.725 SD = 33.016 DW = 1.845

IP16 = −13.947 + 2.30E − 05X16(−1) −0.0352 KP16(−5) + 19.762 PX16(−5)/PZ16(−5)
(−0.38) (2.33)* (−0.81) (0.86)
−3.907 INTGB(−1) − 0.135 EXR(−3)
(−1.82) (−2.08)*
R^2ADJ = 0.414 SD = 9.734 DW = 1.566

IP17 = −116.437 + 7.11E + 05 X17(−4) − 0.0162 KP17(−6) + 390.141 PX17(−7)/PZ17(−7)
(−0.21) (2.59)** (−0.425) (1.47)
−66.366 INTGB(−3)
(−3.19)***
R^2ADJ = 0.856 SD = 216.98 DW = 2.523

IP18 = −330.906 +0.000208 XP18 − 0.293 KP18(−3) + 197.144 PX18(−5)/PZ18(−5)
(−1.00) (6.21)*** (−4.99)*** (0.80)
−65.097 INTGB(−2)
(−4.02)***
R^2ADJ = 0.833 SD = 189.41 DW = 2.071

IP19 = −37.175 + 6.12E − 05 X19(−7) − 0.113 KP19(−8) + 30.827 PX19(−6)/PZ19(−6)
(−0.72) (2.97)** (−1.05) (3.64)***
−0.941 INTGB(−3)
(−0.66)
R^2ADJ = 0.366 SD = 10.738 DW = 2.115

IP20 = 61.437 + 3.22E − 05 X20(−6) + 0.0230 KP20(−7) − 51.871 PX20(−1)/PZ20(−1)
(0.55) (1.34) (0.31) (−0.71)
−0.486 EXR + 163.142 DUM99
(−3.01)*** (6.59)***
R^2ADJ = 0.751 SD = 46.408 DW = 0.754

IP21 = −547.773 + 0.000147 X21 − 0.125 KP21(−3) + 49.228 PX21/PZ21 + 0.00215 CP(−1)
(−2.59)** (4.21)*** (−2.62)** (0.91) (3.69)***
R^2ADJ = 0.384 SD = 59.237 DW = 1.355

IP22 = −71.751 + 8.84E − 05 X22(−1) − 0.0154 KP22(−6) + 24.048 PX22(−3)/PZ22(−3)
(−0.52) (2.91)*** (−0.47) (0.25)
−8.377 INTGB(−2) + 5.68E − 06 IGXSUM(−4)
(−1.06) (1.02)
R^2ADJ = 0.583 SD = 55.119 DW = 1.151

(*Continued*)

Table A3.2. (*Continued*)

$$IP23 = 108.509 + 3.55E-06\ X23(-1) - 0.0512\ KP23(-4) - 57.998\ PX23(-1)/PZ23(-1)$$
(1.17) (0.79) (−0.82) (−0.91)

$$-10.250\ INTGB(-1) + 7.59E-06\ IGXSUM(-2)$$
(−0.91) (3.05)***

$R^2ADJ = 0.786$ SD = 49.804 DW = 1.321

$$IP24 = 6.858 + 2.83E-06\ X24 - 0.0531 KP24(-3) - 2.904\ PX24(-2)/PZ(-2) - 2.194\ INTGB(-2)$$
(0.36) (3.78)*** (−0.67) (−0.19) (−2.90)**

$R^2ADJ = 0.305$ SD = 5.329 DW = 1.178

$$IP25 = 12.803 + 2.05E-05 X25(-2) - 0.102\ KP25(-4) + 123.835\ PX25(-4)/PZ25(-4)$$
(0.14) (2.01)* (−5.72)** (1.40)

$$-7.650\ INTGB(-2)$$
(−3.12)***

$R^2ADJ = 0.499$ SD = 26.269 DW = 1.607

$$IP26 = 103.170 + 3.04E-05\ X26(-2) - 0.300\ KP26(-4) - 10.284\ INTGB(-2)$$
(2.30)* (2.16)* (−3.86)*** (−2.03)*

$$+6.07E-06\ IGXSUM(-2)$$
(1.73)

$R^2ADJ = 0.704$ SD = 36.974 DW = 1.415

$$IP27 = -969.549 + 0.000186\ X27 - 0.0548\ KP27(-2) + 752.589\ PX27(-1)/PZ27(-1)$$
(−1.27) (6.23)*** (−1.69) (1.73)

$$-54.800\ INTGB(-2)$$
(−3.89)***

$R^2ADJ = 0.876$ SD = 207.78 DW = 1.554

$$IP28 = -94.933 + 0.000107\ X28 - 0.0377\ KP28(-2) + 34.003\ PX28(-6)/PZ28(-6)$$
(−0.18) (6.05)*** (−1.59) (0.09)

$$-59.699\ INTGB(-2)$$
(−3.70)***

$R^2ADJ = 0.894$ SD = 222.09 DW = 1.394

$$IP29 = 194.533 + 3.99E-05 X29 - 0.0261\ KP29(-1) + 39.979\ PX29(-1)/PZ29(-1)$$
(1.16) (0.59) (−2.65)* (0.58)

$$-15.472\ INTGB(-3)$$
(−2.02)*

$R^2ADJ = 0.274$ SD = 42.276 DW = 1.940

$$IP30 = 785.681 + 2.37E-05\ X30 + 0.0357\ KP30(-5) - 368.042\ PX30(-5)/PZ30(-5)$$
(2.87)** (1.39) (0.54) (−2.37)*

$$-22.948\ INTGB(-3)$$
(−2.21)*

$R^2ADJ = 0.527$ SD = 97.453 DW = 1.283

$$IP31 = 2901.763 + 0.000177\ X31 - 0.217\ KP31(-4) - 456.750\ PX31(-1)/PZ31(-1)$$
(2.36)* (2.74)** (−4.09)*** (−0.752)

$$-111.112\ INTGB(-3) + 3.56E-05\ IGXSUM$$
(−0.75) (1.82)

$R^2ADJ = 0.787$ SD = 316.42 DW = 1.315

$$IP32 = -607.427 + 9.95E-05\ X32(-1) - 0.0633\ KP32(-2) + 310.327\ PX32(-7)/PZ32(-7)$$
(0.48) (2.51)** (−1.55) (0.56)

$$-12.980\ INTGB(-2) + 4.54E-06\ IGXSUM(-2)$$
(−0.50) (0.38)

$R^2ADJ = 0.864$ SD = 240.50 DW = 1.740

(*Continued*)

Table A3.2. (*Continued*)

$$IP33 = -74.547 + 0.000165\ X33 - 0.0951\ KP33(-2) + 116.007\ PX33(-6)/PZ33(-6)$$
(−0.32) (5.27)*** (−1.50) (0.56)

$$-21.102\ INTGB(-2)$$
(−2.95)***

$R^2ADJ = 0.707$ $SD = 80.909$ $DW = 1.279$

$$IP34 = 173.139 + 9.26E-05X34 - 0.0209KP34(-2) + 153.280\ PX34(-1)/PZ34(-1)$$
(0.42) (6.87)*** (−0.48) (0.37)

$$-59.284\ INTGB(-2)$$
(−3.18)***

$R^2ADJ = 0.926$ $SD = 320.85$ $DW = 1.180$

$$IP35 = -401.504 + 0.000103X35(-1) - 0.0205\ KP35(-4) + 316.935\ PX35(-1)/pz35(-1)$$
(−1.485) (4.47)*** (−0.82) (2.31)*

$$-23.781\ INTGB(-2) + 5.19E-06\ IGXSUM$$
(−5.10)*** (1.12)

$R^2ADJ = 0.776$ $SD = 76.978$ $DW = 1.415$

$$IP36 = -668.752 + 0.000264\ X36 - 0.0140\ KP36(-4) - 1.985\ PX36/PZ36 - 60.805\ INTGB(-3)$$
(−1.076) (4.614)*** (−0.560) (−0.703) (−3.518)***

$$2.06E-05\ IGXSUM(-3) + 1.987\ EXR(-1)$$
(2.587)** (2.642)**

$R^2ADJ = 0.833$ $SD = 194.26$ $DW = 1.392$

$$IP37 = -531.499 + 0.000184X37(-1) - 0.0150KP37(-2) + 918.372\ PX37(-1)/PZ37(-1)$$
(−0.89) (2.44)** (−0.63) (2.89)**

$$-46.910\ INTGB(-5)$$
(−2.01)*

$R^2ADJ = 0.437$ $SD = 182.22$ $DW = 1.882$

$$IP38 = -2778.922 + 0.000150X38 - 0.00322KP38(-1) + 2157.175PX38/PZ38$$
(−4.56)*** (6.07)*** (−0.13) (4.79)***

$$-81.906\ INTGB(-2) - 2.60E-06\ IGXSUM$$
(−3.92)*** (−0.20)

$R^2ADJ = 0.829$ $SD = 270.95$ $DW = 2.115$

$$IP40 = 367.121 + 7.38E-05\ X40 - 0.112\ KP40(-5) + 270.941\ PX40(-2)/PZ40(-2)$$
(0.66) (0.79) (−2.19)* (0.87)

$$-101.722\ INTGB(-2) + 3.64E-05\ IGXSUM(-4)$$
(−4.37)*** (2.76)**

$R^2ADJ = 0.890$ $SD = 328.82$ $DW = 0.975$

$$IP41 = 588.945 + 7.46E-05X41 - 0.00644\ KP41(-2) - 265.630\ PX41/PZ41$$
(0.64) (3.20)*** (−0.20) (−0.57)

$$-74.927\ INTGB(-2) + 1.46E-05\ IGXSUM(-3)$$
(−2.40)* (0.80)

$R^2ADJ = 0.846$ $SD = 360.579$ $DW = 0.931$

$$IP42 = 51.595 + 0.000151\ X42 + 0.0308\ KP42(-3) - 0.0184\ PX42/PZ42 + 0.1736\ EXR(-2)$$
(0.34) (4.53)*** (0.40) (−0.009) (0.34)

$R^2ADJ = 0.808$ $SD = 148.71$ $DW = 1.018$

$$IP43 = 593.311 + 7.62E-05X43 - 0.0325\ KP43(-2) + 31.826\ PX43(-1)/PZ43(-2)$$
(1.41) (12.26)*** (−2.81)** (0.13)

$$-114.186\ INTGB(-3)$$
(−7.09)***

$R^2ADJ = 0.968$ $SD = 492.88$ $DW = 2.130$

(*Continued*)

Table A3.2. (*Continued*)

IP44 = 83.844 + 0.000110 X44 − 0.155 KP44(−3) + 879.205 PX44/PX44(−2)
(0.08) (5.67)*** (−2.79)** (1.32)

−145.272 INTGB(−3) + 0.00241 IGX71(−1) + 817.390 DUM91
(−1.87) (2.47)** (2.27)*

R^2ADJ = 0.942 SD = 1300.76 DW = 1.463

IP45 = −180.297 + 1.78E − 05 X45 − 0.0293 KP45(−3) + 206.018 PX45(−1)/PZ(−1)
(−0.89) (1.79) (−1.33) (1.30)

+0.200 EXR(−6) + 0.000127 IGX71(−1) + 273.860 DUM86
(1.22) (1.31) (8.51)***

R^2ADJ = 0.783 SD = 66.891 DW = 1.459

IP46 = 218.857 + 0.000159 X46(−2) − 0.0826 KP46(−3) − 47.937 INTGB(−3)
(1.55) (6.69)*** (−1.87) (−3.16)***

+9.49E − 06 IGXSUM(−5)
(1.08)

R^2ADJ = 0.864 SD = 187.16 DW = 0.917

IP47 = −137.064 + 0.000131 X47(−1) − 0.214 KP47(−3) − 217.137 INTGB(−2) + 4.819 EXR(−1)
(−0.17) (8.04)*** (−4.89)*** (−4.81)*** (2.24)*

+9.41E − 05 IGXSUM(−2)
(3.00)**

R^2ADJ = 0.939 SD = 866.58 DW = 1.795

IP48 = 0.424 + 6.69E − 06X48(−4) − 0.0601 KP48(−7) + 18.411 PX48(−2)/PZ48(−2)
(0.02) (0.92) (−0.87) (1.48)

−2.612 INTGB(−2) + 6.24E − 07 IGXSUM(−2)
(−1.57) (0.84)

R^2ADJ = 0.633 SD = 11.187 DW = 2.518

IP49 = −238.342 + 0.000107 X49(−1) − 0.214 KP49(−2) + 352.423 PX49(−1)/PZ49(−1)
(−3.10)*** (7.19)*** (−4.17)*** (4.19)***

−26.488 INTGB(−3)
(−5.76)***

R^2ADJ = 0.703 SD = 74.6197 DW = 1.853

IP50 = 25.532 + 2.28E − 05 X50(−2) − 0.153 KP50(−4) − 5.472 INTGB(−2)
(0.91) (1.78) (−2.32)* (−2.01)*

+3.62E − 06 IGXSUM
(3.65)***

R^2ADJ = 0.635 SD = 23.094 DW = 1.529

IP51 = −31.977 + 3.25E − 05 X51 − 0.0416 KP51(−3) + 53.069 PX51/PZ51 − 6.094 INTGB(−2)
(−0.61) (3.29)*** (−1.07) (1.64) (3.80)***

R^2ADJ = 0.517 SD = 15.397 DW = 1.227

IP52 = −40.549 + 4.22E − 05 X52(−1) − 0.00555 KP52(−4) + 46.301 PX52(−1)/PZ52(−1)
(−0.21) (2.48)** (−0.39) (0.42)

−10.534 INTGB(−3) + 3.11E − 06 IGXSUM(−3)
(−1.8) (0.79)

R^2ADJ = 0.809 SD = 57.957 DW = 2.011

IP53 = 113.685 + 2.64E − 05 X53(−1) − 0.0443 KP53(−3) − 1.920 EXR − 235.000 PX53/PZ53
(0.35) (3.06)*** (−2.06)* (−3.12)*** (−0.90)

+0.0264 IH(−2)
(2.96)***

R^2ADJ = 0.834 SD = 227.607 DW = 1.081

(*Continued*)

Table A3.2. (*Continued*)

$$\mathrm{IP54} = -442.407 + 2.48\mathrm{E}-05\ \mathrm{X54} - 0.00763\ \mathrm{KP54}(-4) + 0.417\ \mathrm{EXR}(-5) + 0.644\ \mathrm{IP54}(-1)$$
(3.97)*** (5.45)*** (−0.48) (1.55) (7.67)***

R^2ADJ = 0.947 SD = 264.990 DW = 1.381

$$\mathrm{IP55} = -528.524 + 3.76\mathrm{E}-05\ \mathrm{X55}(-2) - 0.1057\ \mathrm{KP55}(-3) + 495.888\ \mathrm{PX55}(-2)/\mathrm{PZ55}(-2)$$
(−1.97) (3.38)*** (−4.82)*** (2.21)*

$$+2.16\mathrm{E}-05\ \mathrm{IGXSUM}$$
(2.36)*

R^2ADJ = 0.823 SD = 175.084 DW = 1.516

$$\mathrm{IP56} = -87.250 + 3.96\mathrm{E}-05\ \mathrm{X56} - 0.0493\ \mathrm{KP56}(-1) - 21.935\ \mathrm{INTGB}(-4) + 2.23\mathrm{E}-05\ \mathrm{IGXSUM}$$
(−0.74) (4.74)*** (−1.71) (−1.87) (3.05)***

R^2ADJ = 0.846 SD = 194.071 DW = 1.338

$$\mathrm{IP57} = 2837.549 + 0.000204(-2) - 0.0742\ \mathrm{KP57}(-13) - 213.758\ \mathrm{INTGB}(-8)$$
(1.88) (1.38) (−1.48) (−3.00)***

$$-1132.734\ \mathrm{DUM0203} + 0.000135\ \mathrm{IGXSUM} - 3.052\ \mathrm{EXR}(-3)$$
(−3.66)*** (4.21)*** (−1.27)

R^2ADJ = 0.921 SD = 816.146 DW = 2.662

$$\mathrm{IP58} = 180.451 + 6.99\mathrm{E}-05\ \mathrm{X58}(-3) - 0.172\ \mathrm{KP58}(-5) + 1.04\mathrm{E}-05\ \mathrm{IGXSUM}(-3)$$
(4.01)*** (1.56) (−2.34)* (2.13)*

R^2ADJ = 0.825 SD = 91.924 DW = 1.495

$$\mathrm{IP60} = 2328.374 + 0.000134\ \mathrm{X61}(-6) - 0.4062\ \mathrm{KP60}(-7) + 176.151\ \mathrm{PX60}/\mathrm{PZ60}$$
(4.10)*** (2.45)** (−3.15)** (0.41)

$$-72.953\ \mathrm{INTGB}(-6) - 4.671\ \mathrm{EXR} + 0.000400\ \mathrm{IGXSUM}$$
(−2.89)** (−461)*** (1.95)

R^2ADJ = 0.675 SD = 190.907 DW = 1.352

$$\mathrm{IP61} = 9157.758 + 9.40\mathrm{E}-05\ \mathrm{X61} - 0.178\ \mathrm{KP61}(-3) - 89.550\ \mathrm{INTGB}(-4) - 24.146\ \mathrm{EXR}$$
(3.51)*** (3.03)*** (−3.56)*** (−0.81) (−4.50)***

R^2ADJ = 0.759 SD = 1420.835 DW = 0.897

$$\mathrm{IP62} = -716.444 + 0.000102\ \mathrm{X62} - 0.0132\ \mathrm{KP62}(-1) + 232.137\ \mathrm{PX62}/\mathrm{PZ62}$$
(−3.40)*** (5.47)*** (−0.30) (1.08)

R^2ADJ = 0.773 SD = 217.344 DW = 1.890

$$\mathrm{IP63} = -1900.885 + 5.70\mathrm{E}-05\mathrm{X63} - 0.0734\ \mathrm{KP63}(-2) + 1734.855\ \mathrm{PX63}(-2)/\mathrm{PZ63}(-2)$$
(−1.16) (1.63) (−1.27) (0.98)

$$-31.618\ \mathrm{INTGB}(-3) + 6.98\mathrm{E}-05\ \mathrm{IGXSUM}(-4)$$
(−0.53) (1.87)

R^2ADJ = 0.796 SD = 601.771 DW = 1.277

$$\mathrm{IP64} = 17.102 + 4.24\mathrm{E}-05\ \mathrm{X64} + 0.0501\ \mathrm{KP64}(-3) + 103.211\ \mathrm{PX64}(-3)/\mathrm{PZ64}(-3)$$
(0.15) (0.26) (2.34)* (0.24)

$$-67.269\ \mathrm{INTGB} + 2.49\mathrm{E}-5\ \mathrm{IGXSUM}$$
(−2.33) (1.52)

R^2ADJ = 0.898 SD = 559.175 DW = 2.220

$$\mathrm{IP65} = 67.899 + 4.27\mathrm{E}-07\ \mathrm{X65} - 0.0321\ \mathrm{KP65}(-6) - 0.521\ \mathrm{EXR}(-2) + 1.23\mathrm{E}-05\ \mathrm{IG82}$$
(0.36) (0.083) (−3.46)*** (−1.38) (2.86)**

$$+163.440\ \mathrm{DUM91}$$
(2.82)**

R^2ADJ = 0.515 SD = 79.628 DW = 1.133

$$\mathrm{IP66} = 394.253 + 2.25\mathrm{E}-06\ \mathrm{X66}(-1) - 0.0536\ \mathrm{KP66}(-2) - 207.435\ \mathrm{PX66}(-4)/\mathrm{PZ66}(-4)$$
(1.24) (0.04) (−1.59) (−1.44)

$$+1.010\ \mathrm{EXR}$$
(1.74)

R^2ADJ = 0.606 SD = 99.653 DW = 1.080

(*Continued*)

Table A3.2. (*Continued*)

$$IP67 = \underset{(-0.68)}{-282.494} + \underset{(0.11)}{7.89}\ X67(-3) + \underset{(0.53)}{0.0242}\ KP67(-5) + \underset{(0.12)}{13.990}\ PX67(-5)/PZ67(-5)$$

$$+\underset{(1.23)}{0.974}\ EXR(-1) + \underset{(2.315)^{*}}{0.000737}\ IGX67 + \underset{(2.96)^{***}}{0.134}\ STOCPR$$

$$R^2ADJ = 0.533 \quad SD = 100.762 \quad DW = 1.579$$

$$IP68 = \underset{(-1.34)}{-92.875} + \underset{(2.15)^{*}}{2.14E-05}X68(-2) - \underset{(-5.60)^{***}}{0.0522}\ KP68(-7) - \underset{(-1.62)}{12.165}\ INTGB(-5)$$

$$+\underset{(4.51)^{***}}{1.81E-05}\ IGXSUM$$

$$R^2ADJ = 0.669 \quad SD = 66.659 \quad DW = 1.645$$

$$IP69 = \underset{(-2.91)^{**}}{-5636.149} + \underset{(1.97)^{*}}{0.000232}\ X69(-4) - \underset{(-1.72)}{0.0642}\ KP69(-5) - \underset{(-0.44)}{64.292}\ INTGB(-3)$$

$$+\underset{(6.60)^{***}}{0.000202}\ IG82 + \underset{(1.59)}{899.916}DUM7086$$

$$R^2ADJ = 0.835 \quad SD = 1304.636 \quad DW = 1.382$$

$$IP70 = \underset{(-0.19)}{-107.124} + \underset{(2.27)^{*}}{4.27E-05}X70(-2) - \underset{(-4.74)^{***}}{0.283}\ KP70(-5) - \underset{(-3.31)^{***}}{169.939}\ INTGB(-2) + \underset{(4.11)^{***}}{0.0140}\ CP(-1)$$

$$+\underset{(1.71)}{6.36E-05}\ IGXSUM(-4)$$

$$R^2ADJ = 0.927 \quad SD = 796.474 \quad DW = 1.108$$

$$IP71 = \underset{(0.46)}{792.926} + \underset{(2.54)^{**}}{0.000105}\ X71 - \underset{(-3.75)^{***}}{0.254}\ KP71(-5) - \underset{(-0.67)}{980.633}\ PX71(-3)/PZ71(-3)$$

$$-\underset{(-3.52)^{***}}{373.832}\ INTGB(-3) + \underset{(2.37)^{*}}{0.00375}\ IGX71$$

$$R^2ADJ = 0.755 \quad SD = 819.678 \quad DW = 0.847$$

$$IP72 = \underset{(0.41)}{149.696} + \underset{(3.37)^{***}}{6.70E-05}\ X72 - \underset{(-1.13)}{0.0384}\ KP72(-3) + \underset{(1.75)}{295.652}\ PX72/PZ72$$

$$-\underset{(-2.76)^{**}}{93.655}\ INTGB(-3) + \underset{(2.07)^{*}}{1.70E-05}\ IGXSUM$$

$$R^2ADJ = 0.920 \quad SD = 503.119 \quad DW = 1.008$$

$$IP73 = \underset{(0.38)}{748.046} + \underset{(4.68)^{***}}{0.000212}\ X74 - \underset{(-0.60)}{0.03124}\ KP73(-3) - \underset{(-0.25)}{546.4052}\ PX73(-6)/PZ73(-6)$$

$$-\underset{(-1.51)}{370.0439}\ INTGB(-2)$$

$$R^2ADJ = 0.923 \quad SD = 3141.980 \quad DW = 1.591$$

$$IP79 = \underset{(0.988)}{2564.489} + \underset{(3.62)^{***}}{0.000128}\ X79(-1) - \underset{(-1.68)}{0.066907}\ KP79(-4) - \underset{(-1.11)}{1474.978}\ PX79(-4)/PZ79(-4)$$

$$-\underset{(-1.72)}{161.352}\ INTGB(-4)$$

$$R^2ADJ = 0.874 \quad SD = 912.859 \quad DW = 2.382$$

Notes: (1) ***, ** and * present the level of significance at 1%, 5% and 10%, respectively.

(2) Sector classification: please see notes of Table A3.1.

Table A3.3. Regression results of wage and salaried employees by sector.

$$\ln \mathrm{LW01} = \underset{(1.04)}{6.67279} + \underset{(0.26)}{0.08394} \ln \mathrm{X01} - \underset{(-2.28)^{*}}{0.39380} \ln \mathrm{W01}(-1)/\mathrm{PX01}(-5) + \underset{(2.38)^{**}}{0.47839} \ln \mathrm{LW01}(-1)$$
$$R^2\mathrm{ADJ} = 0.712 \quad \mathrm{SD} = 0.154 \quad \mathrm{DW} = 1.210$$

$$\ln \mathrm{LW02} = -\underset{(0.99)}{1.682} + \underset{(1.90)^{*}}{0.23119} \ln \mathrm{X02}(-5) - \underset{(-1.03)}{0.0773} \ln \mathrm{W02}(-2)/\mathrm{PX02}(-2) + \underset{(13.18)^{***}}{0.8931} \ln \mathrm{LW02}(-1)$$
$$R^2\mathrm{ADJ} = 0.867 \quad \mathrm{SD} = 0.107 \quad \mathrm{DW} = 1.456$$

$$\ln \mathrm{LW03} = -\underset{(-2.71)^{**}}{11.966} + \underset{(2.91)^{**}}{1.2001} \ln \mathrm{X03} - \underset{(-3.58)^{***}}{0.3875} \ln \mathrm{W03}/\mathrm{PX03} + \underset{(9.98)^{***}}{0.9301} \ln \mathrm{LW03}(-1)$$
$$R^2\mathrm{ADJ} = 0.931 \quad \mathrm{SD} = 0.111 \quad \mathrm{DW} = 1.365$$

$$\ln \mathrm{LW04} = -\underset{(-1.44)}{1.73375} + \underset{(1.83)^{*}}{0.24673} \ln \mathrm{X04} - \underset{(-1.33)}{0.07998} \ln \mathrm{W04}/\mathrm{PX04} + \underset{(7.14)^{***}}{0.80378} \ln \mathrm{LW04}(-1)$$
$$R^2\mathrm{ADJ} = 0.963 \quad \mathrm{SD} = 0.143 \quad \mathrm{DW} = 1.248$$

$$\ln \mathrm{LW05} = \underset{(2.48)^{**}}{8.94637} + \underset{(1.60)}{0.41753} \ln \mathrm{X05} - \underset{(-4.87)^{***}}{0.75729} \ln \mathrm{W05}/\mathrm{PX05} + \underset{(1.83)^{*}}{0.275623} \ln \mathrm{LW05}(-1)$$
$$R^2\mathrm{ADJ} = 0.929 \quad \mathrm{SD} = 0.135 \quad \mathrm{DW} = 0.951$$

$$\ln \mathrm{LW06} = \underset{(1.43)}{6.54954} + \underset{(2.14)^{*}}{0.80238} \ln \mathrm{X06} - \underset{(-12.43)^{***}}{0.88612} \ln \mathrm{W06}/\mathrm{PX06}$$
$$R^2\mathrm{ADJ} = 0.896 \quad \mathrm{SD} = 0.147 \quad \mathrm{DW} = 1.078$$

$$\ln \mathrm{LW07} = \underset{(-0.19)}{-0.16698} + \underset{(4.65)^{***}}{0.56601} \ln \mathrm{X07} - \underset{(-4.86)^{***}}{0.43625} \ln \mathrm{W07}/\mathrm{PX07} + \underset{(8.35)^{***}}{0.67540} \ln \mathrm{LW07}(-1)$$
$$R^2\mathrm{ADJ} = 0.974 \quad \mathrm{SD} = 0.053 \quad \mathrm{DW} = 1.077$$

$$\ln \mathrm{LW08} = \underset{(-6.69)^{***}}{4.83326} + \underset{(3.98)^{***}}{1.07477} \ln \mathrm{X08} - \underset{(-11.07)^{***}}{0.98847} \ln \mathrm{W08}/\mathrm{PX08} + \underset{(1.01)}{0.08974} \ln \mathrm{LW08}(-1)$$
$$R^2\mathrm{ADJ} = 0.996 \quad \mathrm{SD} = 0.098 \quad \mathrm{DW} = 0.516$$

$$\ln \mathrm{LW09} = \underset{(4.33)^{***}}{11.7369} + \underset{(0.33)}{0.15542} \ln \mathrm{X09} - \underset{(-3.75)^{***}}{0.89619} \ln \mathrm{W09}/\mathrm{PX09}$$
$$R^2\mathrm{ADJ} = 0.560 \quad \mathrm{SD} = 0.403 \quad \mathrm{DW} = 0.605$$

$$\ln \mathrm{LW10} = \underset{(-2.71)^{**}}{-6.71772} + \underset{(6.33)^{***}}{1.68057} \ln \mathrm{X10} - \underset{(-6.88)^{***}}{0.74967} \ln \mathrm{W10}/\mathrm{PX10} + \underset{(4.71)^{***}}{0.41827} \ln \mathrm{LW10}(-1)$$
$$R^2\mathrm{ADJ} = 0.986 \quad \mathrm{SD} = 0.119 \quad \mathrm{DW} = 0.581$$

$$\ln \mathrm{LW11} = \underset{(8.67)^{***}}{4.47789} + \underset{(9.55)^{***}}{0.79157} \ln \mathrm{X11} - \underset{(-9.30)^{***}}{0.78066} \ln \mathrm{W11}/\mathrm{PX11} + \underset{(2.30)^{**}}{0.20087} \ln \mathrm{LW11}(-1)$$
$$R^2\mathrm{ADJ} = 0.956 \quad \mathrm{SD} = 0.137 \quad \mathrm{DW} = 0.656$$

$$\ln \mathrm{LW12} = \underset{(-0.45)}{-0.52820} + \underset{(8.74)^{***}}{0.96071} \ln \mathrm{X12} - \underset{(-8.85)^{***}}{0.57322} \ln \mathrm{W12}/\mathrm{PX12} + \underset{(5.32)^{***}}{0.31420} \ln \mathrm{LW12}(-1)$$
$$R^2\mathrm{ADJ} = 0.995 \quad \mathrm{SD} = 0.108 \quad \mathrm{DW} = 1.770$$

$$\ln \mathrm{LW13} = \underset{(1.85)^{*}}{2.83567} + \underset{(4.24)^{***}}{0.62413} \ln \mathrm{X13} - \underset{(-5.71)^{***}}{0.60334} \ln \mathrm{W13}/\mathrm{PX13} + \underset{(3.90)^{***}}{0.40042} \ln \mathrm{LW13}(-1)$$
$$R^2\mathrm{ADJ} = 0.929 \quad \mathrm{SD} = 0.095 \quad \mathrm{DW} = 1.058$$

$$\ln \mathrm{LW14} = \underset{(-0.46)}{-0.33118} + \underset{(2.56)^{**}}{0.29813} \ln \mathrm{X14} - \underset{(-2.57)^{**}}{0.14106} \ln \mathrm{W14}/\mathrm{PX14} + \underset{(4.05)^{***}}{0.57348} \ln \mathrm{LW14}(-1)$$
$$R^2\mathrm{ADJ} = 0.856 \quad \mathrm{SD} = 0.055 \quad \mathrm{DW} = 1.302$$

$$\ln \mathrm{LW15} = \underset{(-1.20)}{-2.06064} + \underset{(2.10)^{**}}{0.23520} \ln \mathrm{X15} - \underset{(-0.84)}{0.02624} \ln \mathrm{W15}/\mathrm{PX15} + \underset{(8.61)^{***}}{0.78354} \ln \mathrm{LW15}(-1)$$
$$R^2\mathrm{ADJ} = 0.805 \quad \mathrm{SD} = 0.066 \quad \mathrm{DW} = 1.482$$

(Continued)

Table A3.3. (*Continued*)

$$\ln LW16 = \underset{(0.63)}{0.75418} + \underset{(0.42)}{0.03355} \ln X16 - \underset{(-0.81)}{0.01521} \ln W16/PX16 + \underset{(4.78)^{***}}{0.66428} \ln LW16(-1)$$

$R^2ADJ = 0.476$ SD = 0.048 DW = 1.450

$$\ln LW17 = \underset{(-2.64)^{**}}{-0.33118} + \underset{(3.24)^{***}}{0.29813} \ln X17 - \underset{(-2.08)^{**}}{0.14106} \ln W17/PX17 + \underset{(8.01)^{***}}{0.57348} \ln LW17(-1)$$

$R^2ADJ = 0.951$ SD = 0.037 DW = 1.850

$$\ln LW18 = \underset{(-3.99)^{***}}{-2.39305} + \underset{(8.72)^{***}}{1.11177} \ln X18 - \underset{(-8.08)^{***}}{0.72824} \ln W18/PX18 + \underset{(2.11)^{**}}{0.19600} \ln LW18(-1)$$

$R^2ADJ = 0.841$ SD = 0.038 DW = 1.883

$$\ln LW19 = \underset{(-2.31)^{**}}{-10.8201} + \underset{(2.54)^{**}}{0.95607} \ln X19 - \underset{(-2.77)^{**}}{0.14783} \ln W19/PX19 + \underset{(6.36)^{***}}{0.88092} \ln LW19(-1)$$

$R^2ADJ = 0.938$ SD = 0.049 DW = 1.045

$$\ln LW20 = \underset{(-0.68)}{-2.39979} + \underset{(2.33)^{**}}{0.60186} \ln X20 - \underset{(-3.35)^{***}}{0.34549} \ln W20/PX20 + \underset{(7.21)^{***}}{0.65789} \ln LW20(-1)$$

$R^2ADJ = 0.904$ SD = 0.103 DW = 1.688

$$\ln LW21 = \underset{(-2.99)^{***}}{-6.77813} + \underset{(3.21)^{***}}{0.66797} \ln X21 - \underset{(-1.70)}{0.05402} \ln W21/PX21 + \underset{(4.19)^{***}}{0.587650} \ln LW21(-1)$$

$R^2ADJ = 0.977$ SD = 0.116 DW = 1.438

$$\ln LW22 = \underset{(1.31)}{3.30143} + \underset{(2.21)^{**}}{0.39605} \ln X22 - \underset{(-7.12)^{***}}{0.45708} \ln W22/PX22 + \underset{(6.26)^{***}}{0.56698} \ln LW22(-1)$$

$R^2ADJ = 0.967$ SD = 0.077 DW = 2.068

$$\ln LW23 = \underset{(1.25)}{1.30533} + \underset{(3.44)^{***}}{0.40803} \ln X23 - \underset{(-2.96)^{***}}{0.32209} \ln W23/PX23 + \underset{(5.21)^{***}}{0.54171} \ln LW23(-1)$$

$R^2ADJ = 0.820$ SD = 0.107 DW = 1.134

$$\ln LW24 = \underset{(1.17)}{0.60114} + \underset{(3.54)^{***}}{0.18040} \ln X24 - \underset{(-4.12)^{***}}{0.11845} \ln W24/PX24 + \underset{(5.83)^{***}}{0.68426} \ln LW24(-1)$$

$R^2ADJ = 0.940$ SD = 0.031 DW = 0.869

$$\ln LW25 = \underset{(-2.34)^{**}}{-2.99143} + \underset{(3.34)^{***}}{0.35088} \ln X25 - \underset{(-1.28)}{0.06987} \ln W25/PX25 + \underset{(7.89)^{***}}{0.76534} \ln LW25(-1)$$

$R^2ADJ = 0.985$ SD = 0.039 DW = 1.121

$$\ln LW26 = \underset{(0.28)}{0.22385} + \underset{(4.30)^{***}}{0.37118} \ln X26 - \underset{(-4.33)^{***}}{0.25483} \ln W26/PX26 + \underset{(6.81)^{***}}{0.63750} \ln LW26(-1)$$

$R^2ADJ = 0.939$ SD = 0.045 DW = 1.193

$$\ln LW27 = \underset{(-1.35)}{-0.90177} + \underset{(3.81)^{***}}{0.40844} \ln X27 - \underset{(-3.75)^{***}}{0.24889} \ln W27/PX27 + \underset{(7.24)^{***}}{0.68442} \ln LW27(-1)$$

$R^2ADJ = 0.853$ SD = 0.035 DW = 1.460

$$\ln LW28 = \underset{(1.98)^{*}}{1.39047} + \underset{(1.89)^{*}}{0.22513} \ln X28 - \underset{(-2.21)^{**}}{0.19709} \ln W28/PX28 + \underset{(4.51)^{***}}{0.69105} \ln LW28(-1)$$

$R^2ADJ = 0.911$ SD = 0.039 DW = 0.823

$$\ln LW29 = \underset{(1.14)}{7.74914} + \underset{(0.69)}{0.31777} \ln X29 - \underset{(-2.07)^{**}}{0.16262} \ln W29/PX29 + \underset{(5.19)^{***}}{0.65674} \ln LW29(-1)$$

$R^2ADJ = 0.875$ SD = 0.207 DW = 1.683

$$\ln LW30 = \underset{(1.22)}{0.53422} + \underset{(0.39)}{0.21985} \ln X30 - \underset{(-1.78)^{**}}{0.21907} \ln W30/PX30 - \underset{(-3.97)^{***}}{0.63042} \text{ DUM0203}$$

$R^2ADJ = 0.646$ SD = 0.200 DW = 0.648

$$\ln LW31 = \underset{(0.47)}{1.39138} + \underset{(0.84)}{0.16060} \ln X31 - \underset{(-2.30)^{**}}{0.20435} \ln W31/PX31 + \underset{(6.08)^{***}}{0.82497} \ln LW31(-1)$$

$R^2ADJ = 0.816$ SD = 0.127 DW = 1.502

(*Continued*)

Table A3.3. (*Continued*)

$$\ln LW32 = 2.96124 + 0.34294 \ln X32 - 0.42718 \ln W32/PX32 + 0.66823 \ln LW32(-1)$$
(4.41)*** (6.36)*** (−6.60)*** (7.07)***
$$R^2ADJ = 0.963 \quad SD = 0.034 \quad DW = 2.034$$

$$\ln LW33 = 5.37368 + 0.23790 \ln X33 - 0.42299 \ln W33/PX33 + 0.51450 \ln LW33(-1)$$
(4.49)*** (3.64)*** (−5.60)*** (5.47)***
$$R^2ADJ = 0.884 \quad SD = 0.044 \quad DW = 1.300$$

$$\ln LW34 = 0.80189 + 0.28152 \ln X34 - 0.20156 \ln W34/PX34 + 0.63268 \ln LW34(-1)$$
(1.11) (4.37)*** (−3.86)*** (7.86)***
$$R^2ADJ = 0.976 \quad SD = 0.040 \quad DW = 1.484$$

$$\ln LW35 = -0.81128 + 0.37798 \ln X35 - 0.15723 \ln W35/PX35 + 0.51685 \ln LW35(-1)$$
(−0.98) (3.88)*** (−3.98)*** (4.53)***
$$R^2ADJ = 0.903 \quad SD = 0.046 \quad DW = 1.573$$

$$\ln LW36 = 2.53284 + 0.54029 \ln X36 - 0.53720 \ln W36/PX36 + 0.52142 \ln LW36(-1)$$
(2.03)* (5.20)*** (−6.67)*** (6.65)***
$$R^2ADJ = 0.952 \quad SD = 0.046 \quad DW = 1.125$$

$$\ln LW37 = -13.5298 + 1.56838 \ln X37 - 0.39869 \ln W37/PX37$$
(−1.62) (3.02)*** (−4.87)***
$$R^2ADJ = 0.569 \quad SD = 0.292 \quad DW = 0.424$$

$$\ln LW38 = -2.70874 + 0.28665 \ln X38 - 0.08643 \ln W38/PX38 + 0.88590 \ln LW38(-1)$$
(−1.99)* (4.06)*** (−3.66)*** (9.05)***
$$R^2ADJ = 0.782 \quad SD = 0.027 \quad DW = 1.977$$

$$\ln LW39 = 4.53476 + 0.25121 \ln X39 - 0.29869 \ln W39/PX39$$
(2.61)** (1.92)* (−5.51)***
$$R^2ADJ = 0.493 \quad SD = 0.124 \quad DW = 0.649$$

$$\ln LW40 = -1.42582 + 0.29370 \ln X40 - 0.11110 \ln W40/PX40 + 0.73106 \ln LW40(-1)$$
(−1.32) (2.54)** (−1.85)* (6.10)***
$$R^2ADJ = 0.646 \quad SD = 0.049 \quad DW = 1.293$$

$$\ln LW41 = 1.22379 + 0.42495 \ln X41 - 0.34949 \ln W41/PX41 + 0.57593 \ln LW41(-1)$$
(1.20) (4.05)*** (−4.07)*** (4.94)***
$$R^2ADJ = 0.706 \quad SD = 0.044 \quad DW = 0.688$$

$$\ln LW42 = 1.22379 + 0.42495 \ln X42 - 0.34949 \ln W42/PX42 + 0.57593 \ln LW42(-1)$$
(4.96)*** (5.53)*** (−6.13)*** (7.16)***
$$R^2ADJ = 0.933 \quad SD = 0.109 \quad DW = 1.570$$

$$\ln LW43 = 2.29693 + 0.36615 \ln X43 - 0.35852 \ln W43/PX43 + 0.57178 \ln LW43(-1)$$
(4.21)*** (7.68)*** (−7.56)*** (8.09)***
$$R^2ADJ = 0.929 \quad SD = 0.030 \quad DW = 1.375$$

$$\ln LW44 = -0.33522 + 0.27324 \ln X44 - 0.12709 \ln W44/PX44 + 0.69162 \ln LW44(-1)$$
(−0.77) (2.44)** (−2.18)** (5.89)***
$$R^2ADJ = 0.962 \quad SD = 0.082 \quad DW = 1.023$$

$$\ln LW45 = 5.18623 + 0.14608 \ln X45 - 0.41016 \ln W45/PX45 + 0.66101 \ln LW45(-1)$$
(1.75)* (0.79) (−2.02)* (5.12)***
$$R^2ADJ = 0.803 \quad SD = 0.168 \quad DW = 1.460$$

$$\ln LW46 = 4.36516 + 0.41708 \ln X46 - 0.46653 \ln W46/PX46 + 0.35248 \ln LW46(-1)$$
(4.84)*** (4.61)*** (−5.07)*** (2.85)***
$$R^2ADJ = 0.819 \quad SD = 0.049 \quad DW = 0.823$$

$$\ln LW47 = 3.45672 + 0.28610 \ln X47 - 0.32738 \ln W47/PX47 + 0.50321 \ln LW47(-1)$$
(5.20)*** (4.62)*** (−5.32)*** (4.68)***
$$R^2ADJ = 0.911 \quad SD = 0.049 \quad DW = 1.453$$

(*Continued*)

Table A3.3. (*Continued*)

$$\ln LW48 = \underset{(1.27)}{1.11314} + \underset{(0.24)}{0.01881}\ \ln X48 - \underset{(-0.62)}{0.01940}\ \ln W48/PX48 + \underset{(4.08)^{***}}{0.67963}\ \ln LW48(-1)$$
$$R^2ADJ = 0.532 \quad SD = 0.095 \quad DW = 1.921$$

$$\ln LW49 = \underset{(-2.58)^{**}}{-2.74833} + \underset{(5.60)^{***}}{0.45097}\ \ln X49 - \underset{(-3.15)^{***}}{0.17975}\ \ln W49/PX49 + \underset{(15.68)^{***}}{0.75517}\ \ln LW49(-1)$$
$$R^2ADJ = 0.985 \quad SD = 0.066 \quad DW = 1.382$$

$$\ln LW50 = \underset{(-0.81)}{-0.31181} + \underset{(1.43)}{0.07033}\ \ln X50 - \underset{(-0.43)}{0.01675}\ \ln W50/PX50 + \underset{(8.33)^{***}}{0.90037}\ \ln LW50(-1)$$
$$R^2ADJ = 0.846 \quad SD = 0.074 \quad DW = 2.234$$

$$\ln LW51 = \underset{(0.68)}{0.81111} + \underset{(0.70)}{0.04661}\ \ln X51 - \underset{(-1.18)}{0.03038}\ \ln W51/PX51 + \underset{(8.14)^{***}}{0.73675}\ \ln LW51(-1)$$
$$R^2ADJ = 0.811 \quad SD = 0.059 \quad DW = 1.987$$

$$\ln LW52 = \underset{(1.32)}{1.83247} + \underset{(1.81)^{*}}{0.11241}\ \ln X52 - \underset{(-2.34)^{**}}{0.14951}\ \ln W52/PX52 + \underset{(7.12)^{***}}{0.76531}\ \ln LW52(-1)$$
$$R^2ADJ = 0.906 \quad SD = 0.033 \quad DW = 1.272$$

$$\ln LW53 = \underset{(-3.94)^{***}}{-1.87306} + \underset{(6.18)^{***}}{0.21375}\ \ln X53 - \underset{(-2.15)^{**}}{0.04511}\ \ln W53/PX53 + \underset{(23.78)^{***}}{0.85535}\ \ln LW53(-1)$$
$$R^2ADJ = 0.970 \quad SD = 0.021 \quad DW = 1.451$$

$$\ln LW54 = \underset{(0.86)}{0.61456} + \underset{(1.83)^{*}}{0.10349}\ \ln X54 - \underset{(-2.93)^{***}}{0.12643}\ \ln W54/PX54 + \underset{(17.34)^{***}}{0.94064}\ \ln LW54(-1)$$
$$R^2ADJ = 0.923 \quad SD = 0.042 \quad DW = 1.904$$

$$\ln LW55 = \underset{(2.27)^{**}}{0.88171} + \underset{(4.25)^{***}}{0.33297}\ \ln X55 - \underset{(-3.62)^{***}}{0.24671}\ \ln W55/PX55 + \underset{(10.33)^{***}}{0.62946}\ \ln LW55(-1)$$
$$R^2ADJ = 0.973 \quad SD = 0.027 \quad DW = 1.074$$

$$\ln LW56 = \underset{(-1.73)^{*}}{-1.17749} + \underset{(2.94)^{***}}{0.19940}\ \ln X56 - \underset{(-1.38)}{0.0577}\ \ln W56/PX56 + \underset{(10.88)^{***}}{0.82266}\ \ln LW56(-1)$$
$$R^2ADJ = 0.888 \quad SD = 0.045 \quad DW = 1.072$$

$$\ln LW57 = \underset{(-0.74)}{-0.20949} + \underset{(4.45)^{***}}{0.09120}\ \ln X57 - \underset{(-2.36)^{**}}{0.08039}\ \ln W57/PX57 + \underset{(18.76)^{***}}{1.00211}\ \ln LW57(-1)$$
$$R^2ADJ = 0.961 \quad SD = 0.021 \quad DW = 1.634$$

$$\ln LW58 = \underset{(0.31)}{0.05034} + \underset{(3.25)^{***}}{0.06886}\ \ln X58 - \underset{(-0.91)}{0.03540}\ \ln W58/PX58 + \underset{(6.27)^{***}}{0.87486}\ \ln LW58(-1)$$
$$R^2ADJ = 0.961 \quad SD = 0.022 \quad DW = 2.047$$

$$\ln LW59 = \underset{(1.88)^{*}}{3.20408} + \underset{(1.52)}{0.09268}\ \ln X59 - \underset{(-2.15)^{**}}{0.10683}\ \ln W59/PX59 + \underset{(10.33)^{***}}{0.97256}\ \ln LW59(-1)$$
$$R^2ADJ = 0.837 \quad SD = 0.043 \quad DW = 1.883$$

$$\ln LW60 = \underset{(3.47)^{***}}{2.02952} + \underset{(3.12)^{***}}{0.19186}\ \ln X60 - \underset{(-3.55)^{***}}{0.17588}\ \ln W60/PX60 + \underset{(7.00)^{***}}{0.61124}\ \ln LW60(-1)$$
$$R^2ADJ = 0.983 \quad SD = 0.029 \quad DW = 1.453$$

$$\ln LW61 = \underset{(2.99)^{***}}{0.91795} + \underset{(3.32)^{***}}{0.31550}\ \ln X61 - \underset{(-2.86)^{***}}{0.20651}\ \ln W61/PX61 + \underset{(6.30)^{***}}{0.61631}\ \ln LW61(-1)$$
$$R^2ADJ = 0.969 \quad SD = 0.021 \quad DW = 1.213$$

$$\ln LW62 = \underset{(-3.08)^{***}}{-13.4816} + \underset{(10.61)^{***}}{1.55745}\ \ln X62 - \underset{(-2.05)^{*}}{0.39677}\ \ln W62/PX62$$
$$R^2ADJ = 0.948 \quad SD = 0.131 \quad DW = 1.851$$

$$\ln LW63 = \underset{(1.48)}{1.54845} + \underset{(2.06)^{**}}{0.25361}\ \ln X63 - \underset{(-2.46)^{**}}{0.23217}\ \ln W63/PX63 + \underset{(5.99)^{***}}{0.69533}\ \ln LW63(-1)$$
$$R^2ADJ = 0.977 \quad SD = 0.031 \quad DW = 0.667$$

(*Continued*)

Table A3.3. (*Continued*)

$$\ln LW64 = \underset{(1.50)}{-4.87098} + \underset{(1.36)}{0.24625}\ \ln X64 - \underset{(-1.16)}{0.07150}\ \ln W64/PX64 + \underset{(13.33)^{***}}{0.98122}\ \ln LW64(-1)$$
$$R^2 ADJ = 0.955 \quad SD = 0.049 \quad DW = 2.190$$

$$\ln LW65 = \underset{(0.72)}{0.30405} + \underset{(0.93)}{0.02646}\ \ln X65 - \underset{(-1.13)}{0.02735}\ \ln W65/PX65 + \underset{(18.87)^{***}}{0.95933}\ \ln LW65(-1)$$
$$R^2 ADJ = 0.958 \quad SD = 0.030 \quad DW = 1.209$$

$$\ln LW66 = \underset{(4.30)^{***}}{12.9383} + \underset{(1.73)^{*}}{0.38980}\ \ln X66 - \underset{(-16.27)^{***}}{0.88435}\ \ln W66/PX66$$
$$R^2 ADJ = 0.923 \quad SD = 0.091 \quad DW = 0.727$$

$$\ln LW67 = \underset{(0.46)}{0.09070} + \underset{(0.87)}{0.02364}\ \ln X67 - \underset{(-0.67)}{0.02035}\ \ln W67/PX67 + \underset{(8.64)^{***}}{0.81848}\ \ln LW67(-1)$$
$$R^2 ADJ = 0.951 \quad SD = 0.024 \quad DW = 1.349$$

$$\ln LW68 = \underset{(2.13)^{**}}{2.68605} + \underset{(7.18)^{***}}{2.68605}\ \ln X68 - \underset{(-8.32)^{***}}{0.66022}\ \ln W68/PX68 + \underset{(3.15)^{***}}{0.29519}\ \ln LW68(-1)$$
$$R^2 ADJ = 0.953 \quad SD = 0.104 \quad DW = 1.302$$

$$\ln LW69 = \underset{(1.88)^{*}}{2.48313} + \underset{(1.12)}{0.09722}\ \ln X69 - \underset{(-1.46)}{0.15253}\ \ln W69/PX69 + \underset{(3.84)^{***}}{0.74120}\ \ln LW69(-1)$$
$$R^2 ADJ = 0.921 \quad SD = 0.043 \quad DW = 2.374$$

$$\ln LW70 = \underset{(9.09)^{***}{}^{*}}{4.447116} + \underset{(7.03)^{***}}{0.60753}\ \ln X70 - \underset{(-4.91)^{***}}{0.46981}\ \ln W70/PX70$$
$$R^2 ADJ = 0.726 \quad SD = 0.061 \quad DW = 1.047$$

$$\ln LW71 = \underset{(-1.29)}{-6.44372} + \underset{(6.43)^{***}}{1.16002}\ \ln X71 - \underset{(-2.91)^{***}}{0.51016}\ \ln W71/PX71$$
$$R^2 ADJ = 0.732 \quad SD = 0.210 \quad DW = 0.509$$

$$\ln LW72 = \underset{(-12.99)^{***}}{-5.85891} + \underset{(41.40)^{***}}{0.80764}\ \ln X72 - \underset{(-1.51)}{0.03784}\ \ln W72/PX72$$
$$R^2 ADJ = 0.984 \quad SD = 0.101 \quad DW = 0.956$$

$$\ln LW73 = \underset{(0.93)}{0.70383} + \underset{(2.16)^{**}}{0.38857}\ \ln X73 - \underset{(-2.55)^{**}}{0.24696}\ \ln W73/PX73 + \underset{(2.74)^{**}}{0.52926}\ \ln LW73(-1)$$
$$R^2 ADJ = 0.979 \quad SD = 0.061 \quad DW = 0.821$$

$$\ln LW74 = \underset{(4.64)^{***}}{0.70383} + \underset{(2.61)^{**}}{0.38857}\ \ln X74 - \underset{(-9.88)^{**}}{0.24696}\ \ln W74/PX74 + \underset{(10.06)^{***}}{0.52926}\ \ln LW74(-1)$$
$$R^2 ADJ = 0.989 \quad SD = 0.098 \quad DW = 0.894$$

$$\ln LW75 = \underset{(5.30)^{***}}{3.67060} + \underset{(6.12)^{***}}{0.2668}\ \ln X75 - \underset{(-5.99)^{**}}{0.30825}\ \ln W75/PX75 + \underset{(6.29)^{***}}{0.55706}\ \ln LW75(-1)$$
$$R^2 ADJ = 0.804 \quad SD = 0.016 \quad DW = 1.451$$

$$\ln LW76 = \underset{(4.71)^{***}}{4.47871} + \underset{(7.31)^{***}}{0.81370}\ \ln X76 - \underset{(-7.88)^{***}}{0.75115}\ \ln W76/PX76 + \underset{(1.55)}{0.17493}\ \ln LW76(-1)$$
$$R^2 ADJ = 0.980 \quad SD = 0.029 \quad DW = 0.906$$

$$\ln LW77 = \underset{(1.10)}{0.55269} + \underset{(0.62)}{0.04934}\ \ln X77 - \underset{(-0.90)}{0.08257}\ \ln W77/PX77 + \underset{(12.47)^{***}}{0.98857}\ \ln LW77(-1)$$
$$R^2 ADJ = 0.904 \quad SD = 0.019 \quad DW = 1.155$$

$$\ln LW78 = \underset{(5.17)^{***}}{5.21837} + \underset{(5.73)^{***}}{0.45522}\ \ln X78 - \underset{(-6.27)^{***}}{0.56311}\ \ln W78/PX78 + \underset{(5.31)^{***}}{0.45052}\ \ln LW78(-1)$$
$$R^2 ADJ = 0.961 \quad SD = 0.042 \quad DW = 0.686$$

(*Continued*)

Table A3.3. (*Continued*)

$$\ln LW79 = \underset{(-1.99)^{**}}{-0.53666} + \underset{(2.89)^{***}}{0.12353} \ln X79 - \underset{(-0.81)}{0.03732} \ln W79/PX79 + \underset{(23.39)^{***}}{0.87088} \ln LW79(-1)$$

$R^2ADJ = 0.996 \quad SD = 0.019 \quad DW = 1.764$

$R^2ADJ = 0.996 \quad SD = 0.019 \quad DW = 1.764$

Notes: (1) ***, ** and * present the level of significance at 1%, 5% and 10%, respectively.
(2) Sector classification: please see notes of Table A3.1.

Table A3.4. Regression results of sectoral wage rates.

$$\ln W01 = \underset{(3.57)^{***}}{3.9099} + \underset{(6.56)^{***}}{0.7174} \ln(X01/LW01)/(X82/LW82) + \underset{(8.82)^{***}}{1.08223} \ln(W)$$

$R^2ADJ = 0.737 \quad SD = 0.3768 \quad DW = 0.497$

$$\ln W02 = \underset{(-0.56)}{-0.7758} + \underset{(3.69)^{***}}{0.4389} \ln(X02/LW02)/(X82/LW82) + \underset{(10.31)^{***}}{1.7753} \ln(W)$$

$R^2ADJ = 0.800 \quad SD = 0.5177 \quad DW = 0.943$

$$\ln W03 = \underset{(3.20)^{***}}{3.1089} + \underset{(2.30)^{*}}{0.2357} \ln(X03/LW03)/(X82/LW82) + \underset{(11.16)^{***}}{1.3290} \ln(W)$$

$R^2ADJ = 0.823 \quad SD = 0.494 \quad DW = 1.004$

$$\ln W04 = \underset{(1.26)}{2.2232} + \underset{(4.37)^{***}}{0.9853} \ln(X04/LW04)/(X82/LW82) + \underset{(6.10)^{***}}{1.3495} \ln(W)$$

$R^2ADJ = 0.714 \quad SD = 0.703 \quad DW = 0.574$

$$\ln W05 = \underset{(12.37)^{***}}{8.0105} + \underset{(40.00)^{***}}{0.91199} \ln(X05/LW05)/(X82/LW82) + \underset{(11.79)^{***}}{0.9047} \ln(W)$$

$R^2ADJ = 0.982 \quad SD = 0.970 \quad DW = 1.209$

$$\ln W06 = \underset{(18.13)^{***}}{10.9028} + \underset{(7.83)^{***}}{1.13077} \ln(X06/LW06)/(X82/LW82) + \underset{(6.56)^{***}}{1.13073} \ln(W)$$

$R^2ADJ = 0.918 \quad SD = 0.460 \quad DW = 0.918$

$$\ln W07 = \underset{(3.87)^{***}}{6.3542} + \underset{(4.42)^{***}}{0.436999} \ln(X07/LW07)/(X82/LW82) + \underset{(6.81)^{***}}{0.87192} \ln(W)$$

$R^2ADJ = 0.868 \quad SD = 0.316 \quad DW = 0.841$

$$\ln W08 = \underset{(7.60)^{***}}{8.3089} + \underset{(10.33)^{***}}{0.6437} \ln(X08/LW08)/(X82/LW82) + \underset{(6.78)^{***}}{0.86381} \ln(W)$$

$R^2ADJ = 0.925 \quad SD = 0.656 \quad DW = 0.504$

$$\ln W09 = \underset{(5.59)^{***}}{12.8227} + \underset{(0.47)}{0.61524} \ln(X09/LW09)/(X82/LW82) + \underset{(0.68)}{0.15912} \ln(W)$$

$R^2ADJ = 0.487 \quad SD = 0.373 \quad DW = 0.907$

$$\ln W10 = \underset{(3.62)^{***}}{4.24368} + \underset{(11.48)^{***}}{0.6437} \ln(X10/LW10)/(X82/LW82) + \underset{(9.11)^{***}}{0.59152} \ln(W)$$

$R^2ADJ = 0.957 \quad SD = 0.886 \quad DW = 0.580$

(*Continued*)

Table A3.4. (*Continued*)

$$\ln W11 = \underset{(4.01)^{***}}{6.33537} + \underset{(29.50)^{***}}{0.9882} \ln(X11/LW11)/(X82/LW82) + \underset{(5.39)^{***}}{1.08456} \ln(W)$$

$R^2ADJ = 0.982$ SD = 0.229 DW = 0.920

$$\ln W12 = \underset{(1.62)}{8.99215} + \underset{(2.41)^{*}}{0.9882} \ln(X12/LW12)/(X82/LW82) + \underset{(1.27)}{0.52773} \ln(W)$$

$R^2ADJ = 0.814$ SD = 0.375 DW = 0.735

$$\ln W13 = \underset{(10.42)^{***}}{9.80720} + \underset{(13.23)^{***}}{0.88031} \ln(X13/LW13)/(X82/LW82) + \underset{(5.64)^{***}}{0.61814} \ln(W)$$

$R^2ADJ = 0.871$ SD = 0.136 DW = 1.034

$$\ln W14 = \underset{(9.76)^{***}}{8.08476} + \underset{(4.65)^{***}}{1.50233} \ln(X14/LW14)/(X82/LW82) + \underset{(6.63)^{***}}{0.68693} \ln(W)$$

$R^2ADJ = 0.742$ SD = 0.177 DW = 0.816

$$\ln W15 = \underset{(1.55)}{12.1439} + \underset{(0.54)}{0.4130} \ln(W)$$

$R^2ADJ = 0.277$ SD = 0.246 DW = 1.902

$$\ln W16 = \underset{(-3.04)^{***}}{-11.858} + \underset{(5.17)^{***}}{2.5470} \ln(X16/LW16)/(X82/LW82) + \underset{(7.14)^{***}}{2.48989} \ln(W)$$

$R^2ADJ = 0.622$ SD = 0.391 DW = 1.633

$$\ln W17 = \underset{(3.75)^{***}}{4.21277} + \underset{(4.15)^{***}}{1.3547} \ln(X17/LW17)/(X82/LW82) + \underset{(9.31)^{***}}{1.27732} \ln(W)$$

$R^2ADJ = 0.760$ SD = 0.175 DW = 1.765

$$\ln W18 = \underset{(13.34)^{***}}{4.05214} + \underset{(4.65)^{***}}{0.69131} \ln(X18/LW18)/(X82/LW82) + \underset{(26.62)^{***}}{1.25499} \ln(W)$$

$R^2ADJ = 0.981$ SD = 0.063 DW = 1.072

$$\ln W19 = \underset{(13.13)^{***}}{16.0563} + \underset{(8.79)^{***}}{1.85611} \ln(X19/LW19)/(X82/LW82) - \underset{(-2.42)^{***}}{0.40947} \ln(W)$$

$R^2ADJ = 0.780$ SD = 0.209 DW = 1.106

$$\ln W20 = \underset{(8.85)^{***}}{6.59268} + \underset{(4.44)^{***}}{0.74822} \ln(X20/LW20)/(X82/LW82) + \underset{(8.38)^{***}}{0.92032} \ln(W)$$

$R^2ADJ = 0.870$ SD = 0.157 DW = 1.631

$$\ln W21 = \underset{(1.59)}{5.70965} + \underset{(3.64)^{***}}{1.8749} \ln(X21/LW21)/(X82/LW82) + \underset{(2.62)^{**}}{1.10051} \ln(W)$$

$R^2ADJ = 0.490$ SD = 0.693 DW = 1.388

$$\ln W22 = \underset{(15.72)^{***}}{10.6466} + \underset{(10.12)^{***}}{1.07015} \ln(X22/LW22)/(X82/LW82) + \underset{(6.80)^{***}}{0.55703} \ln(W)$$

$R^2ADJ = 0.859$ SD = 0.138 DW = 1.304

$$\ln W23 = \underset{(6.12)^{***}}{7.07047} + \underset{(8.55)^{***}}{1.01626} \ln(X23/LW23)/(X82/LW82) + \underset{(6.69)^{***}}{0.96201} \ln(W)$$

$R^2ADJ = 0.703$ SD = 0.161 DW = 1.356

$$\ln W24 = \underset{(4.60)^{***}}{3.36801} + \underset{(7.30)^{***}}{0.91303} \ln(X24/LW24)/(X82/LW82) + \underset{(15.73)^{***}}{1.39191} \ln(W)$$

$R^2ADJ = 0.903$ SD = 0.108 DW = 1.214

(*Continued*)

Table A3.4. (*Continued*)

$$\ln W25 = 4.78763 + 0.86899 \ln(X25/LW25)/(X82/LW82) + 1.20553 \ln(W)$$
(2.52)** (0.89) (5.58)***

$R^2ADJ = 0.903$ $SD = 0.108$ $DW = 1.214$

$$\ln W26 = 5.95645 + 0.71259 \ln(X26/LW26)/(X82/LW82) + 1.08708 \ln(W)$$
(16.97)*** (5.10)*** (25.69)***

$R^2ADJ = 0.960$ $SD = 0.074$ $DW = 1.009$

$$\ln W27 = 7.57604 + 0.73126 \ln(X27/LW27)/(X82/LW82) + 0.86902 \ln(W)$$
(19.62)*** (3.24)*** (17.50)***

$R^2ADJ = 0.931$ $SD = 0.082$ $DW = 1.393$

$$\ln W28 = 5.53396 + 1.65384 \ln(X28/LW28)/(X82/LW82) + 1.15381 \ln(W)$$
(18.77)*** (10.88)*** (32.47)***

$R^2ADJ = 0.974$ $SD = 0.063$ $DW = 0.806$

$$\ln W29 = 4.21031 + 1.00063 \ln(X29/LW29)/(X82/LW82) + 1.17045 \ln(W)$$
(2.72)** (8.92)*** (5.93)***

$R^2ADJ = 0.861$ $SD = 0.319$ $DW = 0.970$

$$\ln W30 = 2.32226 + 0.78787 \ln(X30/LW30)/(X82/LW82) + 1.30283 \ln(W)$$
(4.18)*** (11.53)*** (17.68)***

$R^2ADJ = 0.962$ $SD = 0.118$ $DW = 0.749$

$$\ln W31 = 6.28275 + 0.33238 \ln(X31/LW31)/(X82/LW82) + 1.00642 \ln(W)$$
(3.51)*** (1.76) (4.38)***

$R^2ADJ = 0.726$ $SD = 0.263$ $DW = 0.693$

$$\ln W32 = 15.4137 + 1.25978 \ln(X32/LW32)/(X82/LW82) - 0.12125 \ln(W)$$
(22.38)*** (8.57)*** (−1.24)

$R^2ADJ = 0.850$ $SD = 0.100$ $DW = 0.660$

$$\ln W33 = 10.1662 + 1.12621 \ln(X33/LW33)/(X82/LW82) + 0.59227 \ln(W)$$
(17.49)*** (4.64)*** (8.43)***

$R^2ADJ = 0.746$ $SD = 0.124$ $DW = 0.690$

$$\ln W34 = 10.1662 + 1.12621 \ln(X34/LW34)/(X82/LW82) + 0.59227 \ln(W)$$
(17.30)*** (2.26)** (7.18)***

$R^2ADJ = 0.624$ $SD = 0.123$ $DW = 0.572$

$$\ln W35 = 2.09979 + 1.36796 \ln(X35/LW35)/(X82/LW82) + 1.50621 \ln(W)$$
(2.62)** (5.00)*** (16.22)***

$R^2ADJ = 0.900$ $SD = 0.145$ $DW = 0.612$

$$\ln W36 = 8.40429 + 0.81242 \ln(X36/LW36)/(X82/LW82) + 0.79854 \ln(W)$$
(17.24)*** (6.90)*** (13.89)***

$R^2ADJ = 0.979$ $SD = 0.054$ $DW = 1.489$

$$\ln W37 = 4.22399 + 0.43543 \ln(X37/LW37)/(X82/LW82) + 0.15923 \ln(W)$$
(1.43) (1.84)* (0.55)

$$0.60417 \ln W37(-1)$$
(3.73)***

$R^2ADJ = 0.462$ $SD = 0.407$ $DW = 1.600$

(*Continued*)

Table A3.4. (*Continued*)

$$\ln W38 = \underset{(8.54)^{***}}{8.76617} + \underset{(3.98)^{***}}{0.94897} \ln(X38/LW38)/(X82/LW82) + \underset{(6.57)^{***}}{0.70700} \ln(W)$$

$R^2ADJ = 0.591$ SD = 0.175 DW = 1.011

$$\ln W39 = \underset{(11.65)^{***}}{12.5090} + \underset{(7.38)^{***}}{1.760614} \ln(X39/LW39)/(X82/LW82) + \underset{(1.00)}{0.13943} \ln(W)$$

$R^2ADJ = 0.713$ SD = 0.221 DW = 1.220

$$\ln W40 = \underset{(17.49)^{***}}{8.11735} + \underset{(12.77)^{***}}{0.85557} \ln(W)$$

$R^2ADJ = 0.843$ SD = 0.118 DW = 0.983

$$\ln W41 = \underset{(17.13)^{***}}{7.56630} + \underset{(5.89)^{***}}{0.84627} \ln(X41/LW41)/(X82/LW82) + \underset{(17.16)^{***}}{0.91212} \ln(W)$$

$R^2ADJ = 0.923$ SD = 0.092 DW = 0.934

$$\ln W42 = \underset{(6.47)^{***}}{20.8979} + \underset{(6.61)^{***}}{0.69330} \ln(X42/LW42)/(X82/LW82) - \underset{(-1.89)^{*}}{0.71591} \ln(W)$$

$R^2ADJ = 0.871$ SD = 0.228 DW = 0.598

$$\ln W43 = \underset{(11.72)^{***}}{8.03975} + \underset{(2.55)^{**}}{0.56515} \ln(X43/LW43)/(X82/LW82) + \underset{(9.84)^{***}}{0.84048} \ln(W)$$

$R^2ADJ = 0.895$ SD = 0.110 DW = 0.550

$$\ln W44 = \underset{(3.89)^{***}}{5.54040} + \underset{(5.63)^{***}}{1.11914} \ln(X44/LW44)/(X82/LW82) + \underset{(7.40)^{***}}{1.27486} \ln(W)$$

$R^2ADJ = 0.890$ SD = 0.231 DW = 0.804

$$\ln W45 = \underset{(11.19)}{4.99263} + \underset{(2.62)^{**}}{0.27493} \ln(X45/LW45)/(X82/LW82) + \underset{(3.94)^{***}}{1.76761} \ln(ROU)$$

$R^2ADJ = 0.552$ SD = 0.077 DW = 1.449

$$\ln W46 = \underset{(11.54)^{***}}{9.60096} + \underset{(4.16)^{***}}{0.48414} \ln(X46/LW46)/(X82/LW82) + \underset{(6.88)^{***}}{0.66390} \ln(W)$$

$R^2ADJ = 0.959$ SD = 0.069 DW = 0.967

$$\ln W47 = \underset{(4.05)^{***}}{13.2453} + \underset{(3.35)^{***}}{0.48414} \ln(X47(-2)/LW47(-2))/(X82(-3)/LW82(-3)) + \underset{(0.40)}{0.66390} \ln(W)$$

$R^2ADJ = 0.717$ SD = 0.203 DW = 0.667

$$\ln W48 = \underset{(2.18)^{*}}{5.69191} + \underset{(4.35)^{***}}{0.92991} \ln(X48/LW48)/(X82/LW82) + \underset{(3.82)^{***}}{1.13653} \ln(W)$$

$R^2ADJ = 0.719$ SD = 0.211 DW = 1.898

$$\ln W49 = \underset{(8.00)^{***}}{9.83819} + \underset{(3.30)^{***}}{0.60132} \ln(X49/LW49)/(X82/LW82) + \underset{(4.18)^{***}}{0.63594} \ln(W)$$

$R^2ADJ = 0.739$ SD = 0.198 DW = 1.334

$$\ln W50 = \underset{(4.61)^{***}}{12.0809} + \underset{(3.51)^{***}}{1.02696} \ln(X50/LW50)/(X82/LW82) + \underset{(1.07)}{0.34608} \ln(W)$$

$R^2ADJ = 0.661$ SD = 0.324 DW = 1.759

$$\ln W51 = \underset{(2.29)^{**}}{5.25566} + \underset{(4.00)^{***}}{1.18919} \ln(W) \quad (1.07)$$

$R^2ADJ = 0.379$ SD = 0.467 DW = 0.795

(*Continued*)

Table A3.4. (*Continued*)

$$\ln W52 = 7.95659 + 0.61439\ \ln(X52/LW52)/(X82/LW82) + 0.84663\ \ln(W)$$
(10.81)*** (3.60)*** (9.30)***
$R^2ADJ = 0.933$ SD = 0.097 DW = 1.177

$$\ln W53 = 2.47676 + 0.63755\ \ln(X53/LW53)/(X82/LW82) + 1.51210\ \ln(W)$$
(2.71)** (3.34)*** (13.73)***
$R^2ADJ = 0.929$ SD = 0.109 DW = 1.079

$$\ln W54 = 3.91688 + 3.91690\ \ln(X54/LW54)/(X82/LW82) + 1.35351\ \ln(W)$$
(2.88)** (2.61)** (8.48)***
$R^2ADJ = 0.758$ SD = 0.198 DW = 0.777

$$\ln W55 = 5.10816 + 1.03931\ \ln(X55/LW55)/(X82/LW82) + 1.22215\ \ln(W)$$
(11.39)*** (7.73)*** (22.33)***
$R^2ADJ = 0.943$ SD = 0.093 DW = 1.123

$$\ln W56 = 2.83304 + 0.53343\ \ln(X56/LW56)/(X82/LW82) + 1.47949\ \ln(W)$$
(3.07)*** (2.12)** (13.45)***
$R^2ADJ = 0.901$ SD = 0.171 DW = 1.588

$$\ln W57 = 7.60701 + 0.15213\ \ln(X57/LW57)/(X82/LW82) + 0.96980\ \ln(W)$$
(9.81)*** (0.49) (6.89)***
$R^2ADJ = 0.901$ SD = 0.120 DW = 1.579

$$\ln W58 = 7.02892 + 0.35265\ \ln(X58/LW58)/(X82/LW82) + 1.00703\ \ln(W)$$
(8.27)*** (2.99)*** (8.98)***
$R^2ADJ = 0.959$ SD = 0.087 DW = 1.132

$$\ln W59 = 7.31362 + 0.74260\ \ln(X59/LW59)/(X82/LW82) + 0.92803\ \ln(W)$$
(9.79)*** (3.35)*** (9.85)***
$R^2ADJ = 0.832$ SD = 0.156 DW = 0.812

$$\ln W60 = 7.29636 + 0.28812\ \ln(X60/LW60)/(X82/LW82) + 1.01600\ \ln(W)$$
(10.99)*** (1.34) (12.65)***
$R^2ADJ = 0.855$ SD = 0.138 DW = 1.031

$$\ln W61 = .02644 + 1.13927\ \ln(X61/LW61)/(X82/LW82) + 0.93954\ \ln(W)$$
(23.76)*** (9.82)*** (25.79)***
$R^2ADJ = 0.974$ SD = 0.059 DW = 1562

$$\ln W62 = 1.344860 + 0.87162\ \ln(X62/LW62)/(X82/LW82) + 1.65580\ \ln(W)$$
(1.63) (16.80)*** (17.27)***
$R^2ADJ = 0.928$ SD = 0.147 DW = 1.538

$$\ln W63 = 5.89099 + 0.71990\ \ln(X63/LW63)/(X82/LW82) + 1.10005\ \ln(W)$$
(9.57)*** (3.30)*** (13.11)***
$R^2ADJ = 0.925$ SD = 0.081 DW = 0.448

$$\ln W64 = 8.48464 + 0.67666\ \ln(X64/LW64)/(X82/LW82) + 0.82865\ \ln(W)$$
(8.46)*** (3.08)*** (6.73)***
$R^2ADJ = 0.627$ SD = 0.149 DW = 0.999

$$\ln W65 = 6.42563 + 1.02892\ \ln(X65/LW65)/(X82/LW82) + 1.14229\ \ln(W)$$
(9.59)*** (7.66)*** (13.45)***
$R^2ADJ = 0.862$ SD = 0.140 DW = 1.154

(*Continued*)

Table A3.4. (*Continued*)

$$\ln W66 = \underset{(14.67)^{***}}{6.42563} + \underset{(8.96)^{***}}{0.76024} \ln(X66/LW66)/(X82/LW82) + \underset{(8.62)^{***}}{0.68469} \ln(W)$$
$R^2ADJ = 0.916 \quad SD = 0.119 \quad DW = 1.119$

$$\ln W67 = \underset{(2.12)^{*}}{4.37653} + \underset{(0.46)}{0.108834} \ln(X67/LW67)/(X82/LW82) + \underset{(5.18)^{***}}{1.35080} \ln(W)$$
$R^2ADJ = 0.885 \quad SD = 0.170 \quad DW = 1.168$

$$\ln W68 = \underset{(10.25)^{***}}{6.52804} + \underset{(18.79)^{***}}{0.98345} \ln(X68/LW68)/(X82/LW82) + \underset{(13.83)^{***}}{1.05032} \ln(W)$$
$R^2ADJ = 0.943 \quad SD = 0.134 \quad DW = 1.118$

$$\ln W69 = \underset{(17.85)^{***}}{9.41328} + \underset{(13.90)^{***}}{0.94138} \ln(X69/LW69)/(X82/LW82) + \underset{(11.69)^{***}}{0.74302} \ln(W)$$
$R^2ADJ = 0.974 \quad SD = 0.079 \quad DW = 1.201$

$$\ln W70 = \underset{(14.12)^{***}}{7.32818} + \underset{(5.98)^{***}}{0.397837} \ln(X70/LW70)/(X82/LW82) + \underset{(15.96)^{***}}{0.98817} \ln(W)$$
$R^2ADJ = 0.948 \quad SD = 0.093 \quad DW = 1.079$

$$\ln W71 = \underset{(4.60)^{***}}{6.65471} + \underset{(3.21)^{***}}{0.47658} \ln(X71/LW71)/(X82/LW82) + \underset{(5.86)^{***}}{0.89567} \ln(W)$$
$R^2ADJ = 0.522 \quad SD = 0.208 \quad DW = 0.758$

$$\ln W72 = \underset{(6.67)^{***}}{9.36508} + \underset{(4.47)^{***}}{1.69780} \ln(X72/LW72)/(X82/LW82) + \underset{(4.52)^{***}}{0.75693} \ln(W)$$
$R^2ADJ = 0.856 \quad SD = 0.288 \quad DW = 1.659$

$$\ln W73 = \underset{(13.61)^{***}}{6.37045} + \underset{(9.30)^{***}}{1.25189} \ln(X73/LW73)/(X82/LW82) + \underset{(18.96)^{***}}{1.07246} \ln(W)$$
$R^2ADJ = 0.936 \quad SD = 0.100 \quad DW = 1.525$

$$\ln W75 = \underset{(10.50)^{***}}{5.04049} + \underset{(3.06)^{***}}{0.36052} \ln(X75/LW75)/(X82/LW82) + \underset{(22.73)^{***}}{1.27232} \ln(W)$$
$R^2ADJ = 0.968 \quad SD = 0.080 \quad DW = 1.365$

$$\ln W76 = \underset{(12.42)^{***}}{5.92877} + \underset{(4.29)^{***}}{0.71737} \ln(X76/LW76)/(X82/LW82) + \underset{(18.77)^{***}}{1.19989} \ln(W)$$
$R^2ADJ = 0.943 \quad SD = 0.081 \quad DW = 1.354$

$$\ln W77 = \underset{(18.76)^{***}}{6.68936} + \underset{(2.64)^{**}}{0.27347} \ln(X77/LW77)/(X82/LW82) + \underset{(25.14)^{***}}{1.04032} \ln(W)$$
$R^2ADJ = 0.964 \quad SD = 0.068 \quad DW = 0.800$

$$\ln W78 = \underset{(19.77)^{***}}{6.69640} + \underset{(10.56)^{***}}{0.77554} \ln(X78/LW78)/(X82/LW82) + \underset{(25.28)^{***}}{1.08095} \ln(W)$$
$R^2ADJ = 0.955 \quad SD = 0.069 \quad DW = 0.971$

$$\ln W79 = \underset{(7.78)^{***}}{2.83591} + \underset{(6.19)^{***}}{0.48115} \ln(X79/LW79)/(X82/LW82) + \underset{(32.62)^{***}}{1.44229} \ln(W)$$
$R^2ADJ = 0.973 \quad SD = 0.078 \quad DW = 0.905$

Notes: (1) ***, ** and * present the level of significance at 1%, 5% and 10%, respectively.
(2) Sector classification: please see notes of Table A3.1.

Table A3.5. Regression results of sectoral output price (PX).

$$\ln PX01 = \underset{(-0.43)}{-0.15200} + \underset{(7.36)^{***}}{0.24394} \ln ZN01(-1)/X01(-1) + \underset{(2.33)^{**}}{0.88611} \ln D01/X01$$
$$+ \underset{(1.46)}{0.005209} \ln UR(-4) - \underset{(-0.42)}{0.02389} \ln EXR(-3)$$
$$R^2ADJ = 0.894 \quad SD = 0.039 \quad DW = 1.447$$

$$\ln PX02 = \underset{(-0.33)}{-0.37792} + \underset{(4.64)^{***}}{0.26144} \ln ZN02(-1)/X02(-1) + \underset{(1.32)}{0.11702} \ln D02/X02$$
$$\underset{(-2.05)^{*}}{-0.08768} \ln UR(-1) + \underset{(5.29)^{***}}{0.23429} \ln EXR(-3)$$
$$R^2ADJ = 0.842 \quad SD = 0.056 \quad DW = 1.838$$

$$\ln PX03 = \underset{(-3.63)^{***}}{-1.38485} + \underset{(0.38)}{0.04806} \ln ZN03(-3)/X03(-3) + \underset{(2.32)^{**}}{0.55617} \ln D03(-3)/X03(-3)$$
$$\underset{(-0.47)}{-0.02527} \ln UR(-6) + \underset{(3.82)^{***}}{0.30214} \ln EXR(-1)$$
$$R^2ADJ = 0.830 \quad SD = 0.048 \quad DW = 0.810$$

$$\ln PX04 = \underset{(2.09^{**})}{0.62541} + \underset{(1.55)}{0.05948} \ln ZN04(-4)/X04(-4) + \underset{(1.81)^{*}}{0.26315} \ln D04(-4)/X04(-4)$$
$$+ \underset{(2.56)^{**}}{0.148419} \ln EXR$$
$$R^2ADJ = 0.697 \quad SD = 0.068 \quad DW = 2.159$$

$$\ln PX05 = \underset{(0.29)}{0.00345} + \underset{(0.82)}{0.00682} \ln ZN03(-2)/X03(-2) + \underset{(2.62)^{**}}{4.38004} \ln D03(-3)/X03(-3)$$
$$+ 0.81627 \underset{(15.13)^{***}}{\ln PX05(-1)}$$
$$R^2ADJ = 0.925 \quad SD = 0.031 \quad DW = 2.180$$

$$\ln PX06 = \underset{(-0.42)}{-0.09738} + \underset{(0.38)}{0.23818} \ln ZN06(-1)/X06(-1) + \underset{(4.49)^{**}}{0.42647} \ln D06(-1)/X06(-1)$$
$$\underset{(-1.80)^{*}}{-0.13848} \ln UR(-1) + \underset{(1.28)}{0.05542} \ln EXR(-4)$$
$$R^2ADJ = 0.873 \quad SD = 0.053 \quad DW = 1.919$$

$$\ln PX07 = \underset{(2.71)^{**}}{0.30244} + \underset{(16.01)^{***}}{0.67261} \ln ZN07/X07 + \underset{(3.23)^{***}}{0.45424} \ln D07/X07$$
$$+ \underset{(4.30)^{***}}{0.09821} \ln EXR(-2)$$
$$R^2ADJ = 0.954 \quad SD = 0.035 \quad DW = 1.615$$

$$\ln PX08 = \underset{(1.13)}{0.46040} + \underset{(11.06)^{***}}{0.81484} \ln ZN08(-1)/X08(-1) + \underset{(0.22)}{0.01141} \ln D08/X08$$
$$\underset{(-1.59)}{-0.17607} \ln UR(-1)$$
$$R^2ADJ = 0.897 \quad SD = 0.071 \quad DW = 2.227$$

$$\ln PX09 = \underset{(-2.87)^{***}}{-5.22701} + \underset{(4.74)^{***}}{0.57710} \ln ZN09(-1)/X09(-1) + \underset{(2.84)^{***}}{0.7827} \ln D09(-2)/X09(-2)$$
$$+ \underset{(0.78)}{0.10535} \ln EXR(-3)$$
$$R^2ADJ = 0.779 \quad SD = 0.219 \quad DW = 1.361$$

$$\ln PX10 = \underset{(3.41)^{***}}{0.40445} + \underset{(17.29)^{***}}{1.0428} ZN09(-1)/X09(-1) - \underset{(-1.82)^{*}}{0.04677} UR(-3)$$
$$+ \underset{(1.39)}{0.000432} EXR(-2)$$
$$R^2ADJ = 0.914 \quad SD = 0.085 \quad DW = 0.997$$

(*Continued*)

Table A3.5. (*Continued*)

$$\ln PX11 = \underset{(-1.98)^{*}}{-0.84740} + \underset{(9.18)^{***}}{0.87982}\ \ln ZN11/X11 + \underset{(2.31)^{**}}{0.06605}\ \ln D11(-5)/X11(-5) \underset{(-1.48)}{-0.17626}\ \ln UR(-3) + \underset{(1.86)^{*}}{0.14032}\ \ln EXR(-1)$$

$$R^2 ADJ = 0.916 \quad SD = 0.074 \quad DW = 1.605$$

$$\ln PX12 = \underset{(-1.37)}{-1.66211} + \underset{(4.19)^{***}}{0.75819}\ \ln ZN12(-1)/X12(-1) + \underset{(0.66)}{0.10228}\ \ln D12(-2)/X12(-2) + \underset{(-1.98)^{*}}{0.35220}\ \ln EXR(-3)$$

$$R^2 ADJ = 0.825 \quad SD = 0.179 \quad DW = 1.272$$

$$\ln PX13 = \underset{(1.81)}{0.95380} + \underset{(3.78)^{***}}{0.43660}\ \ln ZN13(-1)/X13(-1) + \underset{(1.72)^{*}}{0.12511}\ \ln D13(-2)/X13(-2) \underset{(-1.76)^{*}}{-0.10529}\ \ln UR + \underset{(1.74)^{*}}{0.1494}\ \ln EXR(-3)$$

$$R^2 ADJ = 0.634 \quad SD = 0.072 \quad DW = 1.168$$

$$\ln PX14 = \underset{(1.40)}{0.04174} + \underset{(4.81)^{***}}{0.62706}\ \ln ZN14(-1)/X14(-1) + \underset{(2.42)^{**}}{0.21344}\ \ln D14(-2)/X14(-2) \underset{(-1.49)}{-0.03931}\ \ln UR(-2)$$

$$R^2 ADJ = 0.867 \quad SD = 0.020 \quad DW = 1.128$$

$$\ln PX15 = \underset{(1.95)^{*}}{1.22867} + \underset{(8.37)^{***}}{0.57897}\ \ln ZN15(-1)/X15(-1) + \underset{(1.10)}{0.03929}\ \ln D15/X15 \underset{(-0.44)}{-0.03228}\ \ln UR + \underset{(2.14)^{**}}{0.24953}\ \ln EXR(-3)$$

$$R^2 ADJ = 0.931 \quad SD = 0.078 \quad DW = 1.558$$

$$\ln PX16 = \underset{(3.60)^{****}}{1.25052} + \underset{(0.45)}{0.05327}\ \ln ZN16(-1)/X16(-1) + \underset{(0.58)}{0.22125}\ \ln D16(-4)/X16(-4) \underset{(-1.60)}{-0.14971}\ \ln UR(-2) + \underset{(3.56)^{**}}{0.20709}\ \ln EXR(-3)$$

$$R^2 ADJ = 0.277 \quad SD = 0.086 \quad DW = 0.396$$

$$\ln PX17 = \underset{(0.44)}{0.11236} + \underset{(3.43)^{***}}{0.58707}\ \ln ZN17(-1)/X17(-1) + \underset{(0.45)}{0.60431}\ \ln D17(-3)/X17(-3) \underset{(-1.16)}{-0.0574}\ \ln UR + \underset{(0.42)}{0.01792}\ \ln EXR(-3)$$

$$R^2 ADJ = 0.427 \quad SD = 0.041 \quad DW = 1.409$$

$$\ln PX18 = \underset{(0.84)}{0.18583} + \underset{(5.50)^{***}}{0.51750}\ \ln ZN18(-1)/X18(-1) + \underset{(0.80)}{0.83642}\ \ln D18(-4)/X18(-4) \underset{(-1.42)}{-0.02609}\ \ln UR(-6)$$

$$R^2 ADJ = 0.715 \quad SD = 0.047 \quad DW = 0.614$$

$$\ln PX19 = \underset{(-0.15)}{-0.07969} + \underset{(4.95)^{***}}{0.71498}\ \ln ZN19(-1)/X19(-1) + \underset{(1.52)}{0.41565}\ \ln D19(-2)/X19(-2) \underset{(-1.41)}{-0.04034}\ \ln UR(-1)$$

$$R^2 ADJ = 0.732 \quad SD = 0.113 \quad DW = 1.870$$

$$\ln PX20 = \underset{(1.60)}{0.86579} + \underset{(6.42)^{***}}{0.51304}\ \ln ZN20(-1)/X20(-1) + \underset{(0.28)}{0.14300}\ \ln D20/X20 \underset{(-4.33)^{***}}{-0.27452}\ \ln UR(-1) + \underset{(1.32)}{0.12943}\ \ln EXR(-3)$$

$$R^2 ADJ = 0.896 \quad SD = 0.081 \quad DW = 1.429$$

(*Continued*)

Table A3.5. (*Continued*)

$$\ln PX21 = \underset{(0.10)}{0.00796} + \underset{(6.69)^{***}}{0.82617} \ln ZN21(-1)/X21(-1) + \underset{(0.31)}{0.03247} \ln D21(-5)/X21(-5) \underset{(-1.61)}{-0.04368} \ln UR(-2)$$

$R^2ADJ = 0.802 \quad SD = 0.053 \quad DW = 1.454$

$$\ln PX22 = \underset{(2.63)^{**}}{0.43021} + \underset{(2.27)^{**}}{0.32241} \ln ZN22(-1)/X22(-1) + \underset{(4.20)^{***}}{0.44385} \ln D22(-3)/X22(-3) \underset{(-2.29)^{**}}{-0.08235} \ln UR(-1) + \underset{(2.53)^{**}}{0.06652} \ln EXR(-3)$$

$R^2ADJ = 0.690 \quad SD = 0.037 \quad DW = 1.876$

$$\ln PX23 = \underset{(4.12)^{***}}{0.6753} + \underset{(8.49)^{***}}{0.78104} \ln ZN23(-1)/X23(-1) + \underset{(1.05)}{0.10518} \ln D23(-1)/X23(-1) \underset{(-0.99)}{-0.05708} \ln UR(-2) + \underset{(3.77)^{***}}{0.12138} \ln EXR(-1)$$

$R^2ADJ = 0.929 \quad SD = 0.038 \quad DW = 2.448$

$$\ln PX24 = \underset{(1.41)}{0.36144} + \underset{(6.08)^{***}}{0.58743} \ln ZN24(-1)/X24(-1) + \underset{(1.02)}{0.00144} \ln D24(-1)/X24(-1) + \underset{(1.66)}{0.07592} \ln EXR(-3)$$

$R^2ADJ = 0.816 \quad SD = 0.044 \quad DW = 1.179$

$$\ln PX25 = \underset{(-1.31)}{-0.18982} + \underset{(32.27)^{***}}{0.95977} \ln ZN25/X25 + \underset{(3.32)^{***}}{0.369611} \ln D25(-2)/X25(-2) \underset{(-2.44)^{**}}{-0.02965} \ln UR(-3) + \underset{(1.10)}{0.02846} \ln EXR(-3)$$

$R^2ADJ = 0.992 \quad SD = 0.011 \quad DW = 1.281$

$$\ln PX26 = \underset{(-3.06)^{***}}{-0.69061} + \underset{(4.47)^{***}}{0.61121} \ln ZN26(-1)/X26(-1) + \underset{(2.41)^{**}}{1.22871} \ln D26(-2)/X26(-2) \underset{(-1.85)^{*}}{-0.09946} \ln UR(-1) + \underset{(3.10)^{***}}{0.14990} \ln EXR(-2)$$

$R^2ADJ = 0.918 \quad SD = 0.041 \quad DW = 1.453$

$$\ln PX27 = \underset{(0.49)}{0.11574} + \underset{(1.96)^{*}}{0.27819} \ln ZN27(-2)/X27(-2) + \underset{(2.10)^{**}}{0.3751} \ln D27/X27 \underset{(-1.35)}{-0.01573} \ln UR$$

$R^2ADJ = 0.319 \quad SD = 0.052 \quad DW = 1.164$

$$\ln PX28 = \underset{(20.74)^{***}}{0.106334} + \underset{(57.27)^{***}}{1.0326} \ln ZN28/X28 + \underset{(2.92)^{***}}{1.41043} \ln D28(-1)/X28(-1) \underset{(-6.92)^{***}}{-0.04543} DUM7584$$

$R^2ADJ = 0.995 \quad SD = 0.014 \quad DW = 1.198$

$$\ln PX29 = \underset{(-0.05)}{-0.2382} + \underset{(4.55)^{***}}{0.70930} \ln ZN29(-1)/X29(-1) + \underset{(1.61)}{0.31708} \ln D29(-4)/X29(-4) \underset{(-1.42)}{-0.04169} \ln UR(-1)$$

$R^2ADJ = 0.796 \quad SD = 0.102 \quad DW = 1.425$

$$\ln PX30 = \underset{(-0.95)}{-0.50453} + \underset{(1.17)}{0.11843} \ln ZN30(-1)/X30(-1) + \underset{(1.11)}{0.05425} \ln D30(-3)/X30(-3) + \underset{(7.73)^{***}}{0.60058} \ln PM$$

$R^2ADJ = 0.941 \quad SD = 0.072 \quad DW = 0.707$

(*Continued*)

Table A3.5. (*Continued*)

$$\ln PX31 = \underset{(0.02)}{0.00693} + \underset{(5.92)^{***}}{0.57478} \ln ZN31(-1)/X31(-1) + \underset{(0.50)}{0.47421} \ln D31/X31$$
$$- \underset{(-0.87)}{0.05921} \ln UR + \underset{(1.40)}{0.02620} \ln EXR(-3)$$
$$R^2ADJ = 0.771 \quad SD = 0.084 \quad DW = 1.079$$

$$\ln PX32 = \underset{(1.23)}{0.05962} + \underset{(0.33)}{0.03016} \ln ZN32(-3)/X32(-3) + \underset{(1.92)^{*}}{0.19707} \ln D32(-2)/X32(-2)$$
$$- \underset{(-5.03)^{***}}{0.14113} \ln UR(-1) + \underset{(7.48)^{***}}{0.00116} EXR$$
$$R^2ADJ = 0.895 \quad SD = 0.034 \quad DW = 0.925$$

$$\ln PX33 = \underset{(1.89)^{*}}{0.36085} + \underset{(9.04)^{***}}{0.73703} \ln ZN33(-1)/X33(-1) + \underset{(0.32)}{0.02742} \ln D32(-1)/X33(-1)$$
$$- \underset{(-0.47)}{0.01773} \ln UR + \underset{(1.84)^{*}}{0.05791} \ln EXR$$
$$R^2ADJ = 0.756 \quad SD = 0.042 \quad DW = 2.523$$

$$\ln PX34 = \underset{(2.35)^{**}}{0.45818} + \underset{(1.50)}{0.04802} \ln ZN34(-3)/X34(-3) + \underset{(0.70)}{0.02742} \ln D34(-3)/X34(-3)$$
$$- \underset{(-1.87)^{*}}{0.04277} \ln UR + \underset{(2.61)^{**}}{0.10912} \ln EXR + \underset{(3.57)^{***}}{0.14542} \ln PM34$$
$$R^2ADJ = 0.487 \quad SD = 0.024 \quad DW = 1.360$$

$$\ln PX35 = \underset{(0.31)}{0.12433} + \underset{(3.87)^{***}}{0.53004} \ln ZN35(-1)/X35(-1) + \underset{(0.33)}{0.03575} \ln D35(-2)/X35(-2)$$
$$- \underset{(-1.55)}{0.04163} \ln UR(-1) + \underset{(1.31)}{0.02495} \ln EXR$$
$$R^2ADJ = 0.341 \quad SD = 0.078 \quad DW = 2.768$$

$$\ln PX36 = \underset{(3.60)^{***}}{0.2740} + \underset{(10.98)^{***}}{0.64039} \ln ZN36(-1)/X36(-1) + \underset{(3.67)^{***}}{0.27445} \ln D36(-2)/X36(-2)$$
$$+ \underset{(2.78)^{**}}{0.044466} \ln EXR + \underset{(1.96)^{*}}{0.06774} \ln PM36$$
$$R^2ADJ = 0.932 \quad SD = 0.026 \quad DW = 1.874$$

$$\ln PX37 = \underset{(-0.32)}{-0.23509} + \underset{(4.75)^{***}}{0.50516} \ln ZN37(-1)/X37(-1) + \underset{(0.26)}{0.58858} \ln D37(-1)/X37(-1)$$
$$- \underset{(-2.45)^{**}}{0.19990} \ln UR(-1) + \underset{(0.90)}{0.11670} \ln EXR(-2)$$
$$R^2ADJ = 0.813 \quad SD = 0.099 \quad DW = 1.189$$

$$\ln PX38 = \underset{(-1.42)}{-0.58987} + \underset{(2.05)^{*}}{0.18284} \ln ZN38(-3)/X38(-3) + \underset{(1.53)}{0.82195} \ln D38/X38$$
$$- \underset{(-1.72)^{*}}{0.09914} \ln UR(-1) + \underset{(1.89)^{*}}{0.17925} \ln EXR + \underset{(2.85)^{***}}{0.29750} \ln PM38$$
$$R^2ADJ = 0.852 \quad SD = 0.048 \quad DW = 1.042$$

$$\ln PX40 = \underset{(3.29)^{***}}{1.05170} + \underset{(1.23)}{0.14783} \ln ZN40(-2)/X40(-2) + \underset{(2.91)^{***}}{0.29638} \ln D40(-1)/X40(-1)$$
$$- \underset{(-2.99)^{***}}{0.13650} \ln UR + \underset{(2.83)^{**}}{0.18553} \ln EXR + \underset{(406)^{***}}{0.27074} \ln PM40$$
$$R^2ADJ = 0.772 \quad SD = 0.049 \quad DW = 1.150$$

$$\ln PX41 = \underset{(2.46)^{**}}{0.38837} + \underset{(6.28)^{***}}{0.29905} \ln ZN41(-1)/X41(-1) + \underset{(2.60)^{**}}{0.91207} \ln D41/X41$$
$$+ \underset{(-2.21)^{**}}{0.0735} \ln EXR + \underset{(3.59)^{***}}{0.21096} \ln PM41$$
$$R^2ADJ = 0.914 \quad SD = 0.030 \quad DW = 1.425$$

(*Continued*)

Table A3.5. (*Continued*)

$$\ln PX42 = \underset{(-1.38)}{-0.66673} + \underset{(6.67)^{***}}{0.62375} \ln ZN42(-1)/X42(-1) + \underset{(2.38)^{**}}{0.20089} \ln D42(-1)/X42(-1)$$
$$\underset{(-1.51)}{-0.16465} \ln UR(-2) + \underset{(2.15)^{**}}{0.20058} \ln EXR(-3)$$
$$R^2ADJ = 0.935 \quad SD = 0.106 \quad DW = 2.298$$

$$\ln PX43 = \underset{(4.05)^{***}}{0.44630} + \underset{(0.82)}{0.03603} \ln ZN43(-3)/X43(-3) + \underset{(3.99)^{***}}{0.23567} \ln D43(-1)/X43(-1)$$
$$+\underset{(5.05)^{***}}{0.11486} \ln EXR + \underset{(6.31)^{***}}{0.55198} \ln PM43$$
$$R^2ADJ = 0.669 \quad SD = 0.029 \quad DW = 2.013$$

$$\ln PX44 = \underset{(3.59)^{***}}{0.47982} + \underset{(2.79)^{**}}{0.49864} \ln ZN43(-)/X43(-1) + \underset{(2.35)^{**}}{0.14849} \ln D43(-3)/X43(-3)$$
$$+\underset{(3.21)^{***}}{0.33930} \ln EXR(-1)$$
$$R^2ADJ = 0.869 \quad SD = 0.074 \quad DW = 2.778$$

$$\ln PX45 = \underset{(-2.99)^{***}}{-1.22261} + \underset{(5.11)^{***}}{0.88257} \ln ZN45(-1)/X45(-1) + \underset{(1.42)}{0.10944} \ln D45(-4)/X45(-4)$$
$$\underset{(-1.21)}{-0.01728} \ln UR(-1) + \underset{(2.72)^{**}}{0.27009} \ln EXR(-3)$$
$$R^2ADJ = 0.963 \quad SD = 0.065 \quad DW = 0.914$$

$$\ln PX46 = \underset{(-0.10)}{-0.01543} + \underset{(3.99)^{***}}{0.32630} \ln ZN46(-1)/X46(-1) + \underset{(2.06)^{*}}{0.10471} \ln D46(-4)/X46(-4)$$
$$\underset{(-0.79)}{-0.02169} \ln UR(-1) + \underset{(1.72)}{0.01958} \ln EXR(-2)$$
$$R^2ADJ = 0.633 \quad SD = 0.335 \quad DW = 1.813$$

$$\ln PX47 = \underset{(-1.18)}{-0.17544} + \underset{(0.13)}{0.01228} \ln ZN47(-3)/X47(-3) + \underset{(1.34)}{0.11600} \ln D47(-6)/X47(-6)$$
$$\underset{(-1.69)}{-0.04999} \ln UR(-1) + \underset{(2.04)^{*}}{0.06250} \ln EXR(-2)$$
$$R^2ADJ = 0.541 \quad SD = 0.335 \quad DW = 1.586$$

$$\ln PX48 = \underset{(-1.93)^{*}}{-1.85541} + \underset{(5.38)^{***}}{0.63116} \ln ZN48(-1)/X48(-1) + \underset{(2.65)^{**}}{5.6837} \ln D48(-1)/X48(-1)$$
$$\underset{(-1.83)^{*}}{-0.23420} \ln UR + \underset{(1.92)^{*}}{0.35608} \ln EXR(-1)$$
$$R^2ADJ = 0.815 \quad SD = 0.156 \quad DW = 2.583$$

$$\ln PX50 = \underset{(-1.36)}{-0.35776} + \underset{(7.98)^{***}}{0.55166} \ln ZN50/X50 + \underset{(3.39)^{**}}{0.7143} \ln D50(-3)/X50(-3)$$
$$\underset{(-1.72)^{*}}{-0.05524} \ln UR(-1)$$
$$R^2ADJ = 0.833 \quad SD = 0.032 \quad DW = 1.627$$

$$\ln PX51 = \underset{(1.02)}{0.45145} + \underset{(1.60)}{0.06929} \ln ZN51(-6)/X51(-6) + \underset{(1.10)}{0.0562} \ln D51(-2)/X51(-2)$$
$$\underset{(-11.74)^{*}}{-0.05195} \ln UR + \underset{(2.41)^{**}}{0.10174} \ln EXR(-1)$$
$$R^2ADJ = 0.427 \quad SD = 0.042 \quad DW = 1.411$$

$$\ln PX52 = \underset{(0.07)}{0.45145} + \underset{(5.79)^{***}}{0.06929} \ln ZN52(-1)/X52(-1) + \underset{(1.43)}{0.0562} \ln D52(-1)/X52(-1)$$
$$\underset{(-1.52)}{-0.05195} \ln UR(-1) + \underset{(1.71)^{*}}{0.10174} \ln EXR(-1)$$
$$R^2ADJ = 0.835 \quad SD = 0.051 \quad DW = 1.910$$

(*Continued*)

Table A3.5. (*Continued*)

$$\ln PX53 = \underset{(2.12)^{**}}{0.12090} + \underset{(9.33)^{***}}{0.74575} \ln ZN53(-1)/X53(-1) + \underset{(1.33)}{0.11835} \ln D53(-4)/X53(-4)$$
$$\underset{(-2.04)^{*}}{-0.08532} \ln UR$$
$$R^2ADJ = 0.859 \quad SD = 0.043 \quad DW = 1.584$$

$$\ln PX54 = \underset{(-2.07)^{*}}{-0.13567} + \underset{(2.74)^{**}}{0.17052} \ln ZN5(-4)/X54(-4) + \underset{(2.34)^{**}}{0.28197} \ln D54/X54$$
$$\underset{(-1.45)}{-0.07557} \ln UR$$
$$R^2ADJ = 0.538 \quad SD = 0.070 \quad DW = 0.771$$

$$\ln PX55 = \underset{(-0.63)}{-0.04246} + \underset{(5.84)^{***}}{0.60203} \ln ZN55(-1)/X55(-1) + \underset{(1.80)^{*}}{0.22334} \ln D55(-2)/X55(-2)$$
$$\underset{(-1.37)}{-0.02085} \ln UR(-1)$$
$$R^2ADJ = 0.726 \quad SD = 0.068 \quad DW = 1.463$$

$$\ln PX56 = \underset{(1.03)}{0.27448} + \underset{(14.18)^{***}}{0.72180} \ln ZN56(-1)/X56(-1) + \underset{(1.01)}{0.0219} \ln D56/X56$$
$$\underset{(-1.29)}{-0.05547} \ln UR(-1)$$
$$R^2ADJ = 0.935 \quad SD = 0.040 \quad DW = 1.847$$

$$\ln PX57 = \underset{(2.10)^{*}}{0.13702} + \underset{(6.01)^{***}}{0.50923} \ln ZN57(-2)/X57(-2) + \underset{(2.81)^{**}}{0.80370} \ln D57(-3)/X57(-3)$$
$$\underset{(-1.31)}{-0.06824} \ln UR + \underset{(4.92)^{***}}{0.24947} \ln PM57$$
$$R^2ADJ = 0.807 \quad SD = 0.077 \quad DW = 1.293$$

$$\ln PX58 = \underset{(6.70)^{***}}{0.27546} + \underset{(5.36)^{***}}{0.67962} \ln ZN58/X58 + \underset{(0.53)}{0.05584} \ln D58/X58$$
$$\underset{(-3.13)^{***}}{-0.11029} \ln UR(-1) + \underset{(1.44)}{0.09858} \ln PM58$$
$$R^2ADJ = 0.935 \quad SD = 0.050 \quad DW = 0.922$$

$$\ln PX61 = \underset{(0.93)}{0.48536} + \underset{(9.25)^{***}}{0.33570} \ln ZN61(-1)/X61(-1) + \underset{(0.92)}{0.05468} \ln D61/X61$$
$$\underset{(-2.25)^{**}}{-0.05096} \ln UR(-1) \qquad (1.44)$$
$$R^2ADJ = 0.908 \quad SD = 0.016 \quad DW = 1.944$$

$$\ln PX62 = \underset{(6.48)^{***}}{1.93470} + \underset{(3.22)^{***}}{0.37822} \ln ZN62(-3)/X62(-3) + \underset{(2.06)^{*}}{0.45979} \ln D62(-2)/X62(-2)$$
$$\underset{(-0.45)}{-0.02821} \ln UR + \underset{(6.90)^{***}}{0.39588} \ln EXR(-1)$$
$$R^2ADJ = 0.863 \quad SD = 0.069 \quad DW = 1.013$$

$$\ln PX63 = \underset{(-4.89)^{***}}{-7.00727} + \underset{(3.91)^{***}}{0.4240} \ln ZN63/X63 + \underset{(5.32)^{***}}{0.42729} \ln D63(-2)/X63(-2)$$
$$\underset{(2.10)^{**}}{+0.08121} \ln EXR(-1)$$
$$R^2ADJ = 0.974 \quad SD = 0.032 \quad DW = 1.715$$

$$\ln PX64 = \underset{(-3.38)^{***}}{-0.06087} + \underset{(0.25)}{0.01774} \ln ZN64/X64 + \underset{(2.16)^{**}}{0.44902} \ln D64(-1)/X64(-1)$$
$$\underset{(4.67)^{***}}{+0.07745} \ln PM64(-4) + \underset{(5.86)^{***}}{10.65520} \ln PM65(-1)$$
$$R^2ADJ = 0.933 \quad SD = 0.049 \quad DW = 0.838$$

(*Continued*)

Table A3.5. (*Continued*)

$$\ln PX65 = \underset{(-3.38)^{***}}{0.05572} + \underset{(0.25)}{0.73523} \ln ZN65(-2)/X65(-2) + \underset{(2.16)^{**}}{0.0470} \ln D65/X65$$

$R^2ADJ = 0.896$ SD = 0.052 DW = 0.749

$$\ln PX66 = \underset{(1.00)}{0.08154} + \underset{(0.81)}{0.11559} \ln ZN66(-4)/X66(-4) + \underset{(1.48)}{0.02245} \ln D66(-3)/X66(-3) + \underset{(1.51)}{0.181461} \ln PM66(-2)$$

$R^2ADJ = 0.129$ SD = 0.074 DW = 1.301

$$\ln PX67 = \underset{(-3.52)^{***}}{-0.26609} + \underset{(31.47)^{***}}{0.82588} \ln ZN67/X67 + \underset{(0.95)}{0.01237} \ln D67(-1)/X67(-1) \underset{(-0.39)}{-0.006801} \ln UR + \underset{(3.74)^{***}}{3.73818} \ln EXR(-1)$$

$R^2ADJ = 0.983$ SD = 0.016 DW = 2.017

$$\ln PX68 = \underset{(5.02)^{***}}{1.47647} + \underset{(2.38)^{**}}{0.18034} \ln ZN68/X68 + \underset{(1.36)}{0.05904} \ln D68(-1)/X68(-1) + \underset{(4.84)^{***}}{0.029927} \ln EXR + \underset{(2.16)^{**}}{1.0958} \ln PM68$$

$R^2ADJ = 0.748$ SD = 0.070 DW = 1.113

$$\ln PX70 = \underset{(-3.74)^{***}}{-0.3340} + \underset{(23.46)^{**}}{0.86688} \ln ZN70/X70 + \underset{(1.49)}{1.78765} \ln D70(-1)/X70(-1) \underset{(-5.47)^{***}}{-0.15795} \ln UR(-1) + \underset{(5.02)^{***}}{0.16565} \ln EXR(-3)$$

$R^2ADJ = 0.960$ SD = 0.038 DW = 1.156

$$\ln PX71 = \underset{(-5.01)^{***}}{-0.3340} + \underset{(5.44)^{**}}{0.86688} \ln ZN71/X71 + \underset{(5.59)^{**}}{1.78765} \ln D71(-2)/X71(-2)$$

$R^2ADJ = 0.974$ SD = 0.039 DW = 1.083

$$\ln PX72 = \underset{(1.85)^{*}}{0.58901} + \underset{(1.95)^{*}}{0.14936} \ln ZN72(-3)/X72(-3) + \underset{(2.30)^{**}}{0.7282} \ln D72(-3)/X72(-3) \underset{(-1.06)}{-0.5944} \ln UR + \underset{(4.50)^{***}}{0.22359} \ln EXR(-1)$$

$R^2ADJ = 0.637$ SD = 0.061 DW = 1.183

$$\ln PX73 = \underset{(2.56)^{**}}{0.41854} + \underset{(4.45)^{***}}{0.1865} \ln ZN73(-2)/X73(-2) + \underset{(1.36)}{0.3964} \ln D73(-2)/X73(-2) \underset{(-1.70)}{-0.55221} \ln UR(-1) + \underset{(3.33)^{***}}{0.16899} \ln EXR(-1)$$

$R^2ADJ = 0.790$ SD = 0.036 DW = 1.677

$$\ln PX74 = \underset{(2.56)^{**}}{4.42338} + \underset{(4.45)^{***}}{0.39310} \ln ZN74(-2)/X74(-2) + \underset{(1.36)}{0.23253} \ln D74(-4)/X74(-4) \underset{(-1.70)}{-0.08333} \ln UR(-2) + \underset{(3.33)^{***}}{0.15826} \ln EXR(-1)$$

$R^2ADJ = 0.901$ SD = 0.033 DW = 1.502

$$\ln PX77 = \underset{(1.31)}{-0.69574} + \underset{(6.74)^{***}}{0.69141} \ln ZN77/X77 + \underset{(2.06)^{**}}{0.4909} \ln D77(-2)/X77(-2) + \underset{(-0.91)}{0.03046} \ln EXR$$

$R^2ADJ = 0.926$ SD = 0.025 DW = 0.778

$$\ln PX78 = \underset{(3.74)^{***}}{0.87750} + \underset{(2.64)^{**}}{0.16466} \ln ZN78(-4)/X78(-4) + \underset{(2.78)^{**}}{0.16689} \ln D78(-1)/X78(-1) \underset{(-1.70)}{-0.5895} \ln UR(-1) + \underset{(4.32)^{***}}{0.20225} \ln EXR$$

$R^2ADJ = 0.867$ SD = 0.043 DW = 1.055

(*Continued*)

Table A3.5. (*Continued*)

$$\ln PX78 = \underset{(5.66)^{***}}{1.2998} + \underset{(4.38)^{***}}{0.31870} \ln ZN78(-3)/X78(-3) + \underset{(1.26)}{0.4308} \ln D78(-3)/X78(-3)$$
$$\underset{(-1.43)}{-0.5726} \ln UR(-1) + \underset{(5.95)^{***}}{0.28344} \ln EXR$$
$$R^2ADJ = 0.916 \quad SD = 0.046 \quad DW = 1.544$$

Notes: (1) ***, ** and * present the level of significance at 1%, 5% and 10%, respectively.
(2) Sector classification: please see notes of Table A3.1.

Table A3.6. Regression results of real exports by sector: Major manufacturing sectors.

$$E30 = \underset{(3.871)^{***}}{153690.3} + \underset{(0.984)}{4.923} TWM - \underset{(-3.212)^{***}}{7.12E+08} PE30/EXR/PEW + \underset{(4.139)^{***}}{0.5590} E30(-1)$$
$$R^2ADJ = 0.806 \quad SD = 75842.4 \quad DW = 1.775$$

$$E31 = \underset{(2.512)^{***}}{354351.4} + \underset{(1.762)^{*}}{156.520} TWM - \underset{(-2.443)^{***}}{4.41E+09} PE31/EXR/PEW + \underset{(2.487)^{***}}{0.398} E31(-1)$$
$$R^2ADJ = 0.981 \quad SD = 425099.2 \quad DW = 1.017$$

$$E32 = \underset{(1.676)}{398167.7} + \underset{(4.249)^{***}}{184.502} TWM - \underset{(-1.236)}{3.43E+09} PE32(-2)/EXR(-2)/PEW(-2) + \underset{(2.208)^{*}}{0.368} E32(-1)$$
$$R^2ADJ = 0.969 \quad SD = 473778.0 \quad DW = 2.128$$

$$E33 = \underset{(2.632)^{**}}{130413.2} + \underset{(2.843)^{***}}{28.269} TWM - \underset{(-1.417)}{1.18E+09} PE33/EXR/PEW + \underset{(5.136)^{***}}{0.658} E33(-1)$$
$$R^2ADJ = 0.857 \quad SD = 92541.0 \quad DW = 1.801$$

$$E34 = \underset{(1.682)}{118183.0} + \underset{(2.697)^{***}}{50.067} TWM - \underset{(-1.995)^{*}}{12.69E+09} PE34(-1)/EXR(-1)/PEW(-1) + \underset{(3.025)^{***}}{0.708} E34(-1)$$
$$R^2ADJ = 0.934 \quad SD = 143472.3 \quad DW = 1.439$$

$$E37 = \underset{(0.644)}{22234.8} + \underset{(0.333)}{0.645} TWM - \underset{(-0.511)}{1.23E+08} PE37(-2)/EXR(-2)/PEW(-2) + \underset{(4.851)^{***}}{0.671} E37(-1)$$
$$R^2ADJ = 0.519 \quad SD = 24053.1 \quad DW = 1.382$$

$$E38 = \underset{(4.225)^{***}}{2535548.1} - \underset{(-3.952)^{***}}{1.81E+10} PE38/EXR/PEW + \underset{(5.022)^{***}}{0.548} E37(-1)$$
$$R^2ADJ = 0.839 \quad SD = 4965.2 \quad DW = 2.003$$

$$E39 = \underset{(0.705)}{14789.3} + \underset{(2.707)^{***}}{8.298} TWM - \underset{(-0.315)}{6.90E+07} PE39/EXR/PEW + \underset{(3.632)^{***}}{0.570} E39(-1)$$
$$R^2ADJ = 0.870 \quad SD = 35642.9 \quad DW = 1.904$$

$$E40 = \underset{(1.369)}{107474.6} + \underset{(2.837)^{***}}{39.808} TWM - \underset{(-1.126)}{1.08E+09} PE40/EXR/PEW + \underset{(4.843)^{***}}{0.632} E40(-1)$$
$$R^2ADJ = 0.919 \quad SD = 175819.7 \quad DW = 1.685$$

$$E41 = \underset{(3.549)^{***}}{708130.5} + \underset{(1.221)}{28.896} TWM - \underset{(-2.962)^{***}}{7.18E+09} PE41/EXR/PEW + \underset{(4.664)^{***}}{0.590} E41(-1)$$
$$R^2ADJ = 0.793 \quad SD = 248719.1 \quad DW = 1.909$$

$$E43 = \underset{(1.399)}{794072.1} + \underset{(2.269)^{*}}{211.703} TWM - \underset{(-0.372)}{2.10E+09} PE43/EXR/PEW + \underset{(6.449)^{***}}{0.714} E43(-1)$$
$$R^2ADJ = 0.928 \quad SD = 1451853.5.1 \quad DW = 2.127$$

(*Continued*)

Table A3.6. (*Continued*)

$$E44 = \underset{(-1.686)}{-1522664.3} + \underset{(3.314)^{***}}{1372.507}\ TWM - \underset{(-0.517)}{3.77E+09}\ PE44/EXR/PEW + \underset{(3.111)^{***}}{0.506}\ E44(-1)$$

$R^2ADJ = 0.981$ SD = 4753483.4 DW = 1.503

$$E46 = \underset{(3.162)^{***}}{744567.5} + \underset{(2.575)^{**}}{49.499}\ TWM - \underset{(-2.524)^{**}}{6.50E+09}\ PE46/EXR/PEW + \underset{(6.247)^{***}}{0.615}\ E46(-1)$$

$R^2ADJ = 0.869$ SD = 251910.2 DW = 1.839

$$E47 = \underset{(3.444)^{***}}{424228.2} + \underset{(3.221)^{***}}{525.245}\ TWM - \underset{(-2.935)^{***}}{5.45E+10}\ PE47/EXR/PEW + \underset{(11.537)^{***}}{0.799}\ E47(-1)$$

$R^2ADJ = 0.932$ SD = 2412331.0 DW = 2.953

Notes: (1) ***, ** and * present the level of significance at 1%, 5% and 10%, respectively.
(2) Sector classification: please see notes of Table A3.1.

Chapter 4

Macroeconomic Model Block

4.1. Macro Model Block in DEMIOS: Linkage Between Macro and Sectoral Variables

In most traditional macro Input–Output (I–O) integrated-type models, real GDP components in the macro model are linked with the final demand components in I–O part, including private final consumption expenditure, government consumption expenditure, housing investment, non-housing investment, inventory changes, exports of goods and services and imports of goods and services. Therefore, the integrated-type model could analyze the macro variables' changes on the sectoral variables through a backward linkage. In addition, the model could analyze the sectoral variable changes with changes in input coefficients, etc., on the macro variables through a forward linkage in the integrated-type model.

On the other hand, unlike those macro and I–O integrated-type models, our KLM-type model explicitly endogenizes many sectoral variables including input coefficient, sectoral prices, wage rates, labor demand, exports and imports, technical progress, and so on. Each specific aggregated value of a sectoral variable has consistently interactions with the corresponding macro variable. Therefore, the macro variables contain dynamic structural changes of sectoral economies in the model. In other words, macro variables endogenously determined in the model implicitly include effects of sectoral variables' changes in sectoral economies.

In the macroeconomic block, the number of macroeconomic variables exceeds one hundred. Accordingly, by and large, all of the macroeconomic variables would be explicitly and implicitly influenced by the changes in the sectoral variables in the model as well as in the real economy.

4.2. Macroeconomic Block: Structure of the Model and Regression Results

The macroeconomic block in DEMIOS consists of eight sub-blocks: (1) the real expenditure block; (2) the nominal expenditure sub-block; (3) the prices and wage rates sub-block; (4) the production and labor force sub-block; (5) the income distribution sub-block; (6) the money and finance sub-block; (7) the government finance sub-block; and (8) the foreign variable and BOP sub-block.

In this section, the structure of behavioral equations and identities is discussed by sub-block.

4.2.1. *Real expenditure sub-block*

It is one of the most important sub-blocks in the macroeconomic block for keeping the direct interaction with I–O block through a backward linkage. Some of the GDP components, including real private final consumption expenditure, real housing investment and real private inventory changes are determined within a behavioral equation in this sub-block. In addition, real government consumption is determined by nominal government consumption and deflator of government consumption within an identity.

On the other hand, real non-housing investment, real exports of goods and services and real imports of goods and services are determined within a statistical equation with aggregated ones derived from sectoral variables. The rest variables like real government investment and government inventory changes are determined exogenously as a policy variable in this sub-block.

4.2.1.1. *Real household final consumption expenditure*

It employs basically the Keynesian-type consumption function based on an absolute income hypothesis. The specification of the behavioral equations which is explained by five variables is presented as follows:

$$\begin{aligned}\mathrm{CP} = f(&(+)\mathrm{YDP}/\mathrm{PCP}^{*}100, (-)\mathrm{PCP}(-1)/\mathrm{PCP}(-2), (-)\mathrm{INTGB}(-2),\\ &(+)\,\mathrm{NP6500}(-1)/\mathrm{NPT}(-1), (+)\mathrm{NPT}(-1)),\end{aligned}$$

where CP is the real private final consumption expenditure, YDP the private disposable income, PCP the implicit deflator of CP, INTGB the

Table 4.1. Regression results of major endogenous variables in the real expenditure sub-block.

(1) Real final consumption expenditure

$$CP = -14264.36 + 0.70927\ YDP/PCP*100 - 5183.64\ PCP(-1)/PCP(-2)$$
(−0.30) (19.72)*** (−2.99)***

$$-758.472\ INTGB(-2) + 422343.7\ NP6500(-1)/NPT(-1) + 0.5497\ NPT(-1)$$
(−1.32) (7.61)*** (1.43)

$R^2ADJ = 0.998$ $SD = 2361.6$ $DW = 1.493$

(2) Real housing investment

$$IH = 36612.87 + 0.13570\ YDH/PCH*100 - 0.099987\ KH(-3) - 18771.74\ PIH(-1)/PCP(-1)$$
(4.11)*** (4.21)*** (−6.04)*** (−2.52)**

$$+1.32933\ STOCKPR(-1) - 451.163\ INTGB(-1) - 34.3152\ EXR(-1)$$
(1.90)* (−2.06)* (−2.74)**

$R^2ADJ = 0.866$ $SD = 1192.3$ $DW = 1.899$

(3) Real inventory changes

$$JP = 7298.727 + 0.03619\ GDP - 0.31396\ KJP(-1) - 73500.292\ EXC(-2)/GDP(-2)$$
(4.09)*** (4.12)*** (−3.56)*** (−3.17)***

$$-39.7924\ INTOR(-1)$$
(−0.34)

$R^2ADJ = 0.556$ $SD = 931.24$ $DW = 1.739$

Note: ***, ** and * present the level of significance at 1%, 5% and 10%, respectively.

government bond yield (10-year), NP6500 the number of population over 65 years old, and NPT the total number of population, respectively.

In the equation, real final household consumption expenditure is explained by real household disposable income ($YDP/PCP * 100$) as an income effect with the positive expected sign condition (+), changes in the deflator with one-year time lag($PCP(-1)/PCP(-2)$) as a price effect with the negative sign condition (−), government bond yield (10-year) as a cost effect with the negative sign condition (−), the ratio of population over 65 years old to total population with one-year time lag ($NP6500(-1)/NPT(-1)$) with the positive sign condition (+) and total population with one-year time lag ($NPT(-1)$) with the positive sign condition (+). The performance of the regression result is fairly good and there would be very important implications in the result.

As shown in Table 4.1, real household final consumption expenditure is heavily dependent on the real disposable income as an income effect and changes in the deflator with one-year time lag as a price effect.[1]

[1] There are some alternatives for consumption functions in considering the asset effects in the macro block. Real household financial assets are also important to explain

In addition, as a demographic factor, the ratio of population over 65 years old to total population with one-year time lag also has a positive impact on the real consumption.

4.2.1.2. *Real housing investment*

Concerning real housing investment, it is mainly explained by real household disposable income (YDP/PCP ∗ 100) as an income effect with the positive sign condition (+), real housing stock with three-year time lag (KH(−3)) as a stock adjustment effect with the negative sign condition (−), and relative deflator of housing investment to private consumption with one-year time lag (PIH(−1)/PCP(−1)) as a price effect with the negative sign condition (−). In addition, stock prices with one-year time lag (STOCKPR(−1)) as an asset effect, government bond yield with one-year time lag (INTGB(−1)) as a cost effect and exchange rate with one-year time lag (EXR(−1)) are also taken into accounts as independent variables in the real housing investment function, as follows:

$$\mathrm{IH} = f((+)\mathrm{YDP/PCP} * 100,\ (-)\mathrm{KH}(-3),\ (-)\mathrm{PIH}(-1)/\mathrm{PCP}(-1),$$
$$(+)\,\mathrm{STOCKPR}(-1),\ (-)\mathrm{INTGB}(-1),\ (-)\mathrm{EXR}(-1)),$$

where IH is the real housing investment, YDP the private disposable income, PCH the deflator of CH, KH the real housing stock, PIH the deflator of housing investment, STOCKPR the stock market price, INTGB the government bond yield (10-year) and EXR the exchange rate (¥/$), respectively.

The regression result of the real housing investment is fairly good, in which the major independent variables with income effects, stock adjustment, price effects and cost effects seem to be fairly significant, as shown in Table 4.1. In addition, exchange rate which explains competitive relations of the prices of imported materials to domestic ones for housing investment is also significant.

4.2.1.3. *Real private inventory changes*

It is explained, as a theoretical model, by four independent variables such as real GDP with the positive sign condition (+), real private

---

real household consumption expenditure as asset effects in place of stock price (see Nakamura, 2013).

inventory stock with one-year time lag (KJP(−1)) with the negative sign condition (−), ratio of real exports of goods to real GDP with two-year time lag (EXC(−2)/GDP(−2)) which explains foreign demands through exports with the negative sign condition (−) and official discount rate with one-year time lag (INTOR(−1)) with the negative sign condition (−) as well. Though the volume of the real inventory changes is very limited in comparison with real GDP, the inventory changes are sensitive to the business cycle and hence one of the very important endogenous variables as a component of real GDP in the macroeconomic model block. The specification of the equation is as follows:

$$\begin{aligned}\mathrm{JP} = f(&(+)\mathrm{GDP},\ (-)\mathrm{KJP}(-1),\ (-)\mathrm{EXC}(-2)/\mathrm{GDP}(-2),\\ &(-)\,\mathrm{INTOR}(-1)),\end{aligned}$$

where JP is the real inventory changes, GDP the real GDP, KJP the real inventory stock, EXC the real merchandise exports, and INTOR the official discount rate, respectively.

According to the regression result as shown in Table 4.1, the major independent variables such as real GDP and real inventory stock significantly explain the real inventory changes. In addition, the ratio of real merchandise exports to real GDP with two-year time lag which implies external demands for the highly efficient manufacturing sector products is significant, as well.

4.2.1.4. *Real government consumption*

As noted above, real government consumption is determined within an identity, dividing the nominal government consumption by its deflator as follows:

$$\mathrm{CG} = \mathrm{CGN}/\mathrm{PCG} \cdot 100,$$

where CG is the real government consumption, CGN the nominal government consumption, and PCG the deflator of CG respectively.

The nominal government consumption and deflator of government consumption are determined in the nominal expenditure sub-block and the prices and wage rates sub-block which will be discussed later.

4.2.1.5. *Real non-housing investment, real exports of goods and services and real imports of goods and services*

As for the other macro real GDP, components like these variables are linked with sum of the sectoral variables determined in the I–O block, in a statistical equation, as follows:

real private non-housing investment:

$$\mathrm{IP} = f\left(\sum \mathrm{IP}_i\right) = \alpha^{\mathrm{IP}} \cdot \sum \mathrm{IP}_i,$$

real exports of goods and services:

$$\mathrm{EGS} = f\left(\sum \mathrm{EGS}_i\right) = \alpha^{\mathrm{EGS}} \cdot \sum \mathrm{EGS}_i,$$

real imports of goods and services:

$$\mathrm{MGS} = f\left(\sum \mathrm{MGS}_i\right) = \alpha^{\mathrm{MGS}} \cdot \sum \mathrm{MGS}_i.$$

Accordingly, in the database, α^{IP}, α^{EGS} and α^{MGS} are defined as a time series variable as follows:

$$\alpha^{\mathrm{IP}} = \mathrm{IP}\Big/\sum \mathrm{IP}_i,$$

$$\alpha^{\mathrm{EGS}} = \mathrm{EGS}\Big/\sum \mathrm{EGS}_i,$$

$$\alpha^{\mathrm{MGS}} = \mathrm{MGS}\Big/\sum \mathrm{MGS}_i,$$

where IP is the real non-housing investment, IP_i the sectoral non-housing investment, EGS the real exports of goods and services, EGS_i the sectoral exports of goods and services, MGS the real imports of goods and services, MGS_i the sectoral imports of goods and services and α the ratio of sum of the sectoral variables to each macro variable.

4.2.2. *Nominal expenditure sub-block*

In the nominal expenditure sub-block, nominal GDP and its component are endogenously determined. Nominal GDP is determined in an identity as sum of nominal GDP components. Except for nominal government consumption, each nominal GDP component is determined by each real value and its deflator in an identity, as follows:

nominal GDP:

$$\mathrm{GDPN} = \mathrm{CPN} + \mathrm{IHN} + \mathrm{IPN} + \mathrm{JPN} + \mathrm{JGN} + \mathrm{EGSN} - \mathrm{MGSN},$$

nominal private final consumption expenditure:

$$\mathrm{CPN} = \mathrm{CH} \cdot \mathrm{PCH}/100,$$

nominal government investment:

$$\mathrm{IGN} = \mathrm{IG} \cdot \mathrm{PIG}/100,$$

nominal private inventory changes:

$$\mathrm{PN} = \mathrm{JP} \cdot \mathrm{PJP}/100,$$

nominal government inventory changes:

$$\mathrm{JGN} = \mathrm{JG} \cdot \mathrm{PJG}/100,$$

nominal exports of goods and services:

$$\mathrm{EGSN} = \mathrm{EGS} \cdot \mathrm{PEFGS}/100,$$

nominal imports of goods and services:

$$\mathrm{MGSN} = \mathrm{MGS} \cdot \mathrm{PMGS}/100,$$

where GDPN is the nominal GDP, GDP the real GDP, PGDP the deflator of GDP, CPN the nominal private final consumption expenditure, CP the real final private consumption expenditure, PCP the deflator of CP, IGN the nominal government investment, IG the real government investment (exogenous variable), PIG the deflator of IG, JPN the nominal inventory changes, JP the real inventory changes, PJP the deflator of JP, JGN the nominal government inventory changes, JG the real inventory changes (exogenous variable), EGSN the nominal exports of goods and services, EGS the real exports of goods and services, PEGS the deflator of EGS, MGSN the nominal imports of goods and services, MGs the real imports of goods and services and PMGS the deflator of MGS, respectively.

On the other hand, nominal government consumption is determined in a behavioral equation, as follows.

Nominal government consumption:

$$\mathrm{CGN} = f((+)\mathrm{WN},\ (+)\mathrm{NP6500},\ (+)\mathrm{CGN}(-1)),$$

where CGN is the nominal government consumption expenditure, WN the nominal wage rates and NP6500 the population over 65 years old, respectively.

Table 4.2. Regression result of nominal government consumption.

(1) Nominal government consumption
$CGN = -7771.83 + 186.832\ WN + 0.403148\ NP6500(-1) + 0.771416\ CGN(-1)$
$(-2.60)^{**}\ (3.97)^{***}\ \ (2.65)^{**}\ \ (12.05)^{***}$
$R^2ADJ = 0.998 \quad SD = 829.3779 \quad DW = 1.307$

Note: ***, ** and * present the level of significance at 1%, 5% and 10%, respectively.

In the equation, nominal government consumption is explained by nominal wage rates with the positive sign condition (+), population over 65 years old with the positive sign condition (+) and the Koyck type (CGN(−1)). As noted above, real government consumption is determined by nominal government consumption and its deflator. The regression result is shown in Table 4.2.

4.2.3. *Prices and wage rates sub-block*

In the prices and wage rates sub-block, deflator of GDP and deflators of GDP components, nominal wage rates and exchange rate (yen rate to US$) are determined as macro endogenous variables. In DEMIOS, the nominal wage rates have significant effects on sectoral wage rates and hence sectoral labor demands and various sectoral prices. This is an important algorithm for the linkage in between the macroeconomic block and the I–O block. In addition, exchange rate (yen rate to US$) is also endogenously determined in this sub-block, which has crucial influences on the domestic prices and hence the terms of trade, real exports and real imports.

Concerning the prices (deflators), the deflator of GDP is determined by real GDP and nominal GDP as the ratio of nominal GDP to real GDP within an identity. Besides, the implicit deflators of macro GDP components are determined by the ratio of sum of sectoral nominal values to sum of sectoral real values in a statistical equation, as follows:

implicit deflator of GDP:

$$PGDP = GDPN/GDP \cdot 100,$$

implicit deflator of CP:

$$PCP = f\left(\sum(PCP_i \cdot CP_i)/\sum CP_i\right),$$

implicit deflator of CG:

$$\mathrm{PCG} = f\left(\sum(\mathrm{PCG}_i \cdot \mathrm{CG}_i)/\sum \mathrm{CG}_i\right),$$

implicit deflator of IH:

$$\mathrm{PIH} = f\left(\sum(\mathrm{PIH}_i \cdot \mathrm{IH}_i)/\sum \mathrm{IH}_i\right),$$

implicit deflator of IP:

$$\mathrm{PIP} = f\left(\sum(\mathrm{PIP}_i \cdot \mathrm{IP}_i)/\sum \mathrm{IP}_i\right),$$

implicit deflator of IG:

$$\mathrm{PIG} = f\left(\sum(\mathrm{PIG}_i \cdot \mathrm{IG}_i)/\sum \mathrm{IG}_i\right),$$

implicit deflator of EGS:

$$\mathrm{PEGS} = f\left(\sum(\mathrm{PEGS}_i \cdot \mathrm{EGS}_i)/\sum \mathrm{EGS}_i\right),$$

implicit deflator of MGS:

$$\mathrm{PMGS} = f\left(\sum(\mathrm{PMGS}_i \cdot \mathrm{MGS}_i)/\sum \mathrm{MGS}_i\right),$$

where PGDP is the implicit deflator of GDP, PCP the implicit deflator of final consumption expenditure, PCG the implicit deflator of government consumption expenditure, PIH the implicit deflator of housing investment, PIP the implicit deflator of non-housing investment, PIG the implicit deflator of government investment, PEGS the implicit deflator of exports of goods and services and PMGS the implicit deflator of imports of goods and services, respectively.

On the other hand, implicit deflator of private inventory changes (PJP) and implicit deflator of government inventory changes (PJG) are exogenously given in the macro block.

As for macro nominal wage rates, the wage rates are explained by implicit deflator of private consumption expenditure with the positive sign condition (+), rate of unemployment with the negative sign condition (−) and the ratio of real GDP to the number of wage and salaried employed as a labor productivity with the positive sign condition (+) in a percentage change (DOT) function, as follows:

Table 4.3. Regression result of nominal wage rates.

(1) Nominal wage rates (WN)

$$\text{DOT(WN)} = \underset{(2.65)^{**}}{2.937} + \underset{(4.11)^{***}}{0.8573}\ \text{DOT(PCP)} - \underset{(-2.51)^{**}}{0.704266}\ \text{UR} + \underset{(4.16)^{***}}{0.3313}\ \text{DOT(GDP/LW)}$$

R^2ADJ = 0.842 SD = 0.894 DW = 1.764

(2) Exchange rate (EXR)

$$\text{EXR} = \underset{(3.52)^{***}}{80.931} + \underset{(2.95)^{***}}{45.53615}\ \text{PX/PGDPUS} - \underset{(-2.23)^{*}}{43.38}\text{INTGB/INTGBUS}$$

$$+ \underset{(2.86)^{**}}{0.3442}\ \text{EXR}(-1) - \underset{(-3.59)^{***}}{44.4125}\ \text{D8586}$$

R^2ADJ = 0.928 SD = 11.8754 DW = 1.851

Note: ***, ** and * present the level of significance at 1%, 5% and 10%, respectively.

nominal wage rates:

$$\text{DOT(WN)} = f((+)\ \text{DOT(PCP)},\ (-)\ \text{UR},\ (+)\ \text{DOT(GDP/LW)})$$

where WN is the nominal wage rates, PCP the deflator of private final consumption expenditure, UR the rate of unemployment, GDP the real GDP and LW the number of wage and salaried employed, respectively.

According to the regression result, as shown in Table 4.3, nominal wage rates are significantly explained by implicit deflator of private consumption with a plausible coefficient at 0.8573 and labor productivity at 0.3313.

With respect to exchange rate (yen rate to US$), in the current DEMIOS, the ordinary specification with two major explanatory variables including purchasing power parity variable and interest rate parity variable is employed as follows:

$$\text{EXR} = f((+)\text{PX/PGDPUS},\ (-)\text{INTGB/INTGBUS},$$
$$(+)\ \text{EXR}(-1), (-)\text{D858}).$$

In the equation, four explanatory variables are taken into account. The first is the ratio of output price to US GDP deflator (PX/PGDPUS) which presents purchasing power parity with the positive expected sign condition (+). The second is the ratio of Japanese government bond yield to US government bond yield (INTGB/INTGBUS) with the negative sign condition (−). In addition, third and fourth ones are the Koyck type (EXR(−1)) and the dummy variable for the Plaza Accord (D8586).

As shown in Table 4.3, exchange rate (yen rate to US$) is significantly explained by mainly purchasing power parity (PX/PGDPUS) and interest

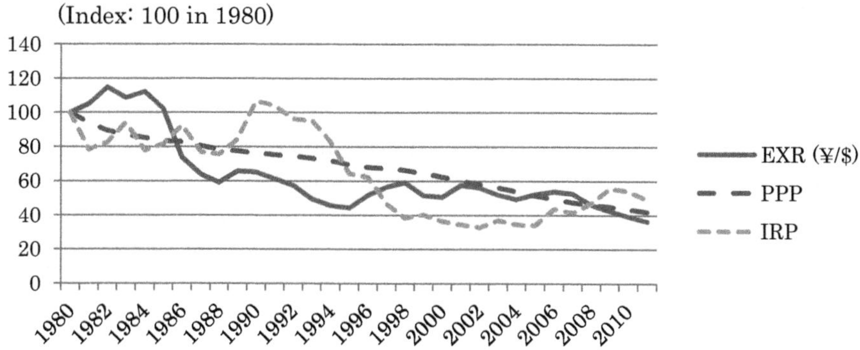

Fig. 4.1. Exchange rate (EXR), purchasing power parity (PPP), and interest rate parity (IRP).

Source: Developed by the authors.

rate parity (INTGB/INTGBUS). In addition, the Plaza Accord dummy variable is also significant at a 1% level. As explained by the regression result, it can be seen that the Japanese yen rate to US$ is dependent on a trend of purchasing parity in a long-run and its fluctuation is explained by an interest rate parity in a short-run, except for its sharp decline (appreciation) after the Plaza Accord, as Fig. 4.1 shows.

4.2.4. *Production and labor force sub-block*

In this section, the following variables are determined; macro real GDP capacity, real capital stock, real depreciation of capital, the number of labor (labor supply), the number of employees, wage and salaried employees, etc. In particular, macro real GDP capacity is estimated by Cobb–Douglas with some adjustments of capital stock, unemployment rate and working hours, on a macro real GDP basis (see Niwa, 2000; Sato, 2001; Shishido, 2004; Nakamura, 2013). Though real sectoral outputs are estimated and determined in the I–O model block, the macro GDP capacity is derived in order to estimate a macro deflationary gap of the Japanese economy in DEMIOS.

In addition, macro labor force (labor supply) is determined by macroeconomic variables when DEMIOS employs the simplified demographic model. Besides, the labor force is determined in the cohort-type demographic population and labor force model, which will be discussed later on, in Chapter 5. Furthermore, the total number of employees (labor demand), including wage and salaried employees and unincorporated companies' workers, are determined in I–O model block, as a sectoral block variable, as discussed earlier.

The first step in estimating capacity real GDP is to regress on real capital stock with utilization rate of capital with the positive sign condition (+), the number of employed with the ratio of actual total working hours to official working hours with the positive sign condition (+) and time trend all under the positive sign condition (+) as follows:

$$\ln(\mathrm{GDP}) = f((+)\ln(\mathrm{KP} * \mathrm{CUR}), \quad (+)\ln((1 - \mathrm{UR}/100) * \mathrm{NL} * \mathrm{RTOH}), (+)\ \mathrm{TIME}),$$

where GDP is the real GDP, KP the real capital stock, CUR the capital utilization rate, UR the unemployment rate, NL the number of labor, RTOH the ratio of total actual working hours to official working hours and TIME the time trend, respectively.

According to the regression result, as shown in Table 4.4, the capital share is 0.3297 and hence the labor share is 0.6703, based on a linear homogeneous production function, with 1% level of significance. In addition, a time trend is also significant with 1.2% technical progress

Table 4.4. Regression results of major endogenous variables in the production and labor force sub-block.

(1) Real GDP (supply side)

$$\underset{(25.44)^{***}}{\ln(\mathrm{GDP}) = 2.4587} + \underset{(10.52)^{***}}{0.3297}\ \ln(\mathrm{KP*CUR}) + \underset{(5.34)^{***}}{0.6703}\ \ln((1-\mathrm{UR}/100)*\mathrm{NL*RTLH})$$

$$+\underset{(2.75)^{**}}{0.012}\ \mathrm{TIME} - \underset{(-3.78)^{***}}{0.05997}\ \mathrm{D2008}$$

R^2ADJ = 0.986 SD = 0.152 DW = 1.268

(2) Real depreciation of capital stock

$$\mathrm{DP} = \underset{(-3.07)^{***}}{-8580.85} + \underset{(2.45)^{**}}{0.02144}\ \mathrm{KP} + \underset{(2.61)^{**}}{0.04043}\ \mathrm{GDP} + \underset{(10.58)^{***}}{0.6661}\ \mathrm{DP}(-1)$$

R^2ADJ = 0.997 SD = 956.486 DW = 1.871

(3) Labor supply (in employing the simplified demographic model)

$$\mathrm{NL} = \underset{(-3.40)^{***}}{-2240.28} + \underset{(3.03)^{***}}{0.0343}\ (\mathrm{NP1564}(-1) + \mathrm{NP6500}(-1)) + \underset{(3.79)^{***}}{5059.89}\ \mathrm{RNLF}(-1))$$

$$+\underset{(3.31)^{***}}{0.471988}\ \mathrm{NL}(-1)\ \underset{(-2.81)^{**}}{-11.128}\ \mathrm{TIME}$$

R^2ADJ = 0.992 SD = 28.328 DW = 1.419

Note: ***, ** and * present the level of significance at 1%, 5% and 10%, respectively.

contribution and the world financial crisis damage is also eliminated by a 2008 dummy variable.

In the second step, GDP capacity is estimated by the adjustment of utilization rate of capital (CUR), rate of unemployment (UR) and the ratio of total actual working hours to official working hours (RTOH) based on the information of the peak of the economy in the asset bubble economy. In the current estimation, the values of these variables are assumed at 100.0% for the rate of capital utilization, 2.0% for the rate of unemployment as a natural rate of unemployment and 1.099 for the ratio of total actual working hours to official working hours, respectively. Accordingly, based on the above assumption, it is estimated that the deflationary gap is fairly large at −8.92% in 2000, at −6.58% in 2005, and −11.07% in 2010, respectively, as shown in Fig. 4.2.

Concerning real private capital stock and depreciation of real capital stock, these variables are defined in an identity for real private capital stock and in a behavioral equation for real depreciation of private capital stock, as follows:

$$\text{KP} = \text{KP}(-1) + \text{IP} - \text{DP},$$

$$\text{DP} = f((+)\text{KP}(+/-)\text{GDP},\ \ (+)\text{DP}(-1)),$$

where KP is the real private capital stock, IP the real private non-housing investment and DP the real depreciation of real capital stock, respectively.

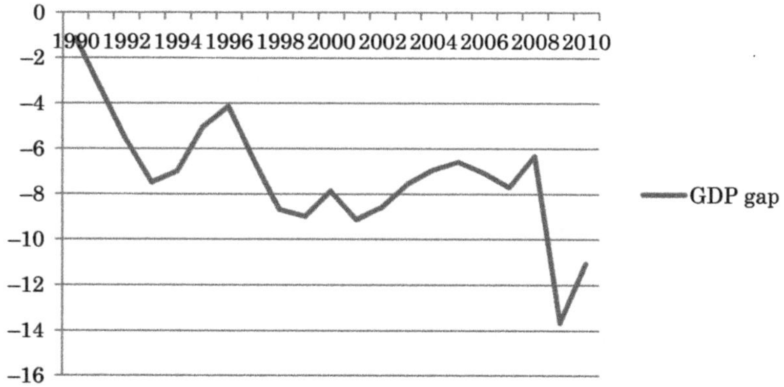

Fig. 4.2. Estimated GDP gap, 1990–2010 (%).

Source: Estimated by the authors.

Note: GDP gap is defined as ((GDP–Capacity GDP) −1) × 100(%).

In the behavioral equation, real depreciation of private capital stock is explained by real capital stock with the positive sign condition (+), real GDP which is to imply effects of business cycle and replacement of capital with the positive or negative sign (+/−) theoretically and the Koyck type (DP(−1)). As for the sign for the second explanatory variable, its causal relation is revealed.

According to the regression result, the sign of the second independent variable is positive and hence the positive causal relation could be seen in this sample period, as shown in Table 4.4. In addition, as considered the coefficient of the Koyck type at 0.666, it is assumed that fairly large depreciation of capital seems to be replaced by the changes in real GDP through the combined coefficient at 0.04043/(1 − 0.6661).

With respect to labor supply, labor supply function is considered in the macro model block when DEMIOS employs the simplified demographic model. On the other hand, total labor force is determined in the demographic and labor force model by age group and gender as discussed later when DEMIOS employs the cohort-type demographic and labor force model for the long-term projections.

The number of labor is explained by five explanatory variables, in which the number of active population and population over 65 years old with one-year time lag is considered as a main independent variable with the positive sign condition (+) in the equation. Recently, many retired persons are participating in job market under the situation of declining in active population. In addition, female labor participation rate with one-year time lag is also introduced as a positive factor. An increase in female labor participation rate is also sustaining the current geriatric society of Japan. Time trend is also taken into account as a recent declining trend of the number of labor in the equation. Based on the causal relations discussed above, the specification of the model is explained as follows:

$$\begin{aligned}\mathrm{NL} = f(&(+)\mathrm{NP1564}(-1) + \mathrm{NP6500}(-1),\ (+)\mathrm{RNLF}(-1),\\ &(+)\,\mathrm{NL}(-1),\ (-)\mathrm{TIME}),\end{aligned}$$

where NL is the number of labor, NP1564 the active population from 15 to 64 years old, NP6500 the population over 65 years old, RNLF the female labor participation rate, and TIME the time trend, respectively.

According to the regression result, the labor supply result performs quite well, as listed in Table 4.4. In particular, the effect of female participation rate is very significant on total labor supply, which implies the recent labor supply could be maintained by increases in female labor participation in labor market. In addition, trend factor is also significant and satisfies the recent declining trend as a negative coefficient in the regression result.

Concerning labor demand, the number of employees is determined in an identity, with sum of sectoral wage and salaried employees and sectoral unincorporated companies' workers, as follows:

$$\text{NLE} = \sum \text{LW}_i + \sum \text{LU}_i,$$

where NLE is the number of employees (labor demand), LW the wage and salaries employees, and LU the unincorporated companies' workers, respectively.

Accordingly, the rate of unemployment is determined in this sub-block. Indeed, the rate of unemployment is very important endogenous variable to determine nominal wage rates, as discussed above and to link the I–O model with the macro model. The rate of unemployment is determined by labor supply and labor demand in an identity, as follows:

$$\text{UR} = (\text{NL} - \text{NLE})/\text{NL} \cdot 100,$$

where UR is the rate of unemployment, GDP the real GDP, WN the nominal wage rates, PGDP the deflator of GDP and TIME the time trend, respectively.

4.2.5. *Income distribution sub-block*

Variables in the income distribution sub-block are also very important since the variables in this sub-block serve an intermediary between the production side national accounts variables and the expenditure (demand) side ones under the principle of three equivalence of national income. In particular, income allocation between wage income (labor share) and corporation income (capital share) is crucial for deciding macro balances, including IS balance, external balance, inflationary and deflationary gap and so on.

Accordingly, the income distribution sub-block is an independent sub-block in the macroeconomic block in DEMIOS. In this sub-block, 11 variables are determined as endogenous variables, including household income, household disposable income, compensation of employee, wage and salaried income, wages and salaries per employee, employer's social contribution, household property income, household dividend income, household interest income, unincorporated enterprise income and corporation income.

Household income and its components are determined in an identity and behavioral equation, as follows:

household income:

$$\mathrm{YH} = \mathrm{YE} + \mathrm{YRH} + \mathrm{YU},$$

compensation of employees:

$$\mathrm{YE} = \mathrm{YW} + \mathrm{ESC},$$

wage and salaried income:

$$\mathrm{YW} = \mathrm{W} \cdot \mathrm{NLW}/100,$$

employer's social contribution:

$$\mathrm{ESC} = f((+)\mathrm{YW},\ (+)\mathrm{ESC}(-1)),$$

household property income:

$$\mathrm{YRH} = \mathrm{YDI} + \mathrm{YRHIR},$$

wages and salaries per employee:

$$\mathrm{W} = f((+)\mathrm{WN},\ (+)\mathrm{WHR},\ (+)\mathrm{W}(-1)),$$

household dividend income:

$$\mathrm{YDI} = f((+)\mathrm{YDIVC},\ (+)\mathrm{YDI}(-1)),$$

household interest income:

$$\mathrm{YRHIR} = f((+)\mathrm{GDPN},\ (+)\mathrm{INTGB}, (+)\mathrm{YRHIR}(-1)),$$

unincorporated enterprise income:

$$\mathrm{YU} = f((+)\mathrm{GDPN}, (-)\mathrm{INTPR}, (+)\mathrm{YU}(-1)),$$

where YH is the household income, YE the compensation of employee, YW the wage and salaried income, ESC the employer's social contribution, W the wages and salaries per employee, WHS the working hours, NLW the number of wage and salaried employee, YRH the household property income, YDI the household dividend income, YRHIR the household interest income, YU the unincorporated enterprise income, GDPN the nominal GDP and INTPR the prime rate, respectively.

As presented above, household income (YH), compensation of employee (YE), wage and salaried income (YW) and household property income (YRH) are defined in an identity. In addition, five variables related to household income are determined in a behavioral equation.

Employer's contribution to society (ESC) is explained by wage and salaried income (YW) with the positive sign condition (+) and the Koyck type (ESC(−1)). Unincorporated enterprise income (YU) is explained by nominal GDP as a proxy for economic climate with the positive sign condition (+), government bond yield (INTGB) as a proxy for a long-term interest rate with a negative sign condition (−) and the Koyck type (YU(−1)).

Wages and salaries per employee (W) are explained by nominal wage rates (WN) as a with a positive sign (+), working hours (WHS) with the positive sign condition (+) and the Koyck type (W(−1)). Household interest income (YRHIR) is explained by nominal GDP as a proxy for economic climate with the positive sign (+), government bond yield (INTGB) with the positive sign condition (+) and the Koyck type (YRHIR(−1)). Household dividend income (YDI) is explained by corporation dividend paid (YDIVC) with the positive sign condition (+) and the Koyck type (YDI(−1)).

In addition, based on the household income, private disposable income is defined in an identity with household income, non-profit institution income and their overall direct tax payment to both the central government and local government.

Private disposable income:

$$\mathrm{YDP} = \mathrm{YH} + \mathrm{YN} - \mathrm{TTP} \quad (\mathrm{TTP} = \mathrm{TI} + \mathrm{TIL}),$$

where YDP is the private sector disposable income, YH the household income, YN the non-profit institution income and TTP household and non-profit institution overall direct tax payment to both the central government and local government, respectively.

Finally, corporation income is determined in a behavioral equation. As a theoretical model, corporation income is explained by nominal GDP as a proxy for economic climate with the positive sign condition (+), prime rate (long-term interest rate for major corporations) with the negative sign condition (−) and wage and salaried income as a total labor cost with the expected coefficient at 1.00 and the negative sign condition (−).

Corporation income:

$$\mathrm{YC} = f((+)\mathrm{GDPN},\ (-)\mathrm{INTPR},\ (-)\mathrm{YW}),$$

Table 4.5. Regression results of major variables in the income distribution sub-block.

(1) Wages and salaries per employee

$$W = -1007.29 + 28.232\ WN + 10.554\ WHS + 0.3480\ W(-1)$$

(−1.25) (5.52)*** (2.45)** (3.20)***

R^2ADJ = 0.935 SD = 2615.10 DW = 1.736

(2) Employer's social contribution

$$ESC = 409.656 + 0.03396\ YW + 0.7664\ ESC(-1)$$

(0.29) (2.47)** (11.52)***

R^2ADJ = 0.981 SD = 1069.71 DW = 1.921

(3) Household dividend income

$$YDI = -482.036 + 0.71092\ YDIVC + 0.72956\ YDI(-1)$$

(−2.33)* (6.15)*** (12.63)***

R^2ADJ = 0.936 SD = 430.5605 DW = 1.109

(4) Household interest income

$$YRHIR = -23724.8 + 0.01755\ GDPN + 4424.93\ INTGB + 0.61878\ YRHIR(-1)$$

(−2.62)** (3.17)*** (5.35)*** (7.54)***

R^2ADJ = 0.968 SD = 2244.90 DW = 1.816

(5) Unincorporated income

$$YU = 13848.6 + 0.01205\ GDP - 677.177\ INTPR + 0.4742\ YU(-1)$$

(2.73)** (2.46)** (−2.56)** (3.79)***

R^2ADJ = 0.945 SD = 1293.12 DW = 1.769

(6) Corporation income

$$YC = 38461.9 + 0.536896\ GDPN - 1274.70\ INTPR - 1.02204\ YW - 3170.84\ D2008$$

(5.61)*** (12.25)*** (−2.99)*** (−12.62)*** (−2.20)**

R^2ADJ = 0.926 SD = 2815.14 DW = 1.346

Note: ***, ** and * present the level of significance at 1%, 5% and 10%, respectively.

where YC is the corporation income, GDPN the nominal GDP, INTPR the prime rate and YW the wage and salaried income, respectively.

Based on the model specification, the regression results are obtained as shown in Table 4.5. According to the regression results, most of the regression results have a strong performance in terms of t-values, R^2 and Durbin–Watson ratio. In general, it may be admitted that modeling the income distribution side is weak, because no good theoretical framework is established yet in comparison with the demand–supply-side models. It is noteworthy, however, that our estimated results in the income distribution sub-block seem to be fairly good, which would be able to link the demand-side with the supply-side model with fairly strong performance within DEMIOS.

In the result of wages and salaries per employee, as shown in Table 4.5, nominal wage rates (WN) and working hours (WHS) are significant despite of highly significant one-year time lag variable of wages and salaries per employee (W(−1)). In addition, the corporation income regression result shows that corporation income (YC) is significantly explained by nominal GDP (GDPN) and long-term interest rate (INTGB). Furthermore, wage and salaried income (YW) has realized the expected coefficient at 1.022 as a total labor cost with the expected negative sign.

4.2.6. *Money and finance sub-block*

The money and finance sub-block is also very important for the policy scenario simulations in DEMIOS. Money stock, stock price (TOPIX) and some interest rates, including call rate, prime rate and government bond yield (10-year), are determined in this sub-block. Official discount rate and base money are given as an exogenous (policy) variable. The model specification of these variables is as follows:

money stock:

$$\mathrm{M2CD} = f((+)\mathrm{GDP},\ (+)\mathrm{MB},\ (-)\mathrm{INTGB}),$$

stock price:

$$\begin{aligned}\mathrm{PSTOCK} = f(&(+)\mathrm{GDP}/((\mathrm{GDP} + \mathrm{GDP}(-1))/2),\\ &(-)\,\mathrm{INTGB} - \mathrm{DOT}(\mathrm{PGDP}), (+)\mathrm{PSTOCK}(-1)),\end{aligned}$$

call rate:

$$\mathrm{INTCR} = f((+)\ \mathrm{INTOR}, (-)\mathrm{M2CD}/\mathrm{GDPN}),$$

prime rate:

$$\mathrm{INTPR} = f((+)\ \mathrm{INTOR}, (-)\mathrm{M2CD}/\mathrm{GDPN}),$$

government bond yield (10 year):

$$\mathrm{INTGB}\, f((+)\mathrm{INTOR},\ (-)\mathrm{M2CD}(-1),\ (+)\mathrm{INTGBUS}, (-)\mathrm{EXR}),$$

where M2CD is the money stock (M2 + CD), GDP real GDP, MB the money stock, INTGB the government bond yield, INTCG the call rate, INTOR the official discount rate, PTOCK the stock price (TOPIX), INTPR the prime rate, PGDP the deflator of GDP and EXR: exchange rate, respectively.

In the money demand function, money stock (M2CD) is explained by real GDP as a proxy of money demand for transaction and pre-cautionary motives with the positive sign condition (+), base money (MB) with the positive sign condition (+) and government bond yield as a proxy of a speculative motive with the negative sign condition (−).

Regarding interest rates as listed above, each interest rate is explained by official discount rate as a policy variable (exogenous variable) with the positive sign condition (+), money stock with the negative sign condition (−). In particular, government bond yield is explained by official discount rate, money stock and two more variables, including US government bond yield (INTGBUS) and exchange rate (EXR) with the positive sign condition (+) and negative sign condition (−), respectively.

According to the regression results based on a model specification (theoretical model), fairly good results are obtained, as Table 4.6 shows. Money stock (M2CD) is significantly explained by three explanatory variables listed above and the world financial crisis dummy variable (D2008). In particular, money supply is heavily dependent on key variables, base money and real GDP, which are highly significant.

The regression result of stock price (PSTOCK) is also relatively good, in which real GDP expected growth (GDP/(GDP + GDP(−1))/2) and the Koyck type (PSTOCK(−1)) are very significant. In addition, government bond yield base real interest rate (INTGB – DOT(PGDP)) is also relatively significant in the stock price function.

Concerning the results of interest rates, call rate, prime rate and government bond yield, as shown in Table 6.6, these three interest rates are significantly explained by official discount rate (INTOR) and money stock (M2CD) with the high determinant coefficient at 0.98–0.99 and acceptable DW. Particularly, Japanese government bond yield is influenced by US government bond yield and yen–dollar exchange rate as a speculative alternatives, as our regression result explains fairly well.

4.2.7. *Government finance sub-block*

In the government finance sub-block, there are 26 endogenous variables for both the central government and local governments. In particular, in the expenditure side, total expenditure and its nine components in the general account of the central government, including social security, local finance, education, economic cooperation, notional defense, foods, public bond, public works and other expenditure and in the revenue

Table 4.6. Regression results of the money and finance sub-block.

(1) Money stock

$$\underset{(-3.03)^{***}}{\text{M2CD} = -252304.8} + \underset{(4.73)^{***}}{0.4444\ \text{MB}} + \underset{(10.82)^{***}}{1.9007\ \text{GDP}} - \underset{(-2.21)^{*}}{9218.47\ \text{INTGB}} + \underset{(4.59)^{***}}{61520.3\ \text{D2008}}$$

R^2 ADJ = 0.995 SD = 13,693.8 DW = 1.767

(2) Stock price

$$\text{PSTOCK} = \underset{(-4.24)^{***}}{-16797.7} + \underset{(4.31)^{***}}{17190.8}\ \text{GDP/(GDP + GDP(}-1))/2))$$

$$\underset{(-2.51)^{**}}{-69.1076\ \text{INTGB}} - \text{DOT(PGDP)} + \underset{(9.82)^{***}}{0.75592\text{PTOCK}(-1)}$$

R^2 ADJ = 0.798 SD = 213.2396 DW = 1.836

(3) Call rate

$$\text{INTCR} = \underset{(1.32)}{0.574357} + \underset{(24.21)^{***}}{1.292\ \text{INTOR}} - \underset{(-1.98)^{*}}{0.5412\ \text{M2CD/GDPN}}$$

R^2 ADJ = 0.995 SD = 0.207981 DW = 1.976

(4) Prime rate

$$\text{INTPR} = \underset{(12.47)^{***}}{4.78264} + \underset{(26.50)^{***}}{0.991\ \text{INTOR}} - \underset{(-8.48)^{***}}{2.2385\ \text{M2CD/GDPN}}$$

R^2 ADJ = 0.992 SD = 0.248799 DW = 1.825

(5) Government bond yield

$$\text{INTGB} = \underset{(4.42)^{***}}{8.70619} + \underset{(12.91)^{***}}{0.\ 73975\ \text{INTORA}} - \underset{(-3.50)^{***}}{0.0000036\ \text{M2CD}(-1)} + \underset{(2.37)^{**}}{0.19640\ \text{INTGBUS}}$$

$$\underset{(-2.94)^{**}}{-1.25499\ \text{ln.EXR}}$$

R^2 ADJ = 0.983 SD = 0.323401 DW = 1.350

Note: ***, ** and * present the level of significance at 1%, 5% and 10%, respectively.

side, total revenue and its components, national tax revenues and non-tax revenues are determined in this sub-block.

Hereby, the revenue side with three national tax revenues, including personal income tax, corporation income tax and consumption tax is discussed because of the space limitation. The model specification of these equations is as follows:

personal income tax revenue:

$$\text{TP} = f((+)\text{YH},\ (+)\,\text{GDPN/GDPN}(-1),\ (+)\,\text{TP}(-1)),$$

corporation tax revenue:

$$\text{TC} = f((+)\text{YC},\ (+)\,\text{CUR}(-n),\ (+)\,\text{INTGB}(-1),$$
$$(+)\,\text{PSTOCK}(-1),\ (-)\text{EXR}(-1),\ (+)\,\text{FDIA}),$$

Consumption tax revenue:

$$\text{TCON} = \beta \cdot \text{CPN},$$

where TP is the personal income tax revenue, YH the household income, GDPN the nominal GDP, TC the corporation tax revenue, YC the corporation income, CUR the capacity rate of utilization of capital, INTGB the government bond yield, PSTOCK the stock price (TOPIX), EXR the exchange rate, FDIA the foreign direct investment abroad, TCON the consumption tax revenue, CPN the nominal final private consumption expenditure and β the rate of consumption tax for the central government, respectively.

As discussed above, personal income tax revenue (TP) is explained by household income (YH) with the positive sign condition (+), changes in nominal GDP as a proxy for explaining changes in the weights of each income tax rate within taxable income by income class in the progressive-type income tax system with the positive sign condition (+), and the Koyck type (TP(−1)). Corporation tax revenue (TC) is explained by corporation income (YC) with the positive sign condition (+), GDP capacity utilization rate of capital (CUR) with the positive sign condition (+) with some year time lag, government bond yield with the positive sign condition (+), stock price (PSTOCK) with the positive sign condition (+), exchange rate to explain terms of trade with the negative sign condition (−) and FDI abroad (asset) so as to explain primary income from abroad with the positive sign condition (+).

On the other hand, consumption tax revenue in the central government is determined by nominal private final consumption expenditure (CPN) and consumption tax rate for the central government (β) in an identity. Therefore, the coefficient (β) is changing as an exogenous variable since the consumption tax rate and allocation ratio to the central government are changing.

As a result of the regression analysis, as shown in Table 4.7, personal income tax revenue (TP) is significantly explained by household income (YH), changes in nominal GDP (GDPN/GDPN(−1)) and the Koyck type (TP(−1)). In particular, personal income tax revenue is very sensitive to the changes in nominal GDP through changes in tax rate by income class in the progressive-type personal income taxation system in Japan. In addition, the result of corporation income tax revenue also has a fairly good performance. Particularly, the tax revenue is highly sensitive to cyclical factors like the rate of capacity utilization (CUR). In addition, the revenue is significantly explained by revenues from bond and stock markets as well as ordinary income. Furthermore, the revenue is very sensitive to changes in exchange rate and FDI to abroad through primary income inflows from FDI destination countries.

Table 4.7. Regression results of personal income tax and corporation tax revenue.

(1) Personal income tax revenue

$$\underset{(-4.92)^{***}}{\mathrm{TP} = -56{,}302.6} + \underset{(2.91)^{**}}{0.0258\ \mathrm{YH}} + \underset{(5.32)^{***}}{53{,}174.8\ \mathrm{GDPN/GDPN}(-1)} + \underset{(7.83)^{***}}{0.6695\ \mathrm{TP}(-1)}$$

R^2ADJ = 0.882 SD = 1294.637 DW = 2.163

(2) Corporation tax revenue

$$\underset{(-2.46)^{**}}{\mathrm{TC} = 18{,}681.55} + \underset{(6.78)^{***}}{0.40109\ \mathrm{YC}} + \underset{(1.73)}{112.816\ \mathrm{CUR}(-4)} + \underset{(6.80)^{***}}{1{,}585.17\ \mathrm{INTGB}(-1)}$$

$$+\underset{(4.60)^{***}}{3.957\ \mathrm{PSTOCK}(-1)} - \underset{(-3.80)^{***}}{27.532\ \mathrm{EXR}(-1)} + \underset{(2.18)^{*}}{0.1576\ \mathrm{FDIA}}$$

R^2ADJ = 0.977 SD = 816.324 DW = 2.462

Note: ***, ** and * present the level of significance at 1%, 5% and 10%, respectively.

4.2.8. *Foreign variables and BOP sub-block*

This sub-block contains real world imports, world import price and variables of balance of payments (BOP). Most of the variables of BOP are exogenously given in this sub-block except for trade balance and its components and service balance and its components. In DEMIOS the project is now planning to improve BOP sub-block based on the framework of IMF-BOP formula version 6 since IMF changed the formula in 2014. Thus, the structure of trade balance and its components: goods exports and imports, and service balance and its components, services exports and imports, are discussed. For the other variables, including income balance and capital balance and hence their components, see the model structure based on the previous version in Nakamura (2013).

In DEMIOS, sectoral exports and imports are determined in the final demand sub-block, as discussed earlier. Accordingly, exports of goods, exports of services, imports of goods and imports of services are determined by sum of nominal sectoral exports and sum of nominal imports in a statistical equation, as follows:
exports of goods in BOP:

$$\mathrm{EG} = \gamma^{\mathrm{EG}} \sum \mathrm{E}_i \cdot \mathrm{PE}_i \quad (i = 1\text{–}52),$$

exports of services in BOP:

$$\mathrm{ES} = \gamma^{\mathrm{ES}} \sum \mathrm{E}_i \cdot \mathrm{PE}_i \quad (i = 53\text{–}80),$$

imports of goods in BOP:

$$\mathrm{MG} = \gamma^{\mathrm{MG}} \sum \mathrm{M}_i \cdot \mathrm{PM}_i \quad (i = 1\text{–}52),$$

imports of services in BOP:

$$MS = \gamma^{MS} \sum M_i \cdot PM_i \quad (i = 53\text{–}80),$$

where EG is the exports of goods in BOP, ES the exports of services in BOP, E_i the sectoral real exports, PE_i the sectoral export prices, MG the imports of goods in BOP, MS the imports of services in BOP, M_i the sectoral real imports, PM_i the sectoral import prices and γ the ratio of BOP base exports of goods and services and imports of goods and services to the sum of sectoral exports and imports in nominal term, respectively.

Therefore, trade balance (TBG) and service balance (TBS) in BOP are determined in an identity, as follows:

trade balance:

$$TBG = EG - MG,$$

service balance:

$$TBS = ES - MS.$$

Chapter 5

Cohort-Type Demographic and Labor Force Block

From the beginning of this project, the KLM project, we have two versions of demographic model, which are: (1) a simplified demographic model and (2) a cohort-type demographic and labor supply model. In particular, the latter one is employed for the long-term scenario simulation, in which the cohort-type demographic variables and labor supply variables by age group and gender have interactive relations with not only macroeconomic variables and sectoral variables in DEMIOS.

No doubt, variables of the number of population and labor and hence their changes have vital effects on both the macroeconomic and sectoral variables and determine macro labor supply and hence macro wage rates. Therefore, this chapter discusses both the simplified demographic model and the cohort-type demographic model.

5.1. Simplified Demographic Model

In the simplified demographic version, seven demographic variables, including the total number of population (NPT), the number of birth (NPB), the number of death (NPD), the number of net immigrants (NPS), the number of active population from 15 to 64 years old (NP15-64), the number of population from 0 to 14 years old (NP0014) and the number of population over 65 years old (NP6500), are determined as endogenous variables. This demographic version is very simple, but the major demographic variables are determined and realize interactive relations with macroeconomic and sectoral economic variables in DEMIOS. Particularly, the relationships with government sector disbursement and final consumption expenditure to the household sector are considered in the model. Theoretical model specification of each equation is defined, as follows:

the number of total population:

$$\mathrm{NPT} = \mathrm{NPT}(-1) + \mathrm{NPB} - \mathrm{NPD} + \mathrm{NPS},$$

the number of population from 15 to 64 years old:

$$\mathrm{NP1564} = \mathrm{NPT} - \mathrm{NP0014} - \mathrm{NP6500},$$

the number of birth:

$$\mathrm{NPB/NPT} = f((+)\mathrm{NP1564}(-2)/\mathrm{NP1564}(-3), (+)\,\mathrm{KH}(-2), (+)\,\mathrm{URATE}(-1), (+)\,\mathrm{CG}(-1)/\mathrm{GDP}(-1)),$$

the number of death:

$$\mathrm{NPD/NPT} = f((+)\mathrm{NP6500/NPT}, (-)\,(\mathrm{CP}(-3) - \mathrm{CP}(-6))/\mathrm{CP}(-6), (-)\,\mathrm{TRGH/GDPN}, (-)\,\mathrm{CG}(-2)/\mathrm{CG}(-3)),$$

the number of net migrants:

$$\mathrm{NPS/NPT} = f((+)(\mathrm{IP}(-1) + \mathrm{IG}(-1))/\mathrm{GDP}(-1), (+)\,(\mathrm{TRGH}(-1) + \mathrm{TRGH}(-2))/\mathrm{GDPN}(-1), (+)\,\mathrm{EXR}),$$

the number of population from 0 to 14 years old:

$$\mathrm{NP0014} = f((+)\Delta(\mathrm{NPT}(-7) + \mathrm{NPT}(-8) + \mathrm{NPT}(-9))/(\mathrm{NPT}(-8) + \mathrm{NPT}(-9) + \mathrm{NPT}(-10)), (+)(\mathrm{KH}(-5) - \mathrm{KH}(-6))/\mathrm{KH}(-6), (-)(\mathrm{URATE}(-8) + \mathrm{URATE}(-9)), (+)\mathrm{CG}(-3)/\mathrm{GDP}(-3)),$$

the number of population over 65 years old:

$$\mathrm{NP6500} = f((+)\,(\mathrm{TRGH}(-7) + \mathrm{TRGH}(-7))/\mathrm{GDPN}(-7), (+)\,\mathrm{CG}(-4)/\mathrm{GDP}(-4), (+)\,(\mathrm{NP1564}(-7) + \mathrm{NP1564}(-8) + \mathrm{NP1564}(-9))/\mathrm{NPT}(-7) + \mathrm{NPT}(-8) + \mathrm{NPT}(-9), (-)\,(\mathrm{NPT}(-4) + \mathrm{NPT}(-5))/\mathrm{NPT}(-5), (-)\,\mathrm{D9700}),$$

where NPT is the total population, NPB the number of birth, NPD the number of death, NPS the number of net immigrants (social increase/decrease), NP0014 the number of population of 0–14 years old, NP1564 the number of population of 15–65 years old (active population), NP6500 the number of population more than 65 years old, IP real non-housing investment, IG the real government investment, TRGH the government transfer to household sector, KH the real housing stock, CG the real government consumption, GDPN the nominal GDP, GDP the real GDP, URATE the unemployment rate and EXR the yen-US$ exchange rate (yen/US$), respectively.

As presented in the model specification, the number of birth (NPB), the number of death (NPD), the number of net migration (NPS), the number of population of 0–14 years old (NP0014) and the number of population 15–64 (NP1564), as an active population are explained by some of macroeconomic variables. In particular, the government transfers to the household sector (TRGH), government consumption expenditure (CG) and government investment (IG) are major important variables to influence to these demographic sector variables and present very remarkable causal relations between the macro sector and the demographic sector in DEMIOS.

For example, in the regression results shown in Table 5.1, fairly high significance of government transfers to the household sector (TRGH) and consumption expenditure (CG) on all demographic variables, including NPB, NPD, NPS, NP0014 and NP6500 could be seen with a specific range of time lags. In addition, some macroeconomic variables which explain economic and business environments like real housing stock (KH), real final consumption expenditure (CP) and real GDP also have significant effects on these demographic variables.

5.2. Cohort-Type Demographic and Labor Supply Model

On the other hand, DEMIOS has a cohort-type demographic and labor supply model for the long-term forecast and scenario simulation analysis. The above demographic model is a simplified model for short- and medium-term forecasts and hence is easier for updating database and regression analysis. However, for longer term forecasts and scenario simulation analysis, the cohort-type demographic and labor supply model has a strong advantage in DEMIOS. Our KLM project developed this cohort-type demographic and labor supply model (see Nakamura and Shishido, 1990).

Table 5.1. Regression results of major demographic variables.

(1) The number of birth

$$NPB/NPT = \underset{(2.103)^{*}}{0.003} + \underset{(5.605)^{***}}{0.0912}\ NP1564(-2)/NP1564(-3) + \underset{(13.420)^{***}}{0.0325}\ KH(-2)$$

$$-\underset{(-3.732)^{***}}{0.00072}\ URATE(-1) + \underset{(5.008)^{***}}{0.00473}\ CG(-3)/GDP(-3)$$

$R^2ADJ = 0.0.9711$ SD = 0.002 DW = 1.949

(2) The number of death

$$NPD/NPT = \underset{(14.343)^{***}}{0.0055} + \underset{(13.014)^{***}}{0.0245}\ NP6500/NPT - \underset{(-1.845)}{0.0016}(CP(-3) - CP(-6))/CP(-6)$$

$$-\underset{(-3.019)^{***}}{0.0134}\ TRGH/GDPN - \underset{(5.008)^{***}}{0.024}\ CG(-2)/CG(-3)$$

$R^2ADJ = 0.9777$ SD = 0.007 DW = 2.274

(3) The number of net immigrants

$$NPS/NPT = \underset{(-2.535)^{**}}{-0.0046} + \underset{(2.175)^{**}}{0.00113}\ (IP(-1) + IG(-1))/GDP(-1)$$

$$+\underset{(2.698)^{***}}{0.0136}\ (TRGH(-1) + TRGH(-2))/GDPN(-1) + \underset{(2.404)^{**}}{4.66E-06}\ EXR$$

$R^2ADJ = 0.813$ SD = 0.0113 DW = 2.296

(4) The number of population from 0 to 14 years old

$$NP0014 = \underset{(-3.955)^{***}}{-0.3488} + \underset{(5.407)^{***}}{8.354}\Delta(NPT(-7) + NPT(-8) + NPT(-9))/(NPT(-8) + NPT(-9) + NPT(-10))$$

$$+\underset{(3.002)^{***}}{0.426}\ (KH(-5) - KH(-6))/KH(-6) - \underset{(-4.097)^{***}}{0.0111}\ (URATE(-8) + URATE(-9))$$

$$+\underset{(6.230)^{***}}{3.196}\ CG(-3)/GDP(-3))$$

$R^2ADJ = 0.920$ SD = 0.028 DW = 1.018

(5) The number of population over 65 years old

$$NP6500/NPT = \underset{(-20.766)^{***}}{-1.384} + 0.354(TRGH(-7) + TRGH(-7))/GDPN(-7) + \underset{(4.176)^{***}}{0.956}\ CG(-4)/GDP(-4)$$

$$+\underset{(20.776)^{***}}{1.995}(NP1564(-7) + NP1564(-8) + NP1564(-9))/(NPT(-7) + NPT(-8) + NPT(-9))$$

$$-\underset{(-4.836)^{***}}{3.705}\ (NPT(-4) + NPT(-5))/NPT(-5) - \underset{(-7.283)^{***}}{0.0075}\ D9700$$

$R^2ADJ = 0.998$ SD = 0.0034 DW = 2.301

Note: ***, ** and * present the level of significance at 1%, 5% and 10%, respectively.

5.2.1. *Population variables*

In the cohort-type demographic model, total population is divided into 18 cohorts, in which most of them are grouped by five years; aged less than one, aged from 1 to 4, aged from 5 to 9, aged from 10 to 14, ... aged over 80 with male and female groups. The breakdown of population, although involving complexities in modeling and forecasting, has a remarkable advantage in the analysis of the structural changes, demographic changes and so on, with respect to age and gender, and hence their effects on the economy.

In principle, incorporated with social increases and decreases by emigration and immigration, population changes are considered by the natural increases (birth) and decreases (death). Therefore the present total population is defined in an identity:

$$\mathrm{NPT}(t) = \mathrm{NPT}(t-1) + \mathrm{NPB}(t) - \mathrm{NPD}(t) + \mathrm{NPM}(t) - \mathrm{NPE}(t),$$

where NPT is the total population, NPB the number of birth, NPD the number of death, NPM the number of immigrants and NPE the number of emigrants, respectively.

Accordingly, it is vital that both the number of birth and the number of death be predicted as accurately as possible for predicting the number of population and its changes in the model. In this demographic model, the number of birth and the number of death are derived from the fertility rate and the death rate by age group.

5.2.1.1. *The number of birth (NPB)*

For the number of births the fertility rates classified by female age groups (BR_i) determine the number of babies with the number of female by age group (NPF_i) in an identity as follows.

$$\begin{aligned}\mathrm{NPB} &= \sum(\mathrm{BR}_i \cdot \mathrm{NPF}_i)\\ &= \mathrm{BR1519} \cdot \mathrm{NPF1519} + \mathrm{BR2014} \cdot \mathrm{NPF2014} + \cdots\\ &\quad + \mathrm{BR4549} \cdot \mathrm{NPF4549}.\end{aligned}$$

As defined above, the number of births (NPB) is obtained the corresponding female population multiplied by each group's fertility rate and then summing these products. Female fertility rates (BR_i) are classified into nine types according to age groups (BR1519, BR2024, BR2529, BR3034, BR3539, BR4044, BR4549, BR5054 and BR5559), each of which is estimated by real wage rates (W/PCP) with a positive sign condition (+), female labor participation rate ($\mathrm{NLF}_i/\mathrm{NPF}_i$) with a positive sign condition (+), average female age at the first marriage (AFM) with a negative sign condition (−) and the Koyck-type ($\mathrm{BR}_i(-1)$)

as follows.

$$BR_i = f((+)W/PCP, (+)\,NLF_i/NPF_i, (-)\,AFM, (+)\,BR_i(-1)),$$

where BR is the fertility rate, W the macro wage and salaries per employee, PCP the deflator of private final consumption expenditure, NLF the number of female labor, NPF the number of female population and AFM the average female age at the first marriage, respectively.

Based on the general model specification discussed above, the regression results of major age group are obtained as shown in Table 5.2. According to the results, these three-aged group fertility rates are depending on the theoretical model except for fertility rate aged 35–39 (BR3539) because of absence of AFM and the performance of the results are very strong with relatively significant coefficients. As shown, the fertility rates for relatively younger generations are very sensitive to real wage and labor participation positively. In addition, younger-aged groups' fertility rates are highly influenced by average female age at the first marriage (AFM).

Table 5.2. Fertility rates regression results by age group, 25–29, 30–34 and 35–39.

(1) Fertility rate of female aged 25–29

$$\underset{(1.98)^{*}}{BR2529 = 0.4587} + \underset{(2.96)^{**}}{0.25745\ W/PCP} + \underset{(3.45)^{***}}{0.3725\ NLF2539/NPF2539} - \underset{(-3.73)^{***}}{0.001726\ AFM} + \underset{(4.60)^{***}}{0.39724\ BR2529(-1)}$$

R^2ADJ = 0.897 SD = 0.0019 DW = 1.897

(2) Fertility rate of female aged 30–34

$$\underset{(1.17)}{BR3034 = 0.7035} + \underset{(3.64)^{***}}{0.2098\ W/PCP} + \underset{(8.71)^{***}}{0.3274\ NLF2539/NPF2539} - \underset{(-4.30)^{***}}{0.00428\ AFM} + \underset{(5.031)^{***}}{0.39724\ BR3034(-1)}$$

R^2ADJ = 0.925 SD = 0.0026 DW = 2.134

(3) Fertility rate of female aged 35–39

$$\underset{(2.00)^{*}}{BR3539 = 0.6921} + \underset{(3.54)^{**}}{0.2384\ W/PCP} + \underset{(2.51)^{***}}{0.2933\ NLF2539/NPF2539} + \underset{(4.80)^{***}}{0.4071\ BR3539(-1)}$$

R^2ADJ = 0.903 SD = 0.0032 DW = 1.537

Note: ***, ** and * present the level of significance at 1%, 5% and 10%, respectively.

5.2.1.2. *The number of deaths*

The one by age group and gender depends on each group's and gender's death rates as follows:

$$\mathrm{DM}_i = \mathrm{DRM}_i \cdot \mathrm{NPM}_i,$$

$$\mathrm{DF}_i = \mathrm{DRF}_i \cdot \mathrm{NPF}_i,$$

where DM_i is the number of death for male by age group, DRM_i the death rates for male by age group, NPM_i the number of male population by age group, DF_i the number of death for female by age group, DRF_i the death rates for female by age group and NPM_i the number of female population by age group, respectively.

Accordingly, in the sub-model death rates for male and female by age group are estimated so as to determine the number of death for male and female by age group. Death rates are explained by average life expectancy for male (ALM) and female (ALF) as follows:

death rates for male:

$$\mathrm{DRM}_i = f((+)1/\mathrm{ALM})$$

death rates for female:

$$\mathrm{DRF}_i = f((+)1/\mathrm{ALF}),$$

where DRM_i is the male death rate by age group, ALM the average life expectancy for male, DRF_i the female death rates and ALF the average life expectancy for female, respectively.

According to the regression results as shown in Table 5.3, the death rates of babies aged zero for male (DRM00) and female (DRF) are explained significantly by the reversed average life expectancy with an expected sign, in which the coefficient of an independent variable of male death rate is a little bit higher than that of female one. Death rates of the population aged 10 to 14 are also explained by the same independent variable, significantly. The coefficient of the independent variable declines to 0.18 for male and 0.13 for female in comparison to that of babies aged zero.

As presented above, the independent variable, average life expectancy, is crucial to determine death rates for all age groups. Accordingly, in the demographic and labor supply sub-block, average life expectancy is also endogenously determined. Both male average life expectancy (ALM) and

Table 5.3. Death rates of babies aged zero and of the population aged 10–14 for male and female.

(1) Death rates aged zero for male

$$DRM00 = -0.13325 + 8.726\ (1/ALM)$$
$$(-29.43)^{***} \quad (30.62)^{***}$$

$R^2ADJ = 0.987$ SD = 0.0015 DW = 2.236

(2) Death rates aged zero for female

$$DRF00 = -0.0931 + 7.058\ (1/ALF)$$
$$(-20.303)^{***} \quad (25.20)^{***}$$

$R^2ADJ = 0.970$ SD = 0.0012 DW = 1.361

(3) Death rates of the population aged 10–14 for male

$$DRM1014 = -0.00192 + 0.1795\ (1/ALM)$$
$$(-18.46)^{***} \quad (22.82)^{***}$$

$R^2ADJ = 0.962$ SD = 0.0028 DW = 2.031

(4) Death rates of the population aged 10–14 for female

$$DRF1014 = -0.00141 + 0.1301\ (1/ALF)$$
$$(-16.34)^{***} \quad (18.06)^{***}$$

$R^2ADJ = 0.973$ SD = 0.0027 DW = 1.985

Note: ***, ** and * present the level of significance at 1%, 5% and 10%, respectively.

female one (ALF) are explained by real government medical expenditure per capita with the positive sign condition (+), as follows:

average life expectancy for male:

$$\ln(ALM) = f((+)\ln(ME/PCP/NPT)),$$

average life expectancy for female:

$$\ln(ALM) = f((+)\ln(ME/PCP/NPT)).$$

As for the regression results of average life expectancy, as shown in Table 5.4, real government medical expenditure per capita explains significantly both the male and female average life expectancies in a log-linear function. It can be seen that the real government expenditure constantly influences the increases in average life expectancy, although

Table 5.4. Regression results of average life expectancy for male and female.

(1) Average male life expectancy

$$\ln(\text{ALM}) = \underset{(81.56)^{***}}{5.2620} + \underset{(19.46)^{***}}{0.08432} \ln(\text{ME/PCP/NPT})$$

R^2ADJ = 0.957 SD = 0.0011 DW = 2.135

(2) Average female life expectancy

$$\ln(\text{ALF}) = \underset{(78.64)^{***}}{5.3286} + \underset{(114.97)^{***}}{0.08643} \ln(\text{ME/PCP/NPT})$$

R^2ADJ = 0.9304 SD = 0.0017 DW = 1.549

Note: ***, ** and * present the level of significance at 1%, 5% and 10%, respectively.

the coefficient (elasticity) is not so high at 0.0843 for male and at 0.0864 for female.

5.2.1.3. *The number of population by age group*

The most crucial issue is how the model estimates population by age group and gender, especially how estimates the movements from babies to children, from children to adults, and from the old aged 75 to 79 to the eldest aged cohort over 80. The cohort at aged zero is explained by total births, as the inflow, and babies' deaths, as the outflow. The specification of the model for the cohort aged zero is as follows:

male population aged zero:

$$\text{NPM00} = f((+)(0.5 \cdot \text{NPB} \cdot (1 - \text{DRM00})))),$$

female population aged zero:

$$\text{NPF00} = f((+)(0.5 \cdot \text{NPB} \cdot (1 - \text{DRF00})))),$$

where NPM00 is the number of male population aged zero, NPB the number of total births, DRM00 the male death rate aged zero, NPF00 the number of female population aged zero and DRF00 the female death rate aged zero, respectively.

Based on the model specification, the fairly good results are obtained (see Table 5.5).

Next, the cohort aged 1 to 4 is calculated with one-fourth of the same cohort in the previous year and the deaths of the same cohort as outflows, and the cohort aged zero as an inflow. Accordingly, the

Table 5.5. Regression results of male and female population aged zero.

(1) Male population aged zero

$$NPM00 = \underset{(2.97)^{***}}{110444.8} + \underset{(22.43)^{***}}{0.90318}\ (0.5 \cdot NPB \cdot (1 - DRM00))$$

$R^2ADJ = 0.957$ SD $= 18431.9$ DW $= 1.673$

(2) Female population aged zero

$$NPF00 = \underset{(3.66)^{***}}{119302.2} + \underset{(21.88)^{***}}{0.8473}\ (0.5 \cdot NPB \cdot (1 - DRF00))$$

$R^2ADJ = 0.941$ SD $= 18984.3$ DW $= 1.205$

Note: ***, ** and * present the level of significance at 1%, 5% and 10%, respectively.

expected coefficient would be 1.0 as a sort of a statistical equation base behavioral equation. The specification of the model is as follows:

male population aged 1 to 4:

$$\begin{aligned} NPM0104 = f((+)((1 - DRM0104) \cdot NPM0104(-1) \\ -1/4(NPM0104(-1) + NPM00(-1)))), \end{aligned}$$

female population aged 1 to 4:

$$\begin{aligned} NPF0104 = f((+)((1 - DRF0104) \cdot NPF0104(-1) \\ -1/4(NPF0104(-1) + NPF00(-1)))), \end{aligned}$$

where NPM0104 is the male population aged 1 to 4, DRM0104 the male death rates aged 1 to 4, NPM00 the male population aged zero, NPF0104 the female population aged 1 to 4, DRF0104 the female death rates aged 1 to 4 and NPF00 the female population aged zero, respectively.

As well as the results of population aged 0 to 4 for male and female, the fairly significant results are obtained as shown in Table 5.6. As discussed above, the coefficients in the results are around 1.0 with 1.0296 for male and at 1.031 for female.

Similarly, each cohort from that aged 5 to 9 to that aged 75 to 79 is explained by the variable with one-fifth of the same cohort in the previous year and deaths in the same cohort as outflows, and one-fifth of younger cohort in the previous year as inflows. Only for the cohort aged 5 to 9, one-fourth is applied to the incoming younger cohort. Accordingly, the model specification is defined as follows:

Table 5.6. Regression results of male and female population aged 1–4.

(1) Male population aged 1–4

$$\underset{(-1.93)^{*}}{\mathrm{NPM0104} = -107935.2} + \underset{(32.87)^{***}}{1.02959}\ (1-\mathrm{DRM0104}\ -1/4)\cdot\mathrm{NPM0104}(-1)+\mathrm{NPM00}(-1))$$

R^2ADJ = 0.8035 SD = 49002.3 DW = 1.295

(2) Female population aged 1–4

$$\underset{(-0.91)}{\mathrm{NPF0104} = -106946.7} + \underset{(24.33)^{***}}{1.03101}\ (1,-\mathrm{DRF0104}\ -1/4)\cdot\mathrm{NPF0104}(-1)+\mathrm{NPF00}(-1))$$

R^2ADJ = 0.897 SD = 51228.7 DW = 1.605

Note: ***, ** and * present the level of significance at 1%, 5% and 10%, respectively.

male population aged 05–09:

$$\begin{aligned}\mathrm{NPM0509} = {} & f((+)((1-\mathrm{DRM0509})\cdot\mathrm{NPM0509}(-1)\\ & -1/4(\mathrm{NPM0509}(-1)+1/4\mathrm{NPM0104}(-1)))),\end{aligned}$$

female population aged 05–09:

$$\begin{aligned}\mathrm{NPF0509} = {} & f((+)((1-\mathrm{DRF0509})\cdot\mathrm{NPF0509}(-1)\\ & -1/4(\mathrm{NPF0509}(-1)+1/4\mathrm{NPF0104}(-1)))),\end{aligned}$$

male population aged 10–14 and 75–79:

$$\begin{aligned}\mathrm{NPM1014} = {} & f((+)((1-\mathrm{DRM1014})\cdot\mathrm{NPM1014}(-1)\\ & -1/4(\mathrm{NPM1014}(-1)+1/5\mathrm{NPM0509}(-1))))\end{aligned}$$

$$\vdots$$

$$\begin{aligned}\mathrm{NPM7579} = {} & f((+)((1-\mathrm{DRM7579})\cdot\mathrm{NPM7579}(-1)\\ & -1/4(\mathrm{NPM7579}(-1)+1/5\mathrm{NPM7074}(-1)))),\end{aligned}$$

female population aged 10–14 and 75–79:

$$\begin{aligned}\mathrm{NPF1014} = {} & f((+)((1-\mathrm{DRF1014})\cdot\mathrm{NPF1014}(-1)\\ & -1/4(\mathrm{NPF1014}(-1)+1/5\mathrm{NPF0509}(-1))))\end{aligned}$$

$$\vdots$$

$$\begin{aligned}\mathrm{NPF7579} = {} & f((+)((1-\mathrm{DRF7579})\cdot\mathrm{NPF7579}(-1)\\ & -1/4(\mathrm{NPF7579}(-1)+1/5\mathrm{NPF7074}(-1)))),\end{aligned}$$

Table 5.7. Regression results of male and female population aged 5–9 and population aged 75–79.

(1) Male population aged 05–09

NPM0509 = −462621.7 + 1.09664 ((1 − DRM0509 − 1/5) NPM0509(−1) + 1/4NPM0104(−1))
(−2.45)** (28.47)***

R^2ADJ = 0.944 SD = 82037.2 DW = 1.561

(2) Female population aged 05–09

NPF0509 = −458735.0 + 1.10350 ((1 − DRF0509 − 1/5) NPF0509(−1) + 1/4 NPF0104(−1))
(−2.17)* (21.75)***

R^2ADJ = 0.958 SD = 108974.4 DW = 1.248

(3) Male population aged 75–79

NPM7579 = −11954.3 + 1.02025 ((1 − DRM7579 − 1/5) NPM7579(−1) + 1/5 NPM7074(−1))
(−1.57) (82.61)***

R^2ADJ = 0.991 SD = 10155.0 DW = 1.621

(4) Female population aged 75–79

NPF7579 = −3472.1 + 0.997 ((1 − DRF7579 − 1/5) NPF7579(−1) + 1/5 NPF7074(−1))
(−1.06) (80.06)***

R^2ADJ = 0.994 SD = 14058.3 DW = 1.762

Note: ***, ** and * present the level of significance at 1%, 5% and 10%, respectively.

where NPM1014 is the male population aged 10 to 14, DRM1014 the male death rates aged 10 to 14, NPF1014 the female population aged 10 to 14 and DRF1014 the female death rates aged 10 to 14, respectively.

Like the results of population aged 5 to 9 for male and female, the fairly significant results are obtained as shown in Table 5.7. In addition, as discussed earlier, the coefficients in the results are at around 1.0 for male and for female.

The cohort aged over 80 is approximated by subtracting deaths of the same cohort in the previous year and by adding one-fifth of the cohort aged 75 to 79. The model specification is as follows:

male population aged over 80:

$$\text{NPM8000} = f((+)((1 - \text{DRM8000}) \cdot \text{NPM8000}(-1) \\ +1/5\text{NPM7579}(-1))),$$

female population aged over 80:

$$\text{NPF8000} = f((+)((1 - \text{DRF8000}) \cdot \text{NPF8000}(-1) \\ +1/5\text{NPF7579}(-1))),$$

Table 5.8. Regression results of male and female population aged over 80.

(1) Male population aged over 80

$$NPM8000 = \underset{(1.478)}{11576.4} + \underset{(80.66)^{***}}{0.9355}\ ((1 - DRM8000) \cdot NPM8000(-1) + 1/5\ NPM7579(-1))$$

$R^2ADJ = 0.992$ SD = 13441.4 DW = 1.011

(2) Female population aged over 80

$$NPF8000 = \underset{(2.15)^{*}}{19758.4} + \underset{(84.37)^{***}}{0.91371}\ ((1 - DRF8000) \cdot NPF8000(-1) + 1/5\ NPF7579(-1))$$

$R^2ADJ = 0.997$ SD = 12469.3 DW = 1.118

Note: ***, ** and * present the level of significance at 1%, 5% and 10%, respectively.

where NPM8000 is the male population aged over 80, DRM8000 the male death rates aged over 80, NPF8000 the female population aged over 80 and DRF8000 the female death rates aged over 80, respectively.

As for the results of regression for male and female population over aged 80, the estimates are very significant, which satisfies the expected results based on the theoretical model discussed above, as shown in Table 5.8.

So far, this section discusses a general approach to estimate each cohort population, which is a very important linkage with economic variables discussed earlier. Unlike the simplified demographic model discussed earlier in this chapter, owing to the cohort-type population model, the cohort-type labor force model has been also developed in DEMIOS.

5.2.2. *Labor supply in the cohort-type demographic and labor supply model*

It is one of the very important features of the current Japanese labor market that the female labor participation rate tends to fluctuate based on business cycle, wage rate fluctuation and taxation system changes. On the other hand, the male labor participation rate still remains fairly rigid without showing fluctuation. Therefore, it is very important to concentrate on the analysis of female participation, as it is essential in forecasting changes in overall labor force participation within changes in business conditions and wage rates changes.

Labor force population is divided into three categories for male: aged 15–24, aged 25–54 and aged over 55, and into four categories for female: aged 15–24, aged 25–39, aged 40–54 and aged 55–64. The specification of male and female labor force population function is as follows:

male labor force group aged 15–24:

$$\mathrm{NLM1524/NPM1524} = f((+)\mathrm{NSM/NPM1524})$$

$$(\mathrm{NPM1524} = \mathrm{NPM1519} + \mathrm{NPM2024}),$$

male labor force group aged 25–54:

$$\mathrm{NLM2554} = f((+)\mathrm{NPM2554})$$

$$(\mathrm{NPM2554} = \mathrm{NPM22529} + \mathrm{NPM3034} + \mathrm{NPM3539} + \cdots + \mathrm{NPM5054}),$$

male labor force group aged over 55:

$$\mathrm{NLM5500} = f((+)\mathrm{NPM5569/NPM5500}, (-)\,\mathrm{PCPP/PCP} \cdot \mathrm{NPM5569})(\mathrm{NPM5569} = \mathrm{NPM5559} + \mathrm{NPM6064} + \mathrm{NPM6569}),$$

female labor force group aged 15–24:

$$\mathrm{NLF1524/NPF1524} = f((+)(\mathrm{GDP} - \mathrm{GDP}(-1)/\mathrm{GDP}(-1), (-)\,\mathrm{NSF/NPF1524}))$$

$$(\mathrm{NPF1524} = \mathrm{NPF1519} + \mathrm{NPF2024}),$$

female labor force group aged 25–39:

$$\mathrm{NLF2539/NPF2539} = f((+)(\mathrm{GDP} - \mathrm{GDP}(-1)/\mathrm{GDP}(-1), (+)\mathrm{W/PCP}, (+)\mathrm{NLF2539}(-1)/\mathrm{NPF2539}(-1)))$$

$$(\mathrm{NPF2539} = \mathrm{NPF2529} + \mathrm{NPF3034} + \mathrm{NPF3539}),$$

female labor force group aged 40–54:

$$\mathrm{NLF4054/NPF4054} = f((+)(\mathrm{GDP} - \mathrm{GDP}(-1)/\mathrm{GDP}(-1), (+)\,\mathrm{W/PCP}, (+)\,\mathrm{NLF4054}(-1)/\mathrm{NPF4054}(-1)))$$

$$(\mathrm{NPF4054} = \mathrm{NPF4044} + \mathrm{NPF4549} + \mathrm{NPF5054}))$$

female labor force group aged 55–64:

$$\mathrm{NLF5564/NPF5564} = f((+)(\mathrm{GDP} - \mathrm{GDP}(-1)/\mathrm{GDP}(-1), (+)\,\mathrm{W/PCP}, (+)\mathrm{NPF5559/NPF5564}))$$

$$(\mathrm{NPF5564} = \mathrm{NPF5559} + \mathrm{NPF6064}),$$

Table 5.9. Regression results of labor force population by age group and by gender.

(1) Male labor force group aged 15–24

$$\text{NLM1524/NPM1524} = \underset{(34.33)^{***}}{1.02641} - \underset{(-14.74)^{***}}{1.0493}\ \text{NSM/NPM1524}$$

$$R^2\text{ADJ} = 0.937 \quad \text{SD} = 0.044 \quad \text{DW} = 1.454$$

(2) Male labor force group aged 25–54

$$\text{NLM2554} = \alpha\text{NPM2554}$$

(3) Male labor force group aged over 50

$$\text{NLM5500} = \underset{(42.64)^{***}}{0.8099} + \underset{(2.54)^{**}}{029541}\ \text{NPM5569/NPM5500} \underset{(-11.33)^{***}}{-196.664}\ \text{PCPP/PCP}\cdot\text{NPM5569}$$

$$R^2\text{ADJ} = 0.917 \quad \text{SD} = 0.025 \quad \text{DW} = 1.035$$

(4) Female labor force group aged 15–24

$$\text{NLF1524/NPF1524} = \underset{(18.33)^{***}}{0.78532} + \underset{(2.66)^{**}}{0.2186}\ (\text{GDP} - \text{GDP}(-1)/\text{GDP}(-1)) \underset{(-6.88)^{***}}{-0.56836}\ \text{NSF/NPF1524}$$

$$R^2\text{ADJ} = 0.933 \quad \text{SD} = 0.015 \quad \text{DW} = 2.269$$

(5) Female labor force group aged 25–39

$$\text{NLF2539/NPF2539} = \underset{(-1.03)}{-0.28970} + \underset{(2.03)^{*}}{0.1599}\ (\text{GDP} - \text{GDP}(-1)/\text{GDP}(-1)) \underset{(2.35)^{**}}{+0.40980}\ \text{W/PCP} + \underset{(3.88)^{***}}{0.76880}\ \text{NLF2539}(-1)/\text{NPF2539}(-1)$$

$$R^2\text{ADJ} = 0.887 \quad \text{SD} = 0.012 \quad \text{DW} = 2.132$$

(6) Female labor force group aged 40–54

$$\text{NLF4054/NPF4054} = \underset{(-0.68)}{-0.01963} + \underset{(1.99)^{*}}{0.013360}\ (\text{GDP} - \text{GDP}(-1)/\text{GDP}(-1)) \underset{(2.99)^{***}}{+0.1733}\ \text{W/PCP} + \underset{(3.20)^{***}}{0.85446}\ \text{NLF4054}(-1)/\text{NPF4054}(-1)$$

$$R^2\text{ADJ} = 0.901 \quad \text{SD} = 0.011 \quad \text{DW} = 1.988$$

(7) Female labor force group aged 55–64

$$\text{NLF5564/NPF5564} = \underset{(3.61)^{***}}{0.19887} + \underset{(1.95)^{*}}{0.0493}\ (\text{GDP} - \text{GDP}(-1)/\text{GDP}(-1)) \underset{(2.29)^{**}}{+0.1634}\ \text{W/PCP} + \underset{(2.98)^{***}}{0.33602}\ \text{NPF5559/NPF5564}$$

$$R^2\text{ADJ} = 0.722 \quad \text{SD} = 0.009 \quad \text{DW} = 2.205$$

Note: ***, ** and * present the level of significance at 1%, 5% and 10%, respectively.

where NLM1524 is the male labor force population group aged 15–24, NSM the number of male population participating in higher education, NLM2554 the male labor force population group aged 25–54, NLM5000 the male labor force population group aged over 50, PCPP the public pension expenditure per capita, NLF1524 the female labor force population group aged 15–24, NSF the number of female population participating in higher education, NLF2539 the female labor force population group aged 25–39, W the nominal wage rates, PCP the implicit deflator of private final consumption expenditure, NLF4054 the female labor force population group aged 40–54 and NLF5564 the female labor force population group aged 55 to 64, respectively.

Concerning the male labor force, the group aged 15–24 (NLM1524) is greatly dependent on the participation rate in higher education (NSM/NPM1524). Besides, the male group aged 25–54 (NLM2554) remains highly stable. So, in the labor force sub-block, the labor force ratio (α) to the number of population for the male group aged 25–54 is employed every year and extrapolates the latest ratio for the future projection as an exogenous (policy) variable. The male group aged over 55 (NLM5500) is accounted for by the ratio of the male population cohort aged 55–69 (NPM5559 + NPM6064 + NPM6569) to the entire population cohort aged over 55 (NPM5500) and the real public pension benefit per capita (PCPP/PCP).

On the other hand, for female labor participation, as discussed above, the economic variables influence the labor participation. The group aged 15–24 is explained by the business condition (rate of changes in real GDP) and the participation rate in higher education (NSF/NPF1524). The group aged 25–39 and the group aged 40–54 are accounted for by the business condition, real wage rates and the previous year variable of the Koyck type. The group aged 55–64 is explained by the business condition, real wage rates and the ratio of the female population cohort aged 55–59 to the female population cohort of aged 55–64.

Regarding the regression results based on the theoretical model specification discussed above, most of the results are fairly good and particular emphasis is placed on the female labor participation rates, whose parameters are highly dependent on the business condition and real wage rates, as shown in Table 5.9. This is very important for understanding the interdependent feedback between labor force population and the real economy within a scenario simulation analysis as discussed later.

Chapter 6

Scenario Projections by DEMIOS

6.1. National Resilience Plan and its Effects on the Japanese Economy

6.1.1. *Introduction*

The Japanese economy had successfully achieved an economic prosperity after WWII. Particularly in the 1950s and 1960s, the economy recorded a 2-digit economic growth by strengthening both the supply-side and the demand-side economies. In the post-war period, a huge amount government investment had been implemented, which led reconstruction of the Japanese economy.

However, more than 50 years have passed since the period of reconstruction. So, recently, most of the social infrastructures which were constructed in the 1950s and 1960s have been damaged and would meet the replacement period, especially in the major districts of Japan including Tokyo, Osaka, Aichi districts and so on. In addition, several repeated disasters, including the Great East Japan Earthquake and Tsunami and the Kumamoto district earthquake and so on require large-scale reconstruction in Japan. But, reconstruction of these disasters has not significantly implemented because of the limited capacities, especially in construction and civil engineering industry which have been undermined through a reform of public finance and administration by the central government since the middle of the 1990s.

Therefore, this section is to examine the impacts of a large scale fiscal stimulus as a national resilience policy on the Japanese economy by utilizing DEMIOS scenario simulations.

6.1.2. *Assumption of two scenario simulations*

As shown in Table 6.1, the real government investment which is one of the major policy variables in the model is extrapolated exogenously from FY2015 to FY2020 for both the baseline projection and the scenario projection. The deviation between the baseline and the scenario projections is assumed at 7.0 trillion yen in FY2016, 12.0 trillion yen in FY2017 and 17.0 trillion yen in FY2018–2020 and hence the accumulated deviation between both the projections during the five years from FY2016 to FY2020 amounts to 70.0 trillion yen. Therefore, the scenario projections could capture the effects of government investment increases on the economy by comparing both the projections.

The extrapolated government investment is allocated to the sectoral government investment and through a backward linkage the allocated sectoral government investments induce sectoral outputs and other sectoral endogenous variables and then decide the macro endogenous variables in DEMIOS as discussed earlier in this book.

6.1.3. *Simulation results: The effects on the Japanese economy*

According to the scenario projections of the baseline and the government investment increase scenario in FY2016–2020, the significant effects of government investment increases on the economy can be seen, as shown in Fig. 6.1. As shown in Tables 6.2 and 6.3, real GDP will probably rise by 8.3 trillion yen in FY2016, 25.2 trillion yen in FY2018, and it will be increasing gradually to 33.6 trillion yen in FY2020. The largest effects will be seen in the real household consumption expenditure by 14.0 trillion yen in FY2020, next the real private non-housing investment by 7.3 trillion yen in FY2020 and the smallest effects will be the real housing investment by 1.4 trillion yen among the domestic demand

Table 6.1. Real government investment for two scenario projections, FY2015–2020 (in trillions of yen).

	FY2015	2016	2017	2018	2019	2020	FY2016–2020
Baseline	25.0	27.0	29.0	31.0	33.0	34.0	154.0
Scenario	25.0	34.0	41.0	48.0	50.0	51.0	224.0
Deviation*	0.0	7.0	12.0	17.0	17.0	17.0	70.0

*Deviation = Scenario–Baseline.

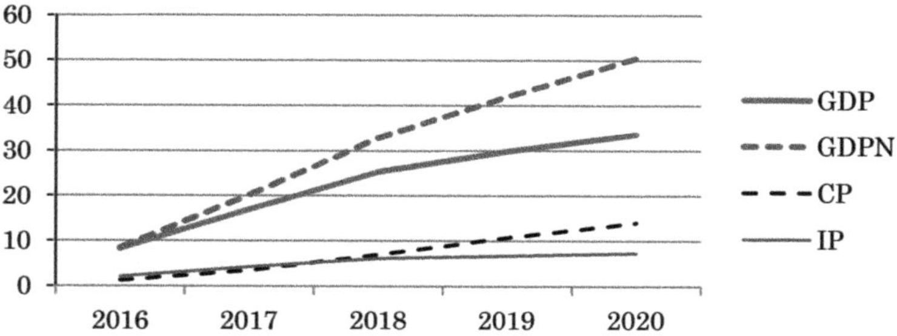

Fig. 6.1. The effects of government investment increases on real GDP, its components and nominal GDP, FY2016–2020.

Note: GDP: real GDP, GDPN: nominal GDP, CP: real household consumption, IP: real private non-housing investment.

components in FY2020. (See Tables A6.1–A6.4 for sectoral output (X), and sectoral wage and salaries employees in both projections.)

The impacts on nominal GDP will be large as well by 8.5 trillion yen to 50.5 trillion yen in FY2016–2020, which will include rises in prices (Shinohara, 1947). Therefore, many indicators which are influenced by nominal GDP will probably have favorable effects during the predicted five years. For example, income tax revenue, corporate tax revenue, indirect tax revenue and hence general government revenue are expected to increase significantly, as shown in Tables 6.2 and 6.3.

In addition, despite large impacts on the economy, rises in prices will probably be limited, because with the large deflationary gap real potential GDP increases will be induced by private non-housing investment increases. Therefore, rises in prices in terms of deflator of private consumption (PCP) will be induced by 0.3% points in FY2018, by 0.6% points in FY2019 and by 0.7% points in FY2020, respectively. With an improvement of economic deflation, exchange rate will be depreciated by 2.3 yen in FY2018, by 4.2 yen in FY2019 and by 6.1 yen in FY2020, which will result in favorable impacts on the Japanese economy. Therefore, the number of employed will have positive effects by 1258–1573 thousands in FY2016–2020, as presented in Tables 6.2 and 6.3.

Based on these two scenario projections, the fairly high dynamic Keynes multiplier in both nominal term and real term can be seen, as shown in Table 6.4. The higher dynamic multiplier in DEMIOS could be induced by both the Keynes multiplier and the Leontief multiplier within a complicated system, which is a remarkable nature in the Keynes–Leontief

Table 6.2. The baseline projection, FY2015–2020.

	2015	2016	2017	2018	2019	2020
Real GDP	563.9	587.2	605.7	615.1	623.5	640.2
(% ch.)	3.8	4.1	3.2	1.6	1.4	2.7
Nominal GDP	529	575.7	630.3	674.6	690.7	701.1
(% ch.)	4.4	8.8	9.5	7	2.4	1.5
Real private consumption	296.8	306.3	314.9	317.4	318.6	323.9
(% ch.)	−0.6	3.2	2.8	0.8	0.4	1.6
Real private investment	72.3	80.1	86.8	89.7	86.8	85.4
(% ch.)	5.9	10.8	8.5	3.3	−3.2	−1.7
Real housing investment	22	23.1	25.5	27.1	27.9	27.5
(% ch.)	43.3	5	10.3	6.1	3.2	−1.7
Real government consumption	108.4	110	111.7	113.3	115.0	116.7
(% ch.)	2	1.5	1.5	1.5	1.5	1.5
Real government investment	25.0	27.0	29.0	31.0	33.0	34.0
(% ch.)	5.0	8.0	7.5	6.9	6.5	3.0
Real exports	110.2	120.3	125.6	127.2	133.7	144.2
(% ch.)	14	9.1	4.4	1.3	5.1	7.9
Real imports	80.1	89.7	100.4	105.5	105.1	104
(% ch.)	7.8	12	12	5	−0.3	−1.1
GDP deflator	93.8	98	104.1	109.7	110.8	109.5
(% ch.)	0.6	4.5	6.1	5.4	1	−1.1
Deflator of CP	97.9	99.8	102.5	105.7	107.8	108.5
(% ch.)	1.2	1.9	2.7	3.1	2	0.6
Government bond yield %	0.3	1.1	2.5	2	1.5	1
(% ch.)	−73.4	277.3	127.9	−18.6	−25.1	−32.1
Wage (1000 yen)	4832	5018	5212	5392	5525	5621
(% ch.)	2.7	3.8	3.9	3.5	2.5	1.7
Employed (1000)	57905	58754	59779	60467	60355	60240
(% ch.)	0.2	1.5	1.7	1.2	−0.2	−0.2
Utilization rate of capital %	78.3	79.9	80.4	79	76.9	75.8
(% ch.)	1.8	2.1	0.6	−1.7	−2.6	−1.5
General government revenue	212441	225114	242904	255521	257390	255932
(% ch.)	9.7	6	7.9	5.2	0.7	−0.6

(*Continued*)

Table 6.2. (*Continued*)

	2015	2016	2017	2018	2019	2020
Net government debt outstanding	447194	386801	353924	332150	334889	325901
(% ch.)	−5	−13.5	−8.5	−6.2	0.8	−2.7
Net government debt to GDPN	82.6	67.2	58	52.1	51.3	48.6
(% ch.)	—	—	—	—	—	—
Real capital stock	614199	627438	646298	665582	678892	688751
(% ch.)	0.9	2.2	3	3	2	1.5
Real residential stock	365820	373072	382413	392917	403843	413803
(% ch.)	1.8	2	2.5	2.7	2.8	2.5
Real government capital stock	269138	270918	274936	282116	290339	298618
(% ch.)	0.2	0.7	1.5	2.6	2.9	2.9
Total population (1000)	129647	129926	130358	130739	131033	131453
(% ch.)	0.2	0.2	0.3	0.3	0.2	0.3
Exchange rate (¥/$)	109.1	91.9	67.5	50.5	56.4	69.4
(% ch.)	2.2	−15.8	−26.6	−25.1	11.6	23.1

Table 6.3. National resilience plan, FY2015–2020.

	2015	2016	2017	2018	2019	2020
Real GDP	563.9	595.5	622.7	640.3	653.3	673.8
(% ch.)	3.8	5.6	4.6	2.8	2.0	3.1
Nominal GDP	529.0	584.2	650.3	707.5	732.7	751.6
(% ch.)	4.4	10.4	11.3	8.8	3.6	2.6
Real private consumption	296.8	307.5	318.4	324.3	329.3	337.9
(% ch.)	−0.6	3.6	3.6	1.9	1.5	2.6
Real private investment	72.3	82.2	91.0	95.8	93.5	92.7
(% ch.)	5.9	13.7	10.8	5.3	−2.4	−0.9
Real housing investment	22.0	23.1	25.9	27.8	29.2	28.9
(% ch.)	43.3	5.0	12.0	7.4	4.7	−1.0
Real government consumption	108.4	110.0	111.7	113.3	115.0	116.7

(*Continued*)

Table 6.3. *(Continued)*

	2015	2016	2017	2018	2019	2020
(% ch.)	2.0	1.5	1.5	1.5	1.5	1.5
Real government investment	25.0	34.0	41.0	48.0	50.0	51.0
(% ch.)	5.0	36.0	20.6	19.5	2.1	1.0
Real exports	110.2	120.2	125.7	128.0	135.2	146.1
(% ch.)	14.0	9.1	4.5	1.8	5.7	8.1
Real imports	80.1	91.8	105.2	113.0	113.8	113.5
(% ch.)	7.8	14.7	14.6	7.3	0.7	−0.3
GDP deflator	93.8	98.1	104.4	110.5	112.2	111.5
(% ch.)	0.6	4.6	6.5	5.8	1.5	−0.5
Deflator of CP	97.9	99.7	102.6	106.1	108.8	110.3
(% ch.)	1.2	1.8	2.9	3.4	2.6	1.3
Government bond yield %	0.3	1.2	2.7	2.2	1.7	1.2
(% ch.)	−73.4	317.4	125.6	−17.3	−24.7	−30.8
Wage (1000 yen)	4832	5049	5292	5536	5732	5894
(% ch.)	2.7	4.5	4.8	4.6	3.5	2.8
Employed (1000)	57905	59034	60321	61256	61265	61253
(% ch.)	0.2	1.9	2.2	1.6	0.0	0.0
Utilization rate of capital %	78.3	81.0	82.6	82.3	80.7	79.7
(% ch.)	1.8	3.5	1.9	−0.4	−2.0	−1.2
General government revenue	212441	227813	250251	267869	273558	275013
(% ch.)	9.7	7.2	9.8	7.0	2.1	0.5
Net government debt outstanding	447194	389674	350707	310117	294395	271443
(% ch.)	−5.0	−12.9	−10.0	−11.6	−5.1	−7.8
Net government debt to GDPN	82.6	66.7	55.6	46.3	42.5	37.9
(% ch.)						
Real capital stock	614199	629764	652993	678214	697449	713262
(% ch.)	0.9	2.5	3.7	3.9	2.8	2.3
Real residential stock	365820	373072	382812	394076	406177	417458
(% ch.)	1.8	2.0	2.6	2.9	3.1	2.8
Real government capital stock	269138	277886	294407	317286	340221	362287
(% ch.)	0.2	3.3	5.9	7.8	7.2	6.5
Total population (1000)	129647	129984	130476	130918	131245	131695

(Continued)

Table 6.3. (*Continued*)

	2015	2016	2017	2018	2019	2020
(% ch.)	0.2	0.3	0.4	0.3	0.2	0.3
Exchange rate (¥/$)	109.1	91.8	68.1	52.8	60.6	75.5
(% ch.)	2.2	−15.9	−25.8	−22.5	14.9	24.5

Table 6.4. The dynamic Keynes multiplier by DEMIOS, FY2016–2020.

	2016	2017	2018	2019	2020
Real	1.19	1.42	1.48	1.75	1.98
Nominal	1.21	1.49	1.56	1.89	2.21

model (KLM) system. In the fifth year, therefore, the multiplier is 1.98 in real term and 2.21 in real term in FY2020. Furthermore, therefore, it is worth noting that the primary balance will probably be improved in the second year in the government investment increase scenario.

6.1.4. *Conclusion*

As discussed above, even now, the Japanese economy has the fairly large Keynes multiplier based on an experiment by DEMIOS. Therefore, it would be a good chance to redevelop social infrastructures with large-scale fiscal policy measures at this moment, which could also contribute to stimulating domestic demands and hence escaping from a long-term economic slump. In addition, optimistic views to overcome the long-term economic deflation based on the large-scale fiscal policy would be very important. The large-scale fiscal policy is applicable to the current long-term deflation by employing an accommodated fiscal policy together with the Bank of Japan as well as implemented in the prewar period. Furthermore, it is noteworthy that employing an appropriate tool like an econometric model is also indispensable to predict future projections as a compass for a voyage.

6.2. Growth Alternatives in Abenomics by DEMIOS

As broadly known in Japan, Abenomics has started since April 2013 as a policy package for redevelopment of the Japanese economy with "Three

Allows": (1) Bolt Monetary Policy, (2) Flexible Fiscal Policy and (3) Growth Strategy to stimulate private sector investment. However, as many studies revealed its limited effectiveness, the assumption of Abenomics would be still weak and ineffective to overcome the long-term economic slump since the middle of the 1990s.[1]

Therefore, this chapter is to examine the appropriate growth strategy in Abenomics and its effectiveness by utilizing DEMIOS as a compass of the Forth Allow to predict the future growth alternatives, as discussed earlier in this book. This kind of *Ex-ante* alternative scenario simulation has often been utilized for predicting the economy. For example, in Japan, the "Income Doubling Plan" planned in 1960 was conducted by utilizing a simple econometric model and scenario simulation analysis for examining growth policies in the 1960s.

6.2.1. *Assumptions of future scenario simulation*

As noted above, this chapter is to predict the future growth alternatives of the Japanese economy. The assumptions in the future growth alternatives consist of three scenarios: (1) Growth alternative scenario with active government expenditures as Scenario 1, (2) Growth alternative scenario as Scenario 2 with Scenario 1 plus expansion of leisure and labor share to induce household sector's final demands and (3) Growth alternative scenario as Scenario 3 with Scenario 1 plus consumption tax rate hikes to 8% from April 2014 and 10% from April 2015.

Given these three assumptions of Abenomics launched in April 2013, this chapter conducts three alternative scenario projections from FY2014 to FY2020, based on the baseline projection conducted in the previous section. More detailed assumptions for policy variables' extrapolation and constant adjustments of related variables are shown, as follows.

---

[1]For instance, Nakamura (2013), Ueda (2012), Honda and Tachibana (2011), Lam (2011), Ugai (2007), Oda and Ueda (2007) analyzed the effectiveness of QE policy measures on the Japanese economy and Nakamura (2014) examines the effects of a bolt monetary policy in Abenomics on the Japanese economy, by employing an econometric model.

6.2.2. *Three growth scenario projections, FY2014–2020*

Scenario 1: Growth scenario

- Base money rises by 6–7 trillion yen every month and achieves 270 trillion yen in December 2014 and remains constant at 270 trillion yen to FY2020.
- Real government consumption expenditure is exogenously assumed at 2.0% annually from 2013 to 2015 and at 1.5% from FY2016 to 2020, as well as in the baseline.
- Real government investment is exogenously extrapolated at 1.3% in 2013, 9.2% in FY2014, 43.3% in FY2015, 34.4% in FY2016 and 5% in FY2017–2020, annually in order to achieve 50 trillion yen government investment in FY2020.
- Policy rate of interest (call-rate) remains at 0.1% from FY2013 to 2020, based on the 0% interest rate policy.
- Corporate tax cut with a reduction of capital duration by 10% from FY2014, based on the baseline.
- Expansion of fiscal investment and loan for business investment by 6 trillion yen for all industries and housing investment by 5 trillion yen from FY2014, based on the baseline.

Scenario 2: Scenario 1 plus leisure expansion scenario

- Paid holiday expansion by 10 hours a month on average in all industries with direct effects on household consumption and housing investment from FY2014.
- Expansion of employment by 3–5% for replacement from FY2014.

Scenario 3: Scenario 1 plus consumption tax rate hike scenario

- Consumption tax rate hike to 8% from FY2014 and 10% from FY2015.

6.2.3. *Simulation results: Major macroeconomic variables and sectoral variables*

Based on the assumptions for scenario simulations discussed above, the three alternative scenario projections are implemented from FY2014 to FY2020. As shown in Fig. 6.2, the first two growth scenario projections will probably achieve higher growth rates in comparison to the baseline projection, in which real GDP in FY2020 is expected to be 715.7

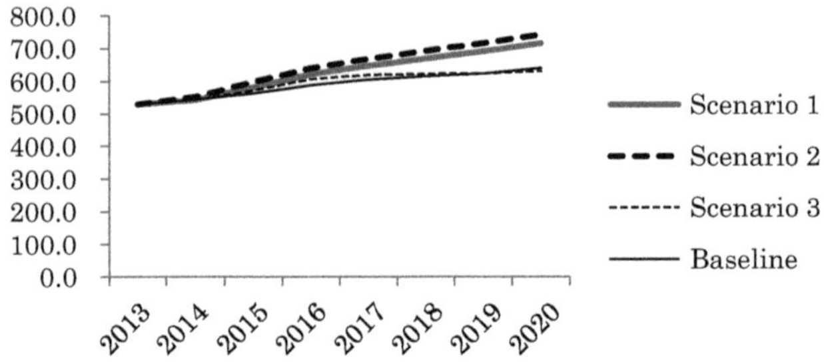

Fig. 6.2. Real GDP in the baseline and three scenario projection, FY2014–2020 (in billions of yen).

trillion yen in Scenario 1 (Growth Scenario) and 742.5 trillion yen in Scenario 2 (Growth plus Leisure Scenario). On the other hand, it is expected that real GDP will be 631.7 trillion yen even in Scenario 3 (Growth plus Consumption Tax Hikes Scenario) because of the strong deflationary pressure to the demand-side economy by consumption tax rate hikes. In comparison to 640.2 trillion yen of real GDP in the baseline projection, it can be seen that the first two growth alternatives will probably achieve a high growth performance and overcome the long-term economic slump by FY2020. (See Tables A6.5–A6.10 for sectoral output (X) and sectoral wage & salaried employees (LW) in Scenario 1, Scenario 2 and Scenario 3.)

In these three growth alternatives, nominal GDP will probably grow strongly up to FY2020. Although nominal GDP in Scenario 3 will probably be stagnant in growth in the latter half of the 2010s because of consumption tax rate hikes to 10%, nominal GDP in Scenario 1 and Scenario 2 will exceed 800 trillion yen in FY2020 (see Tables 6.5–6.7). These strong growth alternatives are mainly attributable to the strong expansion of domestic demands induced by not only increases in government investment and government consumption but also expansion of household consumption expenditures.

In addition, owing to stimulated domestic demands, the economic deflation will probably be improved and hence prices will rise at 3–4% on average in Scenarios 1, 2 and 3 in terms of general deflator of GDP (PGDP), as shown in Tables 6.1–6.3. In particular, the general deflator, PGDP, in Scenario 2 will rise at 4.6% on average in line with the strong GDP growth in the latter half of the 2010s.

Owing to the vital growth performance in both nominal and real GDP, fiscal revenues are also expected to increase drastically through a

Table 6.5. Scenario 1: Growth scenario.

	2014	2015	2016	2017	2018	2019	2020
Real GDP	543.2	581.3	621.2	646.4	669.4	690.9	715.7
(% ch.)	2.6	7..0	6.9	4.1	3.6	3.2	3.6
Nominal GDP	507.8	544.6	612.6	676.8	726.8	771.6	820.7
(% ch.)	1.8	7.2	12.5	10.5	7.4	6.2	6.4
Real private consumption	298.9	302.9	319.5	334.4	344.4	356	369.9
(% ch.)	1.7	1.4	5.5	4.7	3	3.4	3.9
Real private investment	68.1	74.3	84.2	90.4	93.5	93.2	95.3
(% ch.)	2.8	9	13.3	7.4	3.5	−0.4	2.3
Housing investment	15.3	24.8	26.2	31.1	34.3	35.7	35.5
(% ch.)	−0.2	62.3	5.9	18.4	10.5	4	−0.5
Real government consumption	106.3	108.4	110	111.7	113.3	115	116.7
(% ch.)	2	2	1.5	1.5	1.5	1.5	1.5
Real government investment	24.2	34.6	46.6	48.9	51.3	53.9	56.6
(% ch.)	9.2	43.3	34.4	5	5	5	5
Real exports	96.4	110.1	120.4	127.5	135.3	144	152.9
(% ch.)	3.6	14.2	9.3	5.9	6.1	6.4	6.2
Real imports	74.5	83.8	98.1	110.5	115.9	119.6	123.9
(% ch.)	2.6	12.5	17	12.7	4.8	3.2	3.6
GDP deflator	93.5	93.7	98.6	104.7	108.6	111.7	114.7
(% ch.)	−0.8	0.2	5.3	6.2	3.7	2.9	2.7
Deflator of CP	96.7	97.7	100	103.3	107.2	110.6	113.5
(% ch.)	0.9	1	2.3	3.4	3.7	3.2	2.6
CPI (core)	115.2	114.1	114.1	116.1	119	121.9	124.2
(% ch.)	0.2	−1	0	1.7	2.5	2.4	1.9
Government bond yield	2.80%	2.70%	3.70%	4.80%	4.00%	4.10%	3.50%
(% ch.)	−7	−3.9	40.2	29.7	−18.1	2.1	−12.7
Wage (1000 yen)	4699.2	4893.3	5173.4	5447.4	5728.5	6010.7	6280.6
(% ch.)	2.1	4.1	5.7	5.3	5.2	4.9	4.5
Employed (1000)	57810.5	58485.9	59824.4	60822.5	61284	61610.7	62128.6
(% ch.)	0.9	1.2	2.3	1.7	0.8	0.5	0.8
Capital utilization rate	76.80%	80.70%	84.50%	85.70%	85.80%	85.20%	84.70%
(% ch.)	1.3	5	4.7	1.5	0.1	−0.8	−0.5
Government revenue	179.1	191.7	210.6	230.1	242.8	252.6	261.8
(% ch.)	3.7	7	9.9	9.2	5.5	4	3.6
Net government debt outstanding	480.6	468.6	398.6	319.2	254.1	233	208.9
(% ch.)	−6.4	−2.5	−14.9	−19.9	−20.4	−8.3	−10.3

(Continued)

Table 6.5. (*Continued*)

	2014	2015	2016	2017	2018	2019	2020
Debt ratio to GDPN	89.60%	82.90%	64.60%	48.40%	36.40%	31.70%	27.00%
Real capital stock	608.5	616.1	633.7	656.1	678.9	698.4	717.6
(% ch.)	0.2	1.2	2.9	3.5	3.5	2.9	2.7
Real residential stock	359.3	368.5	378.8	393.5	410.9	428.9	445.9
(% ch.)	−0.1	2.6	2.8	3.9	4.4	4.4	4
Real government capital stock	268.1	278.4	300.2	323.1	347	372	398.3
(% ch.)	−0.2	3.8	7.8	7.6	7.4	7.2	7.1
Population (million)	129.4	129.8	130.2	130.5	131	131.5	132.1
(% ch.)	0.2	0.3	0.3	0.3	0.4	0.4	0.5
Exchange rate (¥/$)	104.4	110.4	94.3	77.7	79.6	83.7	84.7
	8.8	5.8	−14.6	−17.6	2.4	5.2	1.1

Table 6.6. Scenario 2: Growth plus leisure expansion scenario.

	2014	2015	2016	2017	2018	2019	2020
Real GDP	552.1	597.3	640.4	667.9	692.5	716.4	742.5
(% ch.)	4.2	8.2	7.2	4.3	3.7	3.5	3.6
Nominal GDP	516.2	562.2	638.4	710.4	767	818.5	874.1
(% ch.)	3.5	8.9	13.6	11.3	8	6.7	6.8
Real private consumption	306.7	316.5	336.9	355.1	367.5	382.2	398
(% ch.)	4.4	3.2	6.4	5.4	3.5	4	4.1
Real private investment	69.1	76.5	87.3	93.7	96.9	96.6	98.6
(% ch.)	4.1	10.8	14.1	7.3	3.4	−0.3	2.1
Housing investment	17.1	28.7	30	34.6	37.6	38.8	38.3
(% ch.)	12	67.5	4.6	15	8.8	3.1	−1
Real government consumption	106.3	108.4	110	111.7	113.3	115	116.7
(% ch.)	2	2	1.5	1.5	1.5	1.5	1.5
Real investment	24.2	34.6	46.6	48.9	51.3	53.9	56.6
(% ch.)	9.2	43.3	34.4	5	5	5	5
Real exports	96.4	110.1	120.3	127.3	135	143.8	152.8
(% ch.)	3.6	14.2	9.3	5.9	6	6.5	6.2
Real imports	76.9	88.9	105	118.5	124.6	128.9	133.4
(% ch.)	5.9	15.6	18.1	12.9	5.1	3.5	3.5
GDP deflator	93.5	94.1	99.7	106.4	110.8	114.2	117.7
(% ch.)	−0.8	0.7	5.9	6.7	4.1	3.1	3
Deflator of CP	96.7	97.9	100.6	104.3	108.6	112.5	115.9

(*Continued*)

Table 6.6. (*Continued*)

	2014	2015	2016	2017	2018	2019	2020
(% ch.)	0.8	1.3	2.7	3.7	4.1	3.6	3
CPI (core)	114.5	113.2	113.3	115.6	118.7	121.9	124.6
(% ch.)	−0.5	−1.1	0.1	2	2.7	2.7	2.3
Government bond yield	2.70%	2.80%	3.80%	4.90%	3.90%	3.90%	3.30%
(% ch.)	−10.4	3.2	39	27.2	−19	−0.5	−16.3
Wage (1,000 yen)	4737.2	4979.3	5302.1	5612.6	5933.5	6259.7	6565.8
(% ch.)	2.9	5.1	6.5	5.9	5.7	5.5	4.9
Employed (1,000)	58173.3	59067.5	60477.4	61530.8	62030.8	62400.5	62929.3
(% ch.)	1.5	1.5	2.4	1.7	0.8	0.6	0.8
Capital utilization rate	78.20%	83.10%	87.30%	88.70%	88.80%	88.20%	87.50%
(% ch.)	3.1	6.2	5.1	1.6	0.1	−0.7	−0.7
Government revenue	185.9	203.8	225.9	248.1	263	274.8	285.6
(% ch.)	7.6	9.6	10.8	9.8	6	4.5	3.9
Net government debt outstanding	476.9	463.9	377.5	289	223.1	202.3	179.6
(% ch.)	−7.1	−2.7	−18.6	−23.4	−22.8	−9.3	−11.2
Debt ratio to GDPN	85.90%	78.30%	58.30%	41.60%	30.20%	26.00%	21.90%
Real capital stock	609.5	619.5	640.3	665.5	690.8	712.4	733.3
(% ch.)	0.3	1.6	3.4	3.9	3.8	3.1	2.9
Real residential stock	361.2	374.3	388.2	406	426.2	446.6	465.7
(% ch.)	0.4	3.6	3.7	4.6	5	4.8	4.3
Real government capital stock	2681	278.4	300.2	323.1	347	372	398.3
(% ch.)	−0.2	3.8	7.8	7.6	7.4	7.2	7.1
Population (million)	129.4	129.9	130.3	130.8	131.3	131.9	132.5
(% ch.)	0.2	0.4	0.3	0.3	0.4	0.4	0.5
Exchange rate (¥/$)	104.3	109.8	93.8	77.6	79.5	84.4	85.1
(% ch.)	8.7	5.3	−14.5	−17.3	2.5	6.1	0.9

natural increase in tax revenue. Therefore, net fiscal debt outstanding in the central government will probably decline from 513.5 trillion yen in FY2013 to 463.9 trillion yen in FY2015 and 179.6 trillion yen in FY2020 and its declines could present changes in terms of the ratio to nominal GDP from 97.6% in FY2013, to 78.3% in FY2015 and 21.9% in FY2020 in Scenario 2 (Growth plus Leisure Expansion scenario).

Table 6.7. Scenario 3: Growth plus consumption tax hikes.

	2014	2015	2016	2017	2018	2019	2020
Real GDP	542.9	572.7	606.5	619.2	622.4	623.2	631.7
(% ch.)	2.5	5.5	5.9	2.1	0.5	0.1	1.4
Nominal GDP	507.6	539.9	609.1	670.3	705.4	720.2	729.3
(% ch.)	1.7	6.4	12.8	10.1	5.2	2.1	1.3
Real private consumption	298.7	297.7	310.2	319.8	320.3	319	319.8
(% ch.)	1.7	−0.3	4.2	3.1	0.2	−0.4	0.2
Real private investment	68.2	73.6	83.5	89.7	90.6	85.8	83.8
(% ch.)	2.8	7.9	13.5	7.4	1.1	−5.3	−2.4
Housing investment	15.3	21.9	23.4	26.7	28.5	29.1	28.6
(% ch.)	−0.2	43.3	6.7	14.4	6.7	2	−1.5
Real government consumption	106.3	108.4	110	111.7	113.3	115	116.7
(% ch.)	2	2	1.5	1.5	1.5	1.5	1.5
Real government investment	24.2	34.6	46.6	48.9	51.3	53.9	56.6
(% ch.)	9.2	43.3	34.4	5	5	5	5
Real exports	96.4	109.7	118	118.8	117.3	118.7	123.8
(% ch.)	3.6	13.8	7.6	0.7	−1.3	1.2	4.3
Real imports	74.6	82.7	97.2	109	111.3	109.7	108.5
(% ch.)	2.7	10.9	17.6	12.1	2.1	−1.4	−1.1
GDP deflator	93.5	94.3	100.4	108.3	113.3	115.6	115.5
(% ch.)	−0.7	0.8	6.5	7.8	4.7	2	−0.1
Deflator of CP	96.8	97.9	100	103.3	106.8	108.8	109.1
(% ch.)	0.9	1.1	2.2	3.3	3.4	1.9	0.2
CPI (core)	115.2	114.8	115.1	117.8	121.7	125	126.5
(% ch.)	0.2	−0.4	0.2	2.4	3.3	2.7	1.2
Government bond yield	2.10%	1.40%	2.60%	3.80%	2.90%	2.90%	2.20%
(% ch.)	−31.2	−32.1	85	47.6	−23.5	−1.6	−23.6
Wage (1000 yen)	4699.4	4862.7	5109.5	5322.4	5492.6	5601.8	5654.2
(% ch.)	2.1	3.5	5.1	4.2	3.2	2	0.9
Employed (1000)	57813.1	58286.8	59766.7	60985.4	61518.4	61510.9	61531.6
(% ch.)	0.9	0.8	2.5	2	0.9	0	0
Capital utilization rate	76.80%	79.40%	82.50%	82.10%	79.70%	76.40%	74.20%
(% ch.)	1.3	3.4	3.8	−0.4	−2.9	−4.1	−2.9
Government revenue	195.5	217.6	237.9	258.8	267.6	267.9	265
(% ch.)	13.1	11.3	9.3	8.8	3.4	0.1	−1.1
Net government debt outstanding	470.8	452.7	382.7	319.5	284.8	309.4	328.7
(% ch.)	−8.3	−3.8	−15.5	−16.5	−10.9	8.6	6.3

(*Continued*)

Table 6.7. (*Continued*)

	2014	2015	2016	2017	2018	2019	2020
Debt ratio to GDPN	88.00%	82.00%	63.60%	50.20%	43.20%	46.00%	48.10%
Real capital stock	608.5	615.3	632.4	654.1	673.9	685.9	694.3
(% ch.)	0.2	1.1	2.8	3.4	3	1.8	1.2
Real residential stock	359.3	365.6	373.1	383.6	395.5	407.5	418.5
(% ch.)	−0.1	1.7	2	2.8	3.1	3	2.7
Real government capital stock	268.2	278.4	300.2	323.1	347	372	398.3
(% ch.)	−0.2	3.8	7.8	7.6	7.4	7.2	7.1
Population (million)	129.4	129.7	130.1	130.3	130.6	130.8	131.2
(% ch.)	0.2	0.3	0.3	0.2	0.2	0.2	0.3
Exchange rate (¥/$)	104.4	105.8	78.9	49.8	39.2	37.2	38.4
(% ch.)	8.8	1.4	−25.4	−36.8	−21.3	−5.2	3.2

6.2.4. *Conclusion*

Unlike Reaganomics in the US conducted in the early 1980s, Abenomics is a policy package which is based on a demand-side economics in order to escape from the long-term economic deflation started from the middle of the 1990s. The original policy package of Abenomics would be a monetary quantity-easing oriented policy package which was evaluated and appreciated by Hamada in 2013 as a grade A for monetary policy, grade B for fiscal stimulus and grade E for growth strategy as a name of ABE. However, the effects of the policies as a policy package are now very limited in reality.

Therefore, the Japanese government should introduce a more dynamic and stronger policy package to stimulate the demand side of the economy as discussed in this chapter. In addition, the government should utilize an appropriate tool like DEMIOS as a compass to predict future projections.

Furthermore, as predicted in the scenario projections, it is worth noting that the Japanese economy will be able to achieve high economic growth with appropriate policy packages. So, it is also very important for us to evaluate the government growth strategy with our critical eyes.

6.3. Analysis of Huge Earthquake Damages of East Japan: Huge Damage and Reconstruction — An Example of Leontief Cross

On March 11, 2011 a huge earthquake hit the north east of the Japanese islands. How much is the damage directly and indirectly hit the Japanese Islands and how fast the Japanese Islands can recover from this deep damages? We can use Leontief regional I–O table and meager direct and indirect damages hit by earthquake by means of Leontief Cross which is available by prefecture. Then we move to national and regional Leontief table developed by the Japanese Government which is available every five years.

The nation-wide damages estimated by regional I–O table in 2011 are then transferred into national damages which are at the next step transferred into DEMIOS which gives us sectoral output, employment and investment as well as fiscal and monetary variables for 2009–2020. This time, DEMIOS is attached to small regional sub-models for eight sub-regions, i.e., Hokkaido, Tohoku, Kanto, Chubu, Kinki, Chugoku, Shikoku and Kyushu in order to see the national and regional results of reconstruction program. These are the outline of DEMIOS and regional damage and economic reconstruction simulation. Now we can see the damage and reconstruction process more closely on regional and national basis by using Leontief cross.

First in Table 6.8, we can see the original damage caused by the earthquake and Tsunami for four prefectures, i.e., Aomori, Iwate, Miyagi, and Fukushima. Table 6.9 indicates the result of direct and indirect damage ratios using Leontief Cross from MITIs Regional I–O table in 2011 for four Tohoku prefectures.

Next, we proceed to nation–wide repercussion of damages of Tohoku based on a Leontief regional I–O table prepared by the Japanese government. In Table 6.8 we must be careful about figures which include both damages due to capacity and demand-side losses of consumption and investment, i.e., direct and indirect loss of capacity and decline in output from final demand. It is a typical Leontief Cross, i.e., multiplication of row vector from right side and, oppositely multiplication of column vector of final demand from right side. This is the typical exercise using "Leontief Cross". In this table, three points can be mentioned as follows.

(1) The highest loss is observed in Tohoku, which is 17.964, with Hokkaido being the second at 0.259 and Kanto being at 0.224. The least hit area is Okinawa, being at 0.034.

Table 6.8. Direct damage ratio: Four prefectures in Tohoku.

	Prefecture			
Sector	Aomori	Iwate	Miyagi	Fukushima
01		0.127	0.127	0.127
02				
03		0.413	0.413	0.413
04				
05	0.300			
06				
07		0.148	0.148	0.148
08				
09				
10				
11				
12				
13				
14		0.148	0.148	0.148
15		0.148	0.148	0.148
16				
17				
18				
19				
20				
21				
22				
23		0.305	0.305	0.305
24				
25				
26		0.148	0.148	0.148
27				

Note: 01 Agriculture, forestry and fishery, 02 Mining. 03 Foods and tobacco, 04 Textile, 05 Pulp and wood products, 06 Chemical products, 07 Oil and coal products, 08 Plastic products, 09 Rubber, 10 Ceramic products, 11 Iron and steel, 12 Non-metal products, 13 Metal products, 14 General machinery, 15 Electric machinery, 16 Automobile, 17 Other transportation equipment, 18 Precise machinery, 19 Other manufactures, 20 Construction, 21 Civil engineering, 22 Other construction, 23 Non-profitable industries, 24 Commerce, 25 Finance and insurance, 26 Transportation, 27 Others.

(2) By industry, except Tohoku, petroleum and coal, chemical products, and agriculture in Hokkaido, and agriculture, plastics, paper, printing and publishing in Kanto area, auto parts, and other manufacturing in Chubu and apparel and other textiles in Chubu, electronic parts in Shikoku.

Table 6.9. The effects of the East Japan disaster on Tohoku four prefectures — Aggregate damage ratio (= 1− damage ratio).

	Prefecture			
Sector	Aomori	Iwate	Miyagi	Fukushima
01	0.997	0.639	0.597	0.603
02	0.997	0.961	0.901	0.892
03	1.000	0.458	0.452	0.454
04	1.000	0.962	0.958	0.967
05	0.538	0.938	0.939	0.924
06	0.999	0.929	0.930	0.936
07	0.999	0.772	0.767	0.748
08	0.998	0.895	0.885	0.895
09	1.000	0.937	0.937	0.917
10	0.999	0.973	0.955	0.952
11	1.000	0.952	0.959	0.945
12	1.000	0.936	0.936	0.964
13	1.000	0.939	0.939	0.921
14	1.000	0.749	0.768	0.745
15	1.000	0.737	0.740	0.735
16	1.000	0.994	0.983	0.898
17	1.000	0.948	0.808	0.878
18	1.000	0.967	0.972	0.968
19	0.999	0.943	0.942	0.902
20	0.999	0.919	0.891	0.892
21	1.000	1.000	1.000	1.000
22	1.000	1.000	1.000	1.000
23	0.993	0.643	0.626	0.622
24	0.999	0.882	0.865	0.876
25	0.999	0.898	0.891	0.885
26	0.998	0.772	0.762	0.758
27	0.999	0.911	0.909	0.895
Total	0.990	0.809	0.774	0.727

Note: 01 Agriculture, forestry and fishery, 02 Mining, 03 Foods and tobacco, 04 Textile, 05 Pulp and wood products, 06 Chemical products, 07 Oil and coal products, 08 Plastic products, 09 Rubber, 10 Ceramic products, 11 Iron and steel, 12 Non-metal products, 13 Metal products, 14 General machinery, 15 Electric machinery, 16 Automobile, 17 Other transportation equipment, 18 Precise machinery, 19 Other manufactures, 20 Construction, 21 Civil engineering, 22 Other Construction, 23 Non-profitable industries, 24 Commerce, 25 Finance and insurance, 26 Transportation, 27 Others.

(3) The sum of these nationwide damages is 1.24% in term of gross production, not value added or GDP, as shown at the right side bottom of this table.

6.3.1. *Nation-wide reconstruction program up to 2020 and its impacts on regional economies*

What about reconstruction program from these nation-wide damages? Here we consider government impacts on reconstruction and regional effects by regional sub-model for the period in 2010–2020.

There are hot debates on policy packages: the first program is to use the reconstruction fund by saving existing fiscal expenses without issuing public bonds, considering the huge public debts of the Japanese government. The second policy package is to issue the huge government bond not only for Tohoku reconstruction, but also for preventing huge earthquake damages all over the Japanese Islands which amount to 50 billion yen contributing also to escaping from chronical deflation since 1990. Regional inequality issues in income and employment are also likely to disappear. Fiscal debt issue is also likely to be solved if the Bank of Japan cooperates by buying the government bond in security market, i.e., accommodated fiscal policy. Regarding regional sub-models for eight regions, regional GDP and population are regressed for each region on national GDP and population estimated by DEMIOS so as to see changes in regional GDP and population.

As shown in Table 6.10, we present the results of DEMIOS forecast for the period in 2011–2020 on the conservative reconstruction program in which reconstruction expenses are mostly financed by cutting existing fiscal investment programs so that only increase is shown for government consumption for medical care and social consumption.

In Table 6.11 we can see another alternative reconstruction program which is more active, especially more ambitious public investment program, amounting to 58 billion yen in real term in 2011–2020, three times as high as that in the conservative program. As regard to private sector, especially for housing and business investment, financial incentive and tax support are provided. Some of the increases in the table are accounted for by the big push in public investment. Employment is also dramatically improved in this scenario, especially

Table 6.10. The baseline forecast, FY2011–2020.

	2011	2012	2013	2014	2015	2016	2017	2018	2019	2020
Real GDP	527.4	535.7	549.2	567.4	586.1	603.0	613.9	618.5	622.2	631.6
(% ch.)	−0.3	1.6	2.5	3.3	3.3	2.9	1.8	0.7	0.6	1.5
Nominal GDP	473.7	471.8	477.7	489.5	509.3	547.5	580.5	604.3	460.3	616.9
(% ch.)	−0.6	−0.4	1.2	2.5	4.0	7.5	6.0	4.1	0.8	1.3
Real private consumption	283.1	282.1	281.3	286.9	294.9	305.7	313.0	314.5	312.8	314.8
(% ch.)	−1.9	−0.3	−0.3	2.0	2.8	3.7	2.4	0.5	−0.5	0.6
Real private investment	70.1	71.8	72.7	76.7	80.4	84.9	87.2	86.9	83.3	81.4
(% ch.)	−3.0	2.5	1.3	5.5	4.8	5.6	2.6	−0.3	−4.2	−2.2
Real housing investment	12.9	13.4	16.7	18.9	19.8	20.6	21.9	22.6	23.0	22.6
(% ch.)	−7.6	4.0	24.5	12.8	5.1	3.7	6.6	3.0	1.7	−1.8
Real government consumption*	102.8	104.9	107.0	109.1	111.3	113.0	114.7	116.4	118.1	119.9
(% ch.)	2.0	2.0	2.0	2.0	2.0	1.5	1.5	1.5	1.5	1.5
Real government investment*	20.9	20.9	20.9	20.9	20.9	20.9	20.9	20.9	20.9	20.9
(% ch.)	3.8	0.0	0.0	0.0	0.0	0.0	0.0	0.0	0.0	0.0
Real exports and services	82.7	92.1	102.0	109.6	117.5	122.7	126.5	129.1	135.0	142.4
(% ch.)	6.8	11.4	10.7	7.5	7.2	4.5	3.0	2.1	4.6	5.5
Real imports and services	52.2	56.6	58.7	62.1	66.2	72.5	77.6	79.1	77.9	77.4
(% ch.)	8.7	8.4	3.7	5.7	6.6	9.5	7.0	1.9	−1.5	−0.6
GDP deflator	89.8	88.1	87.0	86.3	86.9	90.8	94.6	97.7	97.9	97.7
(% ch.)	−0.3	−1.9	−1.2	−0.8	0.7	4.5	4.1	3.3	0.2	−0.2
Deflator of PC	91.4	90.1	90.3	90.8	91.9	93.6	95.8	98.0	99.1	99.2
(% ch.)	−0.6	−1.4	0.2	0.6	1.1	1.9	2.4	2.3	1.1	0.2
Government bond yield (10 years)	2.62	2.21	2.37	2.34	2.33	3.05	4.08	3.61	3.34	3.31
(% ch.)	—	—	—	—	—	—	—	—	—	—
Wage (1000 yen)	4463	4443	4456	4555	4673	4816	4947	5045	5095	5112
(% ch.)	−1.7	−0.5	0.3	2.2	2.6	3.1	2.7	2.0	1.0	0.3
Employment	55324	55903	56209	55687	57137	58010	58589	58863	58609	58576
(% ch.)	−0.1	1.0	0.5	0.9	0.8	1.5	1.0	0.5	−0.4	−0.1
Unemployment rate (%)	6.67	6.89	6.46	6.10	5.69	5.52	5.29	5.36	5.39	5.46
(% ch)	—	—	—	—	—	—	—	—	—	—
Capital utilization rate (%)	75.6	75.6	75.6	75.6	75.6	75.6	75.6	75.6	75.6	75.6

(*Continued*)

Table 6.10. (*Continued*)

	2011	2012	2013	2014	2015	2016	2017	2018	2019	2020
(% ch.)	—	—	—	—	—	—	—	—	—	—
Total tax revenues	153.7	151.5	157.6	163.7	172.4	181.8	191.3	195.5	194.0	191.6
(% ch.)	−1.0	−1.4	4.0	3.9	5.4	5.4	5.2	2.2	−0.8	−1.2
Net government debt outstanding	480.9	519.3	527.5	488.1	449.9	415.9	398.9	381.7	393.1	395.4
(% ch.)	10.8	8.0	1.6	−7.5	−7.8	−7.6	−4.1	−4.3	3.0	0.6
Net government debt to GDP(%)	101.5	108.1	110.4	99.7	88.3	76.0	68.7	63.2	64.5	64.1
(% ch.)	—	—	—	—	—	—	—	—	—	—
Private capital stock	607.2	604.2	602.5	604.9	610.5	619.8	629.8	638.0	641.4	642.4
(% ch.)	−0.9	−0.5	−0.3	0.4	0.9	1.5	1.6	1.3	0.5	0.2
Housing capital stock	362.3	359.7	360.5	363.4	367.1	371.4	377.0	382.8	388.8	394.2
(% ch.)	−0.9	−0.7	0.2	0.8	1.0	1.2	1.5	1.6	1.6	1.4
Government capital stock	274.8	269.9	263.8	261.0	257.0	253.1	249.6	246.3	243.2	240.3
(% ch.)	−1.9	−1.8	−1.7	−1.6	−1.5	−1.5	−1.4	−1.3	−1.3	−1.2
CO_2 emission	1520.6	1434.6	1382.9	1288.5	1244.9	1225.7	1373.7	1496.2	1636.0	1638.5
(% ch.)	5.8	−5.7	−3.6	−6.8	−3.4	−1.5	12.1	8.9	9.3	0.2
Population	128272	128537	128896	129164	129420	129683	129925	130121	130318	130591
(% ch.)	0.02	0.21	0.28	0.21	0.20	0.20	0.19	0.15	0.15	0.21

*: Exogenous variable

Table 6.11. Growth scenario forecast, FY2011–2020.

	2011	2012	2013	2014	2015	2016	2017	2018	2019	2020
Real GDP	559.1	582.8	609.1	637.7	665.8	692.4	713.2	729.9	746.8	767.7
(% ch.)	5.7	4.2	4.5	4.7	4.4	4.0	3.0	2.3	2.3	2.8
Nominal GDP	502.3	519.2	542.2	571.6	611.3	678.3	741.0	796.8	831.6	870.1
(% ch.)	5.4	3.4	4.4	5.4	6.9	11.0	9.2	7.5	4.4	4.6
Real private consumption	288.0	295.4	303.1	316.1	330.9	349.6	365.0	375.7	384.8	396.4
(% ch.)	−0.2	2.6	2.6	4.3	4.7	5.7	4.4	2.9	2.4	3.0
Real private investment	76.3	80.9	84.3	89.9	95.9	102.5	106.5	108.2	106.9	107.2
(% ch.)	5.6	6.1	4.3	6.6	6.7	6.9	3.9	1.6	−1.2	0.3
Real housing investment	17.9	20.0	23.9	26.4	27.3	27.9	29.1	29.7	30.2	30.0

(*Continued*)

Table 6.11. (*Continued*)

	2011	2012	2013	2014	2015	2016	2017	2018	2019	2020
(% ch.)	28.2	11.3	19.8	10.6	3.1	2.3	4.3	2.1	1.6	−0.5
Real government consumption*	104.3	106.4	108.5	110.6	112.8	114.4	116.1	117.9	119.6	121.4
(% ch.)	3.4	2.0	2.0	2.0	2.0	1.5	1.5	1.5	1.5	1.5
Real government investment*	35.9	39.5	41.4	43.5	45.7	48.0	50.4	52.9	55.5	58.3
(% ch.)	78.5	10.0	5.0	5.0	5.0	5.0	5.0	5.0	5.0	5.0
Real exports and services	87.6	99.6	111.4	120.4	129.3	135.5	140.4	144.5	151.0	158 .2
(% ch.)	13.1	13.8	11.8	8.0	7.4	4.8	3.6	2.9	4.5	4.8
Real imports and services	59.2	67.6	72.7	78.7	85.6	95.4	103.9	108.7	110.7	113.3
(% ch.)	23.2	14.2	7.5	8.2	8.8	11.4	9.0	4.5	1.9	2.4
GDP deflator	89.8	89.1	89.0	89.6	91.8	98.0	103.9	109.2	111.4	113.3
(% ch.)	−0.2	−0.8	−0.1	0.7	2.4	6.7	6.1	5.1	2.0	1.8
Deflator of PC	91.1	90.7	91.9	93.8	96.6	100.2	104.3	108.4	111.3	113.2
(% ch.)	−0.9	−0.5	1.4	2.1	3.0	3.7	4.2	3.9	2.6	1.8
Government bond yield (10 years)	3.04	2.69	2.71	2.61	2.59	3.05	3.77	3.31	2.85	2.85
(% ch.)	—	—	—	—	—	—	—	—	—	—
Wage (1000 yen)	4590	4689	4825	5056	5324	5629	5933	6212	6443	6625
(% ch.)	1.1	2.1	2.9	4.8	5.3	5.7	5.4	4.7	3.7	2.8
Employment (1000)	56182	57110	57720	58390	59035	60205	61111	61798	62068	62505
(% ch.)	1.5	1.7	1.1	1.2	1.1	2.0	1.5	1.1	0.4	0.7
Unemployment rate (%)	6.20	5.16	4.89	4.32	3.82	3.56	3.22	3.17	3.14	3.16
(% ch.)	—	—	—	—	—	—	—	—	—	—
Capital utilization rate (%)	75.1	79.0	81.7	84.6	86.4	87.6	87.3	86.0	84.3	83.1
(% ch.)	—	—	—	—	—	—	—	—	—	—
Total tax revenue	161.8	169.0	180.8	194.0	209.1	226.9	244.5	256.9	263.6	269.3
(% ch.)	4.3	4.4	7.0	7.3	7.8	8.5	7.8	5.1	2.6	2.2
Net government debt outstanding	486.3	472.5	421.6	355.3	296.4	253.9	229.5	202.0	202.5	200.6

(*Continued*)

Table 6.11. (*Continued*)

	2011	2012	2013	2014	2015	2016	2017	2018	2019	2020
(% ch.)	11.7	−2.8	−10.8	−15.7	−16.6	−14.3	−9.6	−12.0	0.3	−0.9
Net government debt to GDP (%)	96.8	91.0	77.8	62.2	48.5	37.4	31.0	25.3	24.4	23.1
(% ch.)	—	—	—	—	—	—	—	—	—	—
Private capital stock	613.4	618.8	627.0	639.7	656.6	677.6	699.7	72.4	736.9	751.4
(% ch.)	0.1	0.9	1.3	2.0	2.6	3.2	3.3	3.0	2.3	2.0
Housing capital stock	367.3	370.9	378.4	388.1	398.2	408.4	419.4	430.6	441.7	452.1
(% ch.)	0.5	1.0	2.0	2.6	2.6	2.6	2.7	2.7	2.6	2.4
Government capital stock	289.7	302.4	316.2	331.2	347.5	365.0	383.7	403.8	425.3	448.2
(% ch.)	3.5	4.4	4.6	4.7	4.9	5.0	5.1	5.2	5.3	5.4
CO_2 emission	1396.8	1266.4	1174.1	1068.2	1011.3	977.6	1074.2	1139.4	1164.7	1134.8
(% ch.)	−2.8	−9.3	−7.3	−9.0	−5.3	−3.3	9.9	6.1	2.2	−2.6
Total population	128646	129042	129536	129986	130437	130908	131354	131759	132156	132590
(% ch.)	0.31	0.31	0.38	0.35	0.35	0.36	0.34	0.31	0.30	0.33

*: Exogenous variable

first half of this scenario, during the period of huge damages in Tohoku areas.

Regarding monetary policy of the Bank of Japan, as compared to the conservative policy scenario projection, long-term interest rate keeps fairly stable, despite of growing demand for public and business investment. Regarding capital account side of government it is noticeable that net capital debts are gradually shrinking, reflecting rapidly growing tax revenues. This is a sharp contrast to the conservative scenario where government debts are to start rising. The two contrasting policy scenarios tell us good lesson that an expansionary policy scenario accommodated by the central bank is much better strategy for reducing public debt issues than the conservative long run strategy.

6.3.2. *Regional sub-model*

Finally, we analyze regional implications of the above two policy scenarios. We developed eight sub-models for each region as follows.

Table 6.12. Growth alternatives by the regional sub-model, FY2010–2020: Ratio in 2020/2010.

	Hokkaido	Tohoku	Kanto	Chubu	Kinki	Chugoku	Shikoku	Kyushu
Real GDP								
Growth scenario	1.66	1.74	1.71	1.66	1.72	1.37	1.70	1.43
Baseline	1.16	1.18	1.22	1.24	1.26	1.10	1.32	1.12
Total population								
Growth scenario	1.061	1.074	1.020	1.026	1.001	1.032	1.029	1.027
Baseline	1.002	1.008	1.004	1.014	0.994	1.004	1.004	1.003

Hokkaido, Tohoku, Kanto, Chubu, Kinki, Chugoku, Shikoku and Kyushu.

In each regional sub-model, real GDP and its component, implicit deflator of GDP components which are derived from Japanese macroeconomic block, population inflows and outflows and total population by region with the rest of Japan are endogenized.

As easily understood, the regression analysis is what we call reduced form equation models for each region. Since DEMIOS could endogenize only national economic and demographic variables, the above regional sub-models could give us various ideas of regional economic and demographic changes with regional I–O models. What are the results of above two policy scenarios on a regional basis? The results are summarized in Table 6.12.

Here we are impressed by the declining tendency of "Regional Differences" in active policy scenario in terms of GDP and population. "Regional Differences" decline mostly in Tohoku, followed by Hokkaido and Kanto as compared to the conservative policy scenario. Active reaction of these suffered and depressed areas is mostly due to relatively lower land prices, higher investment profit and active public investment policy. Higher growth response of Kanto area is mostly due to its investment advantage by the government policy decisions.

Appendix

Table A6.1. Sectoral output (X) in the baseline projection for national resilience plan, FY2014–2020.

	X01	X02	X03	X04	X05
2014	7765555	1108535	3339962	117893.6	744049.9
2015	7419921	1127296	3347117	127788.1	726683.2
2016	7977236	1148110	3260614	145661.4	767350.9
2017	8561882	1185510	3216209	140242.6	809335.5
2018	8655582	1167127	3106573	136069.3	814619.1
2019	8470885	1100647	3091901	133557.7	809915.7
2020	8137035	1037872	3062223	137536.9	798696.2
	X06	X07	X08	X09	X10
2014	944767.8	1340590	19577.63	12166.76	95562.21
2015	982160.1	1470994	18902.1	11183.52	96648.89
2016	1066352	1492563	18597.14	10451.25	97412.47
2017	1120017	1518518	19294.84	11762.36	98941.63
2018	1150424	1527229	20827.87	13637.67	101941.7
2019	1168856	1578516	21528.54	13166.65	104766.9
2020	1175384	1603762	22323.67	12331.13	108359.6
	X11	X12	X13	X14	X15
2014	59.56582	11062.5	1261667	5917885	3475789
2015	59.99484	10143.16	1334433	5874020	3742869
2016	62.17826	9212.798	1497926	5495606	3911446
2017	62.50928	10609.76	1640416	5229269	4220098
2018	61.95206	12540.86	1763395	5001755	4380429
2019	63.12517	11432.25	1805678	5059270	4376245
2020	67.93566	9787.962	1830583	5108498	4098577
	X16	X17	X18	X19	X20
2014	2429645	13444760	10952510	1447580	3132948
2015	2405612	13429910	10899870	1437510	3091150
2016	2822969	13863680	10901230	1362604	3039632
2017	3109515	14452420	11105760	1280911	3048718
2018	3323956	14823600	11228270	1204700	3068318
2019	3245228	15180130	11251710	1206597	3061562
2020	3043718	15116390	11120490	1217861	2998778
	X21	X22	X23	X24	X25
2014	822227.8	2069848	2976798	792433.7	2951438
2015	839723.7	2547957	3376152	771666.6	3602705
2016	829150.5	2832278	3862369	744979.9	3850366
2017	826839.5	3007643	4450312	753680.9	4065462

(*Continued*)

Table A6.1. (*Continued*)

2018	828914.6	2718881	4875187	780116.5	4189537
2019	851889.7	2395151	5069757	774465.9	4233399
2020	886857.8	2367276	4877986	713023	4221259
	X26	X27	X28	X29	X30
2014	2835429	10545420	14049310	1236201	10882230
2015	3199204	10864910	14416860	1293752	10795220
2016	3556535	11222570	15197660	1429357	10986190
2017	3857524	11452270	15695170	1534693	11310590
2018	4025441	11548640	15980090	1619639	11582930
2019	4067265	11716550	16068750	1649151	11601070
2020	4080208	11978280	16322700	1687050	11424330
	X31	X32	X33	X34	X35
2014	11955950	23195940	3769563	13158820	4176957
2015	12405180	23745500	4106014	14192440	4352601
2016	12460260	24497660	4391170	15408210	4629630
2017	12300310	25064350	4542544	16346960	4854413
2018	12217110	25361850	4575836	16920490	5103483
2019	12792740	25599580	4671035	17284000	5273779
2020	13621120	25934080	4860953	17875230	5347432
	X36	X37	X38	X39	X40
2014	5303535	5198841	14131360	1992033	5485447
2015	5625151	5494083	15072290	2103671	5692310
2016	5922498	5721236	15924030	2266317	6118233
2017	6115688	5786522	16288720	2387959	6371174
2018	6251620	5749161	16256090	2490448	6577698
2019	6426077	5804620	16325520	2605469	6830079
2020	6621824	5962058	16749360	2673847	7043682
	X41	X42	X43	X44	X45
2014	13432080	2511960	29972270	60247590	7554490
2015	14907270	2603209	31724000	67420830	7009406
2016	16812770	2776040	34676780	76298830	6810529
2017	18594910	2875256	36778110	82175670	6744581
2018	19963930	2904331	38170060	87244080	6458184
2019	20241710	2864708	38223340	90189720	6303042
2020	20399340	2881703	38900110	94051270	6328305
	X46	X47	X48	X49	X50
2014	4761706	52685410	934302.1	3444155	5513064
2015	4984592	61912120	942560.7	3924570	5679807
2016	4866041	69546950	1042559	4204116	5925130
2017	4761734	74244090	1122442	4069769	6031262

(*Continued*)

Table A6.1. (*Continued*)

2018	4419921	74958750	1237817	3702668	5984128
2019	4775778	78469150	1318119	3789126	5899824
2020	5383442	85354630	1314672	4266243	6042186
	X51	X52	X53	X54	X55
2014	1884971	4850530	16564390	21466630	16368770
2015	2095051	5207638	23730730	22444410	17083940
2016	2210171	5596873	25148920	24749120	21850570
2017	2227779	5825624	28358630	26778020	26651910
2018	2111308	5896949	30640110	28075080	30911080
2019	2172662	6087587	32093800	27993210	31764120
2020	2359188	6376365	31810860	28148710	32091570
	X56	X57	X58	X59	X60
2014	11182930	21622520	3357407	4015494	5809044
2015	11804300	22106570	3401489	4119804	6096938
2016	13771040	22979100	3493965	4243000	6441787
2017	15609220	23445990	3598708	4335383	6730717
2018	16843300	24024650	3648097	4347968	6856597
2019	16669690	24422150	3646333	4336583	6921595
2020	16607800	25072120	3627071	4379866	7103812
	X61	X62	X63	X64	X65
2014	1.11E+08	14576120	46607920	8118740	18340580
2015	1.14E+08	14827140	47178080	8166848	18665610
2016	1.19E+08	15984980	48033190	8391965	19302430
2017	1.25E+08	16504530	48597290	8396265	19877100
2018	1.29E+08	16295810	48227890	8450829	20225630
2019	1.31E+08	15030390	47690610	8534188	20429250
2020	1.33E+08	14685490	47515440	8672271	20717500
	X66	X67	X68	X69	X70
2014	5198833	7522691	11636890	22001930	51048980
2015	5377630	7774042	11816100	22921840	50690780
2016	5421608	8008815	12265180	23547220	54667220
2017	5109630	8171810	12627640	25574190	54542140
2018	5072781	8246809	12767450	25699730	54539740
2019	5685662	8329721	12902360	26104060	55945660
2020	6298824	8476526	13366640	26881820	57351050
	X71	X72	X73	X74	X75
2014	96864660	14374430	59499280	16966550	47660260
2015	98813720	14956010	62309030	18482140	48690860
2016	98752270	16291580	68205310	20192920	49493400
2017	97690040	17420570	72949750	21394930	51202550

(*Continued*)

Table A6.1. (*Continued*)

2018	96160620	18006300	75761170	22166780	52436840
2019	95357130	17918770	76614220	22792610	53226930
2020	95611680	18055630	78340190	23759400	54043360
	X76	X77	X78	X79	X80
2014	24956430	48856790	6604074	20455280	2533229
2015	25247250	49393740	4939412	23145920	2632478
2016	25404430	50260270	6466843	25629340	2779067
2017	25909110	51632210	6508945	26795150	2869739
2018	26266770	52355420	6860443	24196100	2930543
2019	26471220	52711180	7144229	20237700	2992075
2020	26696040	53488430	8372620	20636810	3079636
	X81	X82			
2014	4868695	1.12E+09			
2015	5070969	1.18E+09			
2016	5363033	1.25E+09			
2017	5521923	1.3E+09			
2018	5540248	1.33E+09			
2019	5577807	1.34E+09			
2020	5710552	1.37E+09			

Note: Sector classification:
01 General crops, 02 Industrial crops, 03 Livestock for foods, 04 Livestock for fiber, 05 Agriculture services, 06 Forestry, 07 Fishery, 08 Coal mining, 09 Crude petroleum, 10 Natural gas, 11 Iron mining, 12 Non-metal mining, 13 Other mining, 14 Meat and dairy products, 15 Manufactured sea foods, 16 Grain products, 17 Other foods, 18 Beverages, 19 Feedstuff, 20 Tobacco, 21 Natural and chemical textiles, 22 Other textiles, 23 Wearing apparel, 24 Leather and leather products, 25 Wood and wood products, 26 Furniture, 27 Pulp and paper, 28 Printing and publishing, 29 Coal product, 30 Petroleum product, 31 Basic and intermediate chemicals, 32 Fats, oils and final chemicals, 33 Rubber products, 34 Plastic products, 35 Cement, 36 Other ceramics, 37 Iron products, 38 Rolling, casting and forgings, 39 Aluminum (including secondary), 40 Other non-ferrous products, 41 Metal products, 42 Office machinery, 43 Other general machinery, 44 Industrial electrical machinery, 45 Consumer electrical machinery, 46 Precision machinery, 47 Automobile, 48 Railway vehicle, 49 Ship building, 50 Aircraft, 51 Other transport equipment, 52 Miscellaneous manufacturing, 53 Housing construction, 54 Industrial construction, 55 Public construction, 56 Other construction, 57 Electric power, 58 Gas, 59 Water and sanitary service, 60 Waste disposal, 61 Wholesale and retail trade, 62 Automobile mechanical repair, 63 Hotel and restaurant, 64 Railways, 65 Trucks and buses, 66 Water transportation, 67 Air transport, 68 Other transportation, 69 Communications, 70 Finance and insurance, 71 Real estate, 72 Information processing services, 73 Other corporation services, 74 Research and development, 75 Public services, 76 Education, 77 Medical insurance, 78 Other public services, 79 Other services for individuals, 80 Office supplies, 81 Unallocated, 82 total.

Table A6.2. Sectoral wage and salaried employees (LW) in the baseline projection, FY2014–2020.

	LW01	LW02	LW03	LW04	LW05
2014	112.295	50.22578	11.46364	0.427587	24.57138
2015	109.3522	51.81203	12.21688	0.438997	23.01582
2016	98.89326	52.01114	12.83078	0.455693	20.29935
2017	89.06055	52.45218	12.50304	0.466559	16.36852
2018	80.06935	52.52876	10.79596	0.474453	12.1879
2019	72.53572	51.90062	8.620567	0.476867	8.57915
2020	66.3896	51.31604	6.761334	0.479208	6.005247
	LW06	LW07	LW08	LW09	LW10
2014	44.22224	35.13394	1.071752	1.919548	9.946686
2015	44.47209	32.73081	0.922388	1.799309	9.983663
2016	45.5571	30.69801	0.815017	1.658073	9.634348
2017	48.45791	29.30555	0.810868	1.546684	8.967871
2018	50.38411	28.49883	0.898581	1.703377	8.18321
2019	50.60768	28.46879	0.919066	1.942814	7.421228
2020	49.92892	28.93545	0.961782	1.886245	6.894068
	LW11	LW12	LW13	LW14	LW15
2014	7.427376	0.145644	39.85748	163.0298	168.7633
2015	7.939295	0.128777	40.68865	165.3664	171.4422
2016	9.07987	0.110797	43.0291	167.0028	175.1577
2017	9.367975	0.113492	44.03039	167.5467	180.8751
2018	7.954051	0.127578	43.75476	165.0964	186.7698
2019	6.322895	0.121283	43.7387	161.6394	191.531
2020	6.05406	0.102489	46.78481	158.8861	192.7897
	LW16	LW17	LW18	LW19	LW20
2014	21.65843	1000.296	233.5446	19.10463	21.14661
2015	21.65696	996.1877	235.4815	20.00946	21.85638
2016	21.6282	1000.885	229.4881	19.85809	22.12385
2017	21.57315	1012.509	216.8899	18.55903	21.57701
2018	21.49355	1023.803	196.6569	16.43367	20.2032
2019	21.42503	1035.067	176.5635	14.7677	18.559
2020	21.39009	1042.401	163.8487	13.58769	16.90253
	LW21	LW22	LW23	LW24	LW25
2014	33.88885	36.28225	456.7391	56.23804	137.5467
2015	33.89929	28.66852	455.2872	55.8988	148.3606
2016	33.91449	21.82104	458.9622	55.32472	160.9355
2017	33.89129	16.28929	468.364	54.52161	174.405
2018	33.78466	13.55603	479.8322	53.55986	187.207
2019	33.66828	12.38144	495.6941	52.53147	198.7851
2020	33.62651	11.22555	506.5358	51.4893	208.5562

(*Continued*)

Table A6.2. (*Continued*)

	LW26	LW27	LW28	LW29	LW30
2014	201.3612	378.8842	530.5308	9.559439	41.12509
2015	209.8645	388.9725	526.1627	9.254699	42.43014
2016	219.1447	400.8145	520.8488	8.785427	42.89165
2017	226.7624	409.8471	514.306	8.217863	40.60849
2018	231.8418	415.2797	505.0136	7.654238	37.04998
2019	234.9167	418.1657	494.2611	7.137117	34.30417
2020	238.5975	420.4241	482.3646	6.80952	34.17721

	LW31	LW32	LW33	LW34	LW35
2014	124.6813	877.8367	55.23785	602.0514	199.928
2015	124.4262	898.4936	48.66806	616.3033	202.7454
2016	124.7282	919.5475	42.47983	634.404	206.7547
2017	124.356	936.6873	36.50632	650.6496	209.9579
2018	122.1641	953.6862	30.85741	662.0733	211.6439
2019	117.7711	976.8579	25.81582	670.8191	211.6001
2020	113.221	1007.031	21.8111	680.7854	211.0123

	LW36	LW37	LW38	LW39	LW40
2014	269.791	92.51743	232.6769	25.40811	204.1251
2015	276.8251	103.4623	241.9799	24.91842	210.1164
2016	281.8964	114.989	253.0304	24.44067	218.4173
2017	277.3917	120.8324	262.4817	24.44207	226.2434
2018	262.7934	120.5755	268.8967	23.92494	233.3796
2019	247.6844	120.5287	276.8055	23.03159	241.6282
2020	240.027	124.768	288.7501	22.96858	250.0717

	LW41	LW42	LW43	LW44	LW45
2014	1230.708	40.94727	1391.994	2663.462	296.1655
2015	1301.206	39.48438	1433.935	2738.434	283.086
2016	1372.276	40.79353	1433.86	2854.496	277.6012
2017	1404.808	45.14376	1345.33	2986.607	273.2078
2018	1387.093	51.73128	1205.614	3124.996	267.7005
2019	1370.87	58.8097	1132.077	3268.519	263.3696
2020	1381.839	65.52429	1135.077	3426.372	259.0179

	LW46	LW47	LW48	LW49	LW50
2014	286.2027	780.7824	27.33722	135.7591	93.31762
2015	296.6859	791.036	27.2175	154.7851	98.64066
2016	300.4909	836.0889	27.19598	177.3484	104.0846
2017	291.0993	830.3412	27.13709	195.8391	109.4346
2018	274.0117	821.1223	27.05112	204.2378	114.4966
2019	265.2234	808.5611	26.88639	212.4012	119.2312
2020	274.0639	816.6628	26.67381	229.098	123.9988

(*Continued*)

Table A6.2. (*Continued*)

	LW51	LW52	LW53	LW54	LW55
2014	47.41737	262.2799	956.813	1283.354	1315.819
2015	47.87725	262.1372	1014.414	1263.352	1329.294
2016	48.26597	261.4802	1078.252	1239.176	1369.838
2017	48.48385	260.4078	1161.839	1207.925	1414.06
2018	48.45784	258.9721	1254.676	1171.182	1469.729
2019	48.46384	257.3909	1354.638	1131.12	1497.533
2020	48.6274	255.3834	1444.131	1089.884	1512.227
	LW56	LW57	LW58	LW59	LW60
2014	719.7942	320.7992	58.93525	69.00228	298.0878
2015	728.0775	344.8248	59.64235	65.66011	301.2964
2016	753.6235	372.6266	60.27412	61.85571	303.9183
2017	789.818	397.6721	60.96139	57.65192	305.2402
2018	829.5583	419.5612	61.66513	53.23813	304.3627
2019	861.3025	439.341	62.43386	48.75609	302.1431
2020	888.751	458.8149	63.07156	44.23029	300.366
	LW61	LW62	LW63	LW64	LW65
2014	11240.21	269.6282	5193.277	385.7985	2638.238
2015	11327.45	281.5249	5368.578	400.025	2665.154
2016	11456.01	301.2095	5514.439	417.2838	2692.029
2017	11569.6	306.4702	5617.745	439.435	2717.674
2018	11600.08	385.7827	5672.511	464.4622	2739.677
2019	11519.44	443.5127	5704.527	493.1478	2758.766
2020	11397.2	407.3073	5690.292	526.898	2776.978
	LW66	LW67	LW68	LW69	LW70
2014	119.2798	70.7906	866.92	558.4544	2332.53
2015	115.3775	72.10969	909.7761	562.5295	2361.519
2016	119.2264	73.38027	974.6043	564.758	2381.037
2017	124.0578	74.61569	1084.72	565.2108	2352.574
2018	109.8525	75.78544	1189.061	562.5574	2290.644
2019	81.41931	76.8405	1142.513	557.9114	2234.445
2020	62.05412	77.76262	995.7087	552.8138	2139.669
	LW71	LW72	LW73	LW74	LW75
2014	1444.191	952.5082	3163.176	950.8883	2688.656
2015	1507.344	982.8513	3187.583	934.217	2679.772
2016	1522.133	1052.88	3215.91	896.6218	2641.88
2017	1499.682	1110.996	3271.408	858.4766	2586.51
2018	1453.755	1142.327	3343.814	834.0489	2512.911
2019	1418.921	1139.32	3410.694	811.4778	2434.806
2020	1397.825	1148.032	3403.386	760.1299	2365.315

(*Continued*)

Table A6.2. (*Continued*)

	LW76	LW77	LW78	LW79	LW80
2014	3487.332	10378	1930.125	2732.717	0
2015	3388.245	11397	1931.048	2691.021	0
2016	3214.987	12547.55	1797.538	2686.108	0
2017	2978.943	13852.5	1743.738	2703.185	0
2018	2675.111	15336.26	1731.335	2693.119	0
2019	2392.706	17024.26	1659.824	2622.405	0
2020	2192.752	18952.13	1512.449	2554.546	0

	LW81	LW82
2014	0	70214.38
2015	0	71959.21
2016	0	73748.41
2017	0	75441.79
2018	0	76951.45
2019	0	78262.71
2020	0	79612.19

Note: Sector classification, see Table A6.1.

Table A6.3. Sectoral output (X) in the national resilience plan, FY2014–2020.

	X01	X02	X03	X04	X05
2014	7765555	1108535	3339962	117893.6	744049.8
2015	7419921	1127296	3347117	127788.1	726683.2
2016	7910449	1139540	3241762	140415.8	760813
2017	8394477	1176139	3159149	130846.9	792246.3
2018	8401620	1166333	3003722	121183.8	786343
2019	8200823	1113920	2953047	117458.6	774928.3
2020	7888758	1063481	2915962	122042.4	761212.6

	X06	X07	X08	X09	X10
2014	944767.8	1340590	19577.63	12166.76	95562.21
2015	982160.1	1470994	18902.1	11183.52	96648.88
2016	1066352	1479503	18596.39	10446.18	97458.91
2017	1106361	1478214	19185.32	11640	98838.65
2018	1115980	1452696	20424.21	13392.52	101327.5
2019	1110730	1476881	20815.2	12904.09	103563.5
2020	1103386	1498983	21297.81	12086.38	106613.8

	X11	X12	X13	X14	X15
2014	59.56582	11062.51	1261667	5917885	3475789
2015	59.99484	10143.16	1334433	5874020	3742869
2016	62.14208	9212.798	1366412	5481913	3875700

(*Continued*)

Table A6.3. (*Continued*)

2017	62.39187	10474.55	1404068	5174508	4076933
2018	61.7236	12248.18	1453220	4892005	4113106
2019	62.2438	11120.95	1490933	4893766	4019290
2020	65.81358	9470.061	1512098	4928831	3741315
	X16	X17	X18	X19	X20
2014	2429645	13444760	10952510	1447580	3132948
2015	2405612	13429910	10899870	1437510	3091149
2016	2821116	13838840	10871460	1356771	3039726
2017	3065841	14316960	11012540	1270291	3042354
2018	3194039	14520110	11064440	1185930	3048759
2019	3061425	14710980	11016070	1182368	3032124
2020	2829636	14552850	10820960	1193381	2958104
	X21	X22	X23	X24	X25
2014	822227.8	2069848	2976798	792433.7	2951438
2015	839723.7	2547957	3376152	771666.6	3602705
2016	829150.5	2794837	3797688	746839.8	3793659
2017	829417.7	2914528	4251903	762519.1	3931326
2018	832161.8	2560558	4546316	800756.5	3992954
2019	853687	2206634	4655638	809011	4008052
2020	883215.5	2182297	4476562	761774.5	3990446
	X26	X27	X28	X29	X30
2014	2835429	10545420	14049310	1236201	10882230
2015	3199204	10864910	14416860	1293752	10795220
2016	3480556	11144720	15024490	1343931	10986420
2017	3675002	11282970	15348530	1374222	11319890
2018	3748458	11267710	15429270	1402059	11601510
2019	3739307	11362630	15406610	1424937	11637190
2020	3726019	11572980	15579720	1459694	11486510
	X31	X32	X33	X34	X35
2014	11955950	23195940	3769563	13158820	4176957
2015	12405180	23745500	4106014	14192440	4352601
2016	12464120	24447060	4338468	15214310	4405993
2017	12296050	24972720	4440766	15954250	4419012
2018	12169900	25239610	4418352	16318510	4497437
2019	12703320	25468980	4483544	16565490	4629380
2020	13513420	25788370	4652395	17074080	4677576
	X36	X37	X38	X39	X40
2014	5303535	5198840	14131350	1992033	5485447
2015	5625151	5494082	15072290	2103671	5692310
2016	5854137	5668043	15718110	2252204	6095567

(*Continued*)

Table A6.3. (*Continued*)

2017	5968172	5680117	15896880	2343640	6278072
2018	6024143	5578339	15658040	2408071	6406083
2019	6157335	5608011	15650870	2501370	6626682
2020	6332355	5751688	16021800	2560292	6843055
	X41	X42	X43	X44	X45
2014	13432080	2511960	29972270	60247590	7554489
2015	14907270	2603209	31724000	67420830	7009406
2016	16198640	2729195	34013640	75257690	6792051
2017	17525600	2783055	35599930	80250380	6701137
2018	18354130	2770433	36496550	84580900	6386987
2019	18503470	2712571	36482750	87433970	6191603
2020	18501460	2720041	37053210	91232510	6195926
	X46	X47	X48	X49	X50
2014	4761706	52685410	934302.1	3444155	5513064
2015	4984592	61912120	942560.7	3924570	5679807
2016	4814779	69057920	1021259	4172968	5912760
2017	4657428	73119470	1083742	3996542	6009185
2018	4237859	72728280	1177577	3518668	5947655
2019	4498001	75320500	1253437	3511080	5851190
2020	5029464	81555430	1248409	3937813	5979791
	X51	X52	X53	X54	X55
2014	1884971	4850530	16564390	21466630	16368770
2015	2095051	5207638	23730730	22444410	17083940
2016	2192208	5518544	24944810	23740200	17843020
2017	2181611	5665109	27558500	24836620	19208690
2018	2003899	5625992	29323220	25413490	21176270
2019	2011844	5719022	30303680	25179130	22027940
2020	2176226	5940803	29811390	25218190	22353950
	X56	X57	X58	X59	X60
2014	11182930	21622520	3357407	4015494	5809044
2015	11804300	22106570	3401488	4119804	6096938
2016	12921760	22770220	3474215	4214350	6379443
2017	13995810	23022640	3555308	4273688	6600561
2018	14651820	23357850	3579337	4247502	6646213
2019	14400450	23625790	3562923	4207414	6649841
2020	14255620	24192770	3533310	4226595	6775201
	X61	X62	X63	X64	X65
2014	1.11E+08	14576120	46607920	8118740	18340580
2015	1.14E+08	14827140	47178080	8166848	18665610

(*Continued*)

Table A6.3. (*Continued*)

2016	1.18E+08	15683060	47787980	8330511	19093450
2017	1.22E+08	15923830	48020130	8272184	19441050
2018	1.24E+08	15460980	47313360	8226444	19552840
2019	1.25E+08	14096340	46550780	8251003	19632980
2020	1.26E+08	13534710	46228610	8334864	19829680
	X66	X67	X68	X69	X70
2014	5198833	7522691	11636890	22001930	51048980
2015	5377630	7774042	11816100	22921840	50690780
2016	5388561	8002161	12153810	23225990	54037550
2017	5034856	8157198	12388860	24941370	53232490
2018	4873289	8216980	12371640	24711330	52332680
2019	5455675	8284603	12376140	24889790	53144300
2020	6105324	8418357	12735190	25500250	54114540
	X71	X72	X73	X74	X75
2014	96864660	14374430	59499280	16966550	47660260
2015	98813720	14956010	62309030	18482130	48690860
2016	98350800	15960830	66618030	19975790	49475780
2017	96695190	16776070	69847170	20976110	51167280
2018	94340720	17053480	71196520	21534030	52382010
2019	92873290	16827570	71413180	22074320	53163040
2020	92646660	16843210	72573690	22983620	53973840
	X76	X77	X78	X79	X80
2014	24956430	48856790	6604073	20455280	2533229
2015	25247250	49393740	4939411	23145920	2632478
2016	25400030	50212650	6365330	25391980	2747943
2017	25897230	51541600	6245370	26202480	2805010
2018	26233990	52218180	6344925	22924740	2824326
2019	26411460	52535620	6451020	17844610	2859132
2020	26605110	53268570	7552478	17079740	2923972
	X81	X82			
2014	4868695	1.12E+09			
2015	5070969	1.18E+09			
2016	5260236	1.23E+09			
2017	5315959	1.27E+09			
2018	5222173	1.28E+09			
2019	5206956	1.28E+09			
2020	5306665	1.3E+09			

Note: Sector classification, see Table A6.1.

Table A6.4. Sectoral wage and salaried employees (LW) in the national resilience plan, FY2014–2020.

	LW01	LW02	LW03	LW04	LW05
2014	112.295	50.22578	11.46364	0.427587	24.57138
2015	109.3522	51.81203	12.21688	0.438997	23.01582
2016	98.89326	52.01114	12.83078	0.455693	20.29935
2017	89.06055	52.45218	12.50304	0.466559	16.36852
2018	80.06935	52.52876	10.79596	0.474453	12.1879
2019	72.53572	51.90062	8.620567	0.476867	8.57915
2020	66.3896	51.31604	6.761334	0.479208	6.005247
	LW06	LW07	LW08	LW09	LW10
2014	44.22224	35.13394	1.071752	1.919548	9.946686
2015	44.47209	32.73081	0.922388	1.799309	9.983663
2016	45.5571	30.69801	0.815017	1.658073	9.634348
2017	48.45791	29.30555	0.810868	1.546684	8.967871
2018	50.38411	28.49883	0.898581	1.703377	8.18321
2019	50.60768	28.46879	0.919066	1.942814	7.421228
2020	49.92892	28.93545	0.961782	1.886245	6.894068
	LW11	LW12	LW13	LW14	LW15
2014	7.427376	0.145644	39.85748	163.0298	168.7633
2015	7.939295	0.128777	40.68865	165.3664	171.4422
2016	9.07987	0.110797	43.0291	167.0028	175.1577
2017	9.367975	0.113492	44.03039	167.5467	180.8751
2018	7.954051	0.127578	43.75476	165.0964	186.7698
2019	6.322895	0.121283	43.7387	161.6394	191.531
2020	6.05406	0.102489	46.78481	158.8861	192.7897
	LW16	LW17	LW18	LW19	LW20
2014	21.65843	1000.296	233.5446	19.10463	21.14661
2015	21.65696	996.1877	235.4815	20.00946	21.85638
2016	21.6282	1000.885	229.4881	19.85809	22.12385
2017	21.57315	1012.509	216.8899	18.55903	21.57701
2018	21.49355	1023.803	196.6569	16.43367	20.2032
2019	21.42503	1035.067	176.5635	14.7677	18.559
2020	21.39009	1042.401	163.8487	13.58769	16.90253
	LW21	LW22	LW23	LW24	LW25
2014	33.88885	36.28225	456.7391	56.23804	137.5467
2015	33.89929	28.66852	455.2872	55.8988	148.3606
2016	33.91449	21.82104	458.9622	55.32472	160.9355
2017	33.89129	16.28929	468.364	54.52161	174.405
2018	33.78466	13.55603	479.8322	53.55986	187.207
2019	33.66828	12.38144	495.6941	52.53147	198.7851
2020	33.62651	11.22555	506.5358	51.4893	208.5562

(*Continued*)

Table A6.4. (*Continued*)

	LW26	LW27	LW28	LW29	LW30
2014	201.3612	378.8842	530.5308	9.559439	41.12509
2015	209.8645	388.9725	526.1627	9.254699	42.43014
2016	219.1447	400.8145	520.8488	8.785427	42.89165
2017	226.7624	409.8471	514.306	8.217863	40.60849
2018	231.8418	415.2797	505.0136	7.654238	37.04998
2019	234.9167	418.1657	494.2611	7.137117	34.30417
2020	238.5975	420.4241	482.3646	6.80952	34.17721
	LW31	LW32	LW33	LW34	LW35
2014	124.6813	877.8367	55.23785	602.0514	199.928
2015	124.4262	898.4936	48.66806	616.3033	202.7454
2016	124.7282	919.5475	42.47983	634.404	206.7547
2017	124.356	936.6873	36.50632	650.6496	209.9579
2018	122.1641	953.6862	30.85741	662.0733	211.6439
2019	117.7711	976.8579	25.81582	670.8191	211.6001
2020	113.221	1007.031	21.8111	680.7854	211.0123
	LW36	LW37	LW38	LW39	LW40
2014	269.791	92.51743	232.6769	25.40811	204.1251
2015	276.8251	103.4623	241.9799	24.91842	210.1164
2016	281.8964	114.989	253.0304	24.44067	218.4173
2017	277.3917	120.8324	262.4817	24.44207	226.2434
2018	262.7934	120.5755	268.8967	23.92494	233.3796
2019	247.6844	120.5287	276.8055	23.03159	241.6282
2020	240.027	124.768	288.7501	22.96858	250.0717
	LW41	LW42	LW43	LW44	LW45
2014	1230.708	40.94727	1391.994	2663.462	296.1655
2015	1301.206	39.48438	1433.935	2738.434	283.086
2016	1372.276	40.79353	1433.86	2854.496	277.6012
2017	1404.808	45.14376	1345.33	2986.607	273.2078
2018	1387.093	51.73128	1205.614	3124.996	267.7005
2019	1370.87	58.8097	1132.077	3268.519	263.3696
2020	1381.839	65.52429	1135.077	3426.372	259.0179
	LW46	LW47	LW48	LW49	LW50
2014	286.2027	780.7824	27.33722	135.7591	93.31762
2015	296.6859	791.036	27.2175	154.7851	98.64066
2016	300.4909	836.0889	27.19598	177.3484	104.0846
2017	291.0993	830.3412	27.13709	195.8391	109.4346
2018	274.0117	821.1223	27.05112	204.2378	114.4966
2019	265.2234	808.5611	26.88639	212.4012	119.2312
2020	274.0639	816.6628	26.67381	229.098	123.9988

(*Continued*)

Table A6.4. (*Continued*)

	LW51	LW52	LW53	LW54	LW55
2014	47.41737	262.2799	956.813	1283.354	1315.819
2015	47.87725	262.1372	1014.414	1263.352	1329.294
2016	48.26597	261.4802	1078.252	1239.176	1369.838
2017	48.48385	260.4078	1161.839	1207.925	1414.06
2018	48.45784	258.9721	1254.676	1171.182	1469.729
2019	48.46384	257.3909	1354.638	1131.12	1497.533
2020	48.6274	255.3834	1444.131	1089.884	1512.227
	LW56	LW57	LW58	LW59	LW60
2014	719.7942	320.7992	58.93525	69.00228	298.0878
2015	728.0775	344.8248	59.64235	65.66011	301.2964
2016	753.6235	372.6266	60.27412	61.85571	303.9183
2017	789.818	397.6721	60.96139	57.65192	305.2402
2018	829.5583	419.5612	61.66513	53.23813	304.3627
2019	861.3025	439.341	62.43386	48.75609	302.1431
2020	888.751	458.8149	63.07156	44.23029	300.366
	LW61	LW62	LW63	LW64	LW65
2014	11240.21	269.6282	5193.277	385.7985	2638.238
2015	11327.45	281.5249	5368.578	400.025	2665.154
2016	11456.01	301.2095	5514.439	417.2838	2692.029
2017	11569.6	306.4702	5617.745	439.435	2717.674
2018	11600.08	385.7827	5672.511	464.4622	2739.677
2019	11519.44	443.5127	5704.527	493.1478	2758.766
2020	11397.2	407.3073	5690.292	526.898	2776.978
	LW66	LW67	LW68	LW69	LW70
2014	119.2798	70.7906	866.92	558.4544	2332.53
2015	115.3775	72.10969	909.7761	562.5295	2361.519
2016	119.2264	73.38027	974.6043	564.758	2381.037
2017	124.0578	74.61569	1084.72	565.2108	2352.574
2018	109.8525	75.78544	1189.061	562.5574	2290.644
2019	81.41931	76.8405	1142.513	557.9114	2234.445
2020	62.05412	77.76262	995.7087	552.8138	2139.669
	LW71	LW72	LW73	LW74	LW75
2014	1444.191	952.5082	3163.176	950.8883	2688.656
2015	1507.344	982.8513	3187.583	934.217	2679.772
2016	1522.133	1052.88	3215.91	896.6218	2641.88
2017	1499.682	1110.996	3271.408	858.4766	2586.51
2018	1453.755	1142.327	3343.814	834.0489	2512.911
2019	1418.921	1139.32	3410.694	811.4778	2434.806
2020	1397.825	1148.032	3403.386	760.1299	2365.315

(*Continued*)

Table A6.4. (*Continued*)

	LW76	LW77	LW78	LW79	LW80
2014	3487.332	10378	1930.125	2732.717	0
2015	3388.245	11397	1931.048	2691.021	0
2016	3214.987	12547.55	1797.538	2686.108	0
2017	2978.943	13852.5	1743.738	2703.185	0
2018	2675.111	15336.26	1731.335	2693.119	0
2019	2392.706	17024.26	1659.824	2622.405	0
2020	2192.752	18952.13	1512.449	2554.546	0

	LW81	LW82
2012	0	67397.04
2013	0	68780.45
2014	0	70214.38
2015	0	71959.21
2016	0	73748.41
2017	0	75441.79
2018	0	76951.45
2019	0	78262.71
2020	0	79612.19

Table A6.5. Sectoral output (X) in Abenomics scenario 1, FY2014–2020.

	X01	X02	X03	X04	X05
2014	7788251	1111003	3321109	117462.4	745790.2
2015	7684219	1119092	3395892	136565.9	752182.3
2016	8298445	1126062	3380875	155822.6	803772.1
2017	8788784	1118525	3380971	149183	845612.2
2018	8766325	1062303	3371224	145375.4	853610.6
2019	8534487	1011282	3312090	140879.3	850671.7
2020	8284720	960559.2	3199443	139477.1	840909.6

	X06	X07	X08	X09	X10
2014	945465	1333950	20202.12	13167.06	97028.23
2015	976797.8	1483119	19976.8	12826.01	97483.04
2016	1094813	1563469	20212.79	12874.85	98199.46
2017	1172587	1627887	21558.76	14284.35	100711.2
2018	1225851	1709815	23493.03	15645.04	103895.4
2019	1261636	1744306	24339.08	14820.79	106417.6
2020	1274341	1676813	25754.95	14800.76	109775.7

	X11	X12	X13	X14	X15
2014	60.97448	12170.41	1256657	5878191	3461464
2015	61.29839	12186.02	1529830	5930660	3813285
2016	63.11754	12169.8	1751997	5653840	4192240

(*Continued*)

Table A6.5. (*Continued*)

2017	61.8118	13810.63	1801572	5470583	4668116
2018	61.99848	15525.7	1887858	5476298	4941951
2019	67.17455	13988.96	1939241	5433368	4801395
2020	71.48536	13304.43	1981256	5270194	4505688
	X16	X17	X18	X19	X20
2014	2413359	13419450	10924340	1438430	3124733
2015	2386311	13462700	11046220	1456281	3157587
2016	2874703	14141330	11190330	1385837	3140443
2017	3267741	14848720	11431520	1318241	3164177
2018	3496792	15295540	11619830	1299372	3231858
2019	3395476	15631990	11703150	1274237	3198887
2020	3278014	15692940	11648500	1228845	3138777
	X21	X22	X23	X24	X25
2014	828668.8	2033732	2958932	796075.2	2938235
2015	846817.1	2555193	3439293	758418.3	3864035
2016	834037.3	2895123	4082874	708178.7	4186704
2017	834581.9	3117899	4744556	687150.7	4482224
2018	847008.7	2824107	5060307	676987.4	4676510
2019	887010.7	2466198	5119701	625838.4	4744724
2020	926870.1	2535544	4979639	547206.6	4682131
	X26	X27	X28	X29	X30
2014	2824683	10522660	14024110	1235603	10927300
2015	3382216	11033820	14734180	1416767	10775800
2016	3848463	11468180	15643200	1600189	10963740
2017	4172768	11740920	16108720	1645422	11225290
2018	4372100	12020660	16511190	1699745	11292690
2019	4460557	12257510	16786460	1748513	11267590
2020	4530313	12492800	17150550	1799894	11213270
	X31	X32	X33	X34	X35
2014	11887410	23199460	3754495	13137840	4127951
2015	12392890	23884800	4188226	14490290	4666890
2016	12425610	24598750	4504972	15831700	5098470
2017	12411160	25017430	4668681	16746800	5247927
2018	12792270	25275860	4838528	17474100	5509088
2019	13268840	25671500	4996811	18133130	5666905
2020	13715010	26143040	5168215	18848150	5753762
	X36	X37	X38	X39	X40
2014	5287241	5182027	14099720	1981714	5468603
2015	5765323	5593601	15440210	2137064	5743124
2016	6123630	5844497	16374380	2326346	6253761
2017	6343343	5944841	16782820	2481398	6552439

(*Continued*)

Table A6.5. (*Continued*)

2018	6572992	6049662	17109960	2649953	6828742
2019	6763433	6148902	17400610	2745247	7033584
2020	6916898	6251350	17767920	2779222	7182458
	X41	X42	X43	X44	X45
2014	13371160	2504682	29959050	60231400	7576132
2015	15980080	2652321	32581190	68809780	7086891
2016	17936000	2822910	35499960	77842080	6918965
2017	19695710	2882601	36935450	82607710	6833981
2018	20963250	2911825	38102850	87175660	6574398
2019	21593610	2894953	38617310	90574170	6623182
2020	22160930	2929360	39775410	94966570	6590926
	X46	X47	X48	X49	X50
2014	4724012	52602090	927293.1	3414252	5516797
2015	5090327	63114160	986214.2	3950037	5685927
2016	5051766	71209400	1076801	4266282	5953624
2017	4995156	76982120	1180554	4278078	6048241
2018	5206321	82163850	1285111	4468059	6023589
2019	5551886	87985100	1309129	4732484	6081496
2020	5840500	94257660	1337102	5031332	6236760
	X51	X52	X53	X54	X55
2014	1875146	4827920	16458140	21448580	16485190
2015	2108932	5339381	26963950	23867000	22659390
2016	2248468	5792791	28889460	26731160	29705530
2017	2323655	6098615	34132400	27942380	31090890
2018	2435487	6408872	37695630	28760370	32537970
2019	2571272	6690493	39228300	29138910	34048410
2020	2669397	6895510	39098830	29865490	35640630
	X56	X57	X58	X59	X60
2014	11186540	21622010	3365048	4015989	5811837
2015	12872610	22531620	3471626	4190250	6220476
2016	15165660	23588870	3593421	4351671	6632369
2017	16171290	24043580	3697376	4445641	6887989
2018	16791060	24844490	3744573	4498326	7080413
2019	16956260	25465760	3756151	4548151	7292790
2020	17462860	25976920	3772918	4615288	7526756
	X61	X62	X63	X64	X65
2014	1.11E+08	14599260	46560010	8102387	18347890
2015	1.17E+08	15386960	47764950	8309029	19157460
2016	1.24E+08	16665740	48950540	8564794	19985840
2017	1.29E+08	17105060	49531200	8684035	20543470
2018	1.34E+08	17017540	49356840	8839511	21039710

(*Continued*)

Table A6.5. (*Continued*)

2019	1.37E+08	16728660	49117840	8942512	21372250
2020	1.41E+08	17525200	49129610	9084596	21697690
	X66	X67	X68	X69	X70
2014	5177034	7534114	11654450	22004330	50297100
2015	5438656	7814183	12076970	23416720	51720300
2016	5526987	8065876	12674560	24390510	56385720
2017	5363729	8234708	13083020	26279890	56776370
2018	5881422	8352520	13463790	26739120	57918250
2019	6219152	8494049	13934130	28067990	59589990
2020	6409069	8630240	14333280	29351480	61632120
	X71	X72	X73	X74	X75
2014	96846760	14371360	59389430	16952620	47658250
2015	1.01E+08	15460440	65069500	18833940	48722550
2016	1.04E+08	16931640	71882270	20618250	49538900
2017	1.05E+08	17794290	75893090	21682210	50329530
2018	1.04E+08	18324400	78838780	22640750	51125000
2019	1.04E+08	18635320	81130010	23492790	51926700
2020	1.04E+08	19156280	84298290	24497800	52742090
	X76	X77	X78	X79	X80
2014	24955830	48906670	6668022	20592600	2523407
2015	25256320	49645780	5568355	23881930	2684924
2016	25426200	50572200	7222407	27123720	2857453
2017	25595880	51137520	7384654	28953660	2958391
2018	25826260	51539110	8214916	28329370	3067727
2019	26086870	52199870	8530345	28677520	3159070
2020	26353970	52918180	9656560	30837170	3256681
	X81	X82			
2014	4856991	1.12E+09			
2015	5255253	1.21E+09			
2016	5627498	1.3E+09			
2017	5786192	1.35E+09			
2018	5924706	1.39E+09			
2019	6031176	1.42E+09			
2020	6158490	1.46E+09			

Note: Sector classification, see Table A6.1.

Table A6.6. Sectoral wage and salaried employees (LW) in Abenomics scenario 1, FY2014–2020.

	LW01	LW02	LW03	LW04	LW05
2014	112.2329	50.2244	11.39293	0.427091	24.43562
2015	109.5571	51.81417	12.26124	0.444116	22.84957
2016	98.54456	52.04649	13.33526	0.465824	19.76582
2017	87.92853	52.49613	13.6641	0.47962	15.43635
2018	78.49216	52.55418	13.12035	0.488928	11.19304
2019	71.10479	52.0319	11.919	0.492513	7.666597
2020	65.21763	51.47552	10.12762	0.492274	5.114778
	LW06	LW07	LW08	LW09	LW10
2014	44.22323	35.44274	1.168067	1.919911	10.16113
2015	44.51737	33.56704	1.110302	1.931492	10.23816
2016	45.34579	32.29426	1.070195	1.881226	9.760856
2017	49.20588	31.59444	1.153411	1.874401	9.023642
2018	52.20534	31.66038	1.340731	2.043714	8.186747
2019	53.63983	32.32985	1.385299	2.213188	7.26783
2020	53.72544	32.78582	1.494877	2.104046	6.468274
	LW11	LW12	LW13	LW14	LW15
2014	8.532052	0.157562	40.03774	162.9541	168.6081
2015	10.02605	0.155425	42.65663	166.32	172.0437
2016	11.96455	0.151138	46.77839	169.0449	178.3327
2017	11.47454	0.160873	49.13073	170.6337	187.6043
2018	9.592212	0.176562	50.50349	170.3778	197.4541
2019	9.175388	0.163881	52.99955	168.9993	204.1783
2020	9.59262	0.148076	57.37387	167.4459	206.679
	LW16	LW17	LW18	LW19	LW20
2014	21.65905	1000.17	233.9667	18.99437	21.13776
2015	21.66925	998.235	236.91	20.15426	21.57791
2016	21.64227	1008.557	229.4472	20.30966	21.22893
2017	21.58114	1025.969	214.6791	19.49502	19.87163
2018	21.50213	1043.893	195.4018	18.51396	17.74085
2019	21.43809	1060.712	175.746	17.40395	15.4833
2020	21.38806	1073.485	159.9083	15.98058	13.17131
	LW21	LW22	LW23	LW24	LW25
2014	33.90241	36.57972	456.6615	56.27091	137.2063
2015	33.99279	29.68006	458.5841	55.82903	151.1324
2016	34.05875	23.16081	464.1215	54.94303	167.5077
2017	34.05296	17.57125	473.6836	53.69458	185.7153
2018	34.00324	15.09994	484.0741	52.24699	204.3353

(Continued)

Table A6.6. (*Continued*)

2019	33.98394	14.58542	494.1872	50.64142	221.6079
2020	34.00048	13.71885	501.3928	48.82794	235.3107
	LW26	LW27	LW28	LW29	LW30
2014	201.2124	378.6081	530.6494	9.635478	41.08354
2015	212.3908	391.5516	525.7324	9.113577	42.16302
2016	224.2217	406.0074	519.4828	8.487903	43.01143
2017	232.334	417.6771	511.4951	7.95592	40.90738
2018	238.1809	427.7365	501.2828	7.517104	38.16865
2019	241.574	435.107	489.5356	7.191191	37.32646
2020	242.0565	438.867	475.9308	6.949538	37.27842
	LW31	LW32	LW33	LW34	LW35
2012	126.9633	842.9438	66.9245	588.584	197.3072
2013	125.9892	856.3172	61.26611	594.4323	198.0756
2014	124.9302	877.2136	55.40538	601.7647	199.6991
2015	124.8088	897.2385	49.19883	617.9439	205.5891
2016	125.4535	914.7684	43.38203	636.3611	211.9297
2017	124.9521	926.3504	37.6045	647.5736	213.7496
2018	121.914	938.6487	32.08464	651.3075	212.6267
2019	117.1552	944.7492	27.65612	649.8179	209.7237
2020	111.9049	946.4266	24.48285	647.8179	206.9701
	LW36	LW37	LW38	LW39	LW40
2012	255.4425	83.12504	224.2661	26.00289	196.1562
2013	265.158	86.50434	227.0307	25.79356	199.9728
2014	271.9751	92.33404	232.2467	25.48317	203.8868
2015	283.5108	105.3928	242.1528	24.95613	210.0908
2016	290.8872	115.5875	252.1572	24.78652	218.4026
2017	279.565	114.3532	256.3409	24.76905	224.5142
2018	255.3685	105.9621	255.4255	23.83006	228.625
2019	229.5246	95.47378	251.3185	23.45737	231.4696
2020	211.6077	90.10964	246.945	23.41922	233.4934
	LW41	LW42	LW43	LW44	LW45
2012	1154.99	49.79205	1308.542	2675.006	324.6704
2013	1193.435	44.69946	1346.321	2667.573	307.1087
2014	1227.877	40.91354	1385.496	2662.645	296.5238
2015	1312.987	39.9126	1426.407	2746.178	283.5807
2016	1389.882	41.8696	1384.888	2869.188	275.5802
2017	1380.661	46.03639	1221.44	2996.703	268.6368
2018	1310.922	51.15753	1047.61	3122.34	262.6838
2019	1233.708	54.44831	920.1303	3233.838	261.6251
2020	1181.216	53.79611	853.407	3339.416	259.997

(*Continued*)

Table A6.6. (*Continued*)

	LW46	LW47	LW48	LW49	LW50
2014	286.1025	780.5515	27.33322	135.2064	93.3207
2015	298.7699	794.5913	27.24248	154.8523	98.63593
2016	306.0325	842.5145	27.2006	178.5687	104.1276
2017	297.6906	838.5209	27.14992	200.7692	109.5102
2018	289.3864	851.1016	27.04181	224.2574	114.6529
2019	289.9052	855.3962	26.86782	250.4513	119.7076
2020	292.2938	864.2774	26.72938	280.3161	124.7441
	LW51	LW52	LW53	LW54	LW55
2014	47.40469	262.538	955.577	1283.53	1314.587
2015	47.88392	263.1047	1037.698	1262.317	1366.747
2016	48.28874	262.7761	1127.793	1234.178	1445.524
2017	48.54318	261.6792	1250.42	1199.706	1523.664
2018	48.75578	260.0843	1390.673	1159.793	1567.959
2019	48.97002	257.5299	1540.566	1114.976	1568.443
2020	49.11981	254.4428	1679.116	1066.275	1562.873
	LW56	LW57	LW58	LW59	LW60
2014	719.1011	320.8039	58.93611	68.99417	298.143
2015	737.8443	344.9729	59.65235	65.49582	301.9064
2016	773.2722	373.4046	60.36762	61.41345	304.7611
2017	810.461	401.0835	61.1624	56.91537	305.6371
2018	846.4282	429.5494	61.96173	52.16574	304.7155
2019	877.8761	460.2143	62.74832	47.26415	302.8272
2020	908.8328	493.2672	63.40482	42.30489	300.7006
	LW61	LW62	LW63	LW64	LW65
2014	11246.28	269.5033	5189.275	385.8051	2638.181
2015	11393.76	277.0589	5377.078	400.3192	2664.121
2016	11573.78	293.6424	5517.447	420.0177	2689.683
2017	11695.99	325.5506	5610.314	445.6924	2713.444
2018	11708.82	401.5544	5657.446	476.6299	2733.302
2019	11624.38	408.4809	5644.35	514.3212	2750.743
2020	11493.93	369.9287	5582.351	559.6306	2767.122
	LW66	LW67	LW68	LW69	LW70
2014	119.7616	70.8029	874.1353	558.451	2285.029
2015	117.6423	72.1585	937.3721	563.0888	2315.458
2016	118.2564	73.48392	1013.815	565.4938	2324.145
2017	120.1635	74.77162	1072.725	565.5182	2270.11
2018	98.20581	75.9747	1032.326	562.7053	2215.881
2019	79.35247	77.07559	922.8836	558.028	2157.603
2020	72.8685	78.09755	794.0511	552.2722	2086.777

(*Continued*)

Table A6.6. (*Continued*)

	LW71	LW72	LW73	LW74	LW75
2014	1419.572	952.3104	3161.049	951.683	2689.455
2015	1498.78	1009.511	3227.858	929.1856	2673.795
2016	1550.794	1087.338	3277.968	871.2827	2620.911
2017	1567.542	1131.558	3335.699	816.0375	2542.383
2018	1548.671	1159.797	3391.51	774.2371	2449.225
2019	1528.496	1176.812	3383.281	715.6214	2350.894
2020	1501.589	1202.358	3328.051	638.7515	2256.215
	LW76	LW77	LW78	LW79	LW80
2014	3489.861	10377.08	1940.432	2736.246	0
2015	3404.433	11384.15	1954.14	2702.21	0
2016	3192.019	12513.97	1806.917	2709.836	0
2017	2884.282	13789.05	1687.097	2739.455	0
2018	2557.388	15226.6	1528.585	2755.073	0
2019	2256.13	16852.34	1369.889	2763.078	0
2020	2009.568	18699.65	1217.708	2782.546	0
	LW81	LW82			
2014	0	70155.14			
2015	0	72269.04			
2016	0	74248.18			
2017	0	75896.55			
2018	0	77335.66			
2019	0	78557.94			
2020	0	79855.52			

Note: Sector classification, please see Table A6.1.

Table A6.7. Sectoral output (X) in Abenomics scenario 2, FY2014–2020.

	X01	X02	X03	X04	X05
2014	8149516	1085822	3358107	122560.4	778147.1
2015	8072116	1078614	3508527	143584.4	794978.6
2016	8544477	1067719	3517545	164461.3	842518.8
2017	8940632	1047626	3524701	157338	881882.2
2018	8855916	981330.6	3492654	151269.5	886755.9
2019	8588949	918126.2	3438857	145830.3	883099.1
2020	8317371	864444.9	3326555	142540.8	872381.1
	X06	X07	X08	X09	X10
2014	945475.6	1333992	20202.05	13166.34	96951.89
2015	994629.2	1515147	19845.16	12749.3	97022.85

(*Continued*)

Table A6.7. (*Continued*)

2016	1131137	1617502	20313.54	13051.08	98215.22
2017	1219227	1685332	21914.8	14536.13	101200.7
2018	1274707	1747579	24053.69	15919.57	104703.7
2019	1306241	1759099	24994.9	15072.05	107302.8
2020	1314361	1682650	26423.52	14988	110463.4
	X11	X12	X13	X14	X15
2014	60.62921	12171.16	1269612	5929672	3483350
2015	61.28292	12033.38	1557048	6103567	3986815
2016	63.39989	12256.34	1782474	5853672	4502287
2017	62.27376	13969.36	1832316	5675690	5019154
2018	63.11243	15645.4	1915150	5639240	5245153
2019	68.61698	14085.5	1964233	5580321	5051571
2020	73.076	13320.18	2002801	5403067	4732250
	X16	X17	X18	X19	X20
2014	2421459	13492670	11069000	1451066	3106042
2015	2368467	13662440	11365820	1478908	3128044
2016	2917161	14499430	11579600	1404928	3120912
2017	3335935	15448650	11859970	1334022	3146343
2018	3546266	15852720	12080760	1307819	3208564
2019	3422161	16127830	12189310	1284048	3165257
2020	3300524	16184280	12142680	1237017	3097354
	X21	X22	X23	X24	X25
2014	828651.6	2056065	2922054	772546.5	3070954
2015	841743	2621114	3455212	720360.1	4132011
2016	828525.8	2976263	4114569	652469.3	4433640
2017	834697.5	3176002	4728126	608717.4	4652214
2018	854029.5	2865268	4997012	582693.8	4789220
2019	899369.3	2525182	4997280	513332	4803870
2020	941178.8	2630091	4830636	423767.1	4703034
	X26	X27	X28	X29	X30
2014	2911021	10649780	14248800	1247101	10916900
2015	3584920	11245560	15082470	1437207	10821150
2016	4084770	11707280	16055480	1625343	11055370
2017	4393163	11992990	16545460	1672072	11343760
2018	4582375	12279820	16962740	1726741	11432340
2019	4668036	12538050	17286470	1776433	11409810
2020	4731957	12766690	17628670	1827187	11370630
	X31	X32	X33	X34	X35
2014	11905610	23448420	3787254	13283820	4155923
2015	12385500	24161080	4241955	14749290	4739654

(*Continued*)

Table A6.7. (*Continued*)

2016	12396280	24811080	4558305	16125170	5194714
2017	12375590	25219140	4714999	17057550	5355591
2018	12749410	25485870	4879460	17783810	5619289
2019	13230350	25874740	5039534	18442040	5773321
2020	13672530	26346060	5209347	19154650	5855052
	X36	X37	X38	X39	X40
2014	5345462	5211188	14225720	1991717	5477257
2015	5877805	5635962	15647480	2151569	5757117
2016	6248868	5885955	16594390	2350547	6290513
2017	6469196	5974839	16980970	2510236	6580833
2018	6693279	6071135	17283340	2673800	6832200
2019	6880938	6164288	17560590	2764668	7024615
2020	7028450	6253916	17900190	2797136	7168575
	X41	X42	X43	X44	X45
2014	13726190	2522222	30297710	60740350	7695655
2015	16586610	2685516	33163340	69685830	7245656
2016	18662650	2862829	36213560	78804240	7072727
2017	20449220	2916035	37615900	83445170	6987916
2018	21706540	2937874	38750610	87925140	6722276
2019	22308720	2917290	39270980	91289270	6756858
2020	22830800	2946637	40345900	95615160	6719225
	X46	X47	X48	X49	X50
2014	4771450	53831700	945231.9	3413534	5524933
2015	5294285	64803720	1012043	3947260	5702787
2016	5081805	72975420	1117265	4269675	5973554
2017	5057310	78741630	1224244	4282750	6065909
2018	5275952	83925200	1329150	4470199	6040498
2019	5637442	89859470	1354348	4743744	6097419
2020	5924459	96051870	1376901	5043123	6256877
	X51	X52	X53	X54	X55
2014	1876870	4921935	18463900	21448580	16487270
2015	2118133	5497871	31164310	23867000	22664530
2016	2263056	5967643	32954290	26731160	29712700
2017	2354440	6282651	37843560	27942380	31098370
2018	2474134	6593513	41178840	28760370	32545510
2019	2614722	6872471	42483570	29138910	34056250
2020	2712081	7075294	42136240	29865490	35648150
	X56	X57	X58	X59	X60
2014	11306600	21891430	3420444	4071543	5914572

(*Continued*)

Table A6.7. (*Continued*)

2015	13166090	23038730	3577991	4293208	6409775
2016	15576020	24251070	3729377	4480591	6876437
2017	16598190	24823710	3854037	4595547	7177793
2018	17223720	25694720	3916604	4662175	7406828
2019	17405380	26385760	3940935	4723568	7650309
2020	17890660	26966550	3964027	4800252	7899282
	X61	X62	X63	X64	X65
2014	1.13E+08	14949360	47450250	8250838	18686040
2015	1.2E+08	15911570	49428340	8524707	19749040
2016	1.28E+08	17225290	50882640	8856295	20676680
2017	1.34E+08	17619600	51634660	9008993	21280960
2018	1.4E+08	17565370	51582910	9182602	21806430
2019	1.43E+08	17351010	51393370	9303321	22165970
2020	1.47E+08	18253830	51361050	9431886	22480980
	X66	X67	X68	X69	X70
2014	5204591	7586913	11884340	22405760	52064830
2015	5475717	7892195	12474680	24051880	54061920
2016	5567575	8146428	13152900	25129840	59147600
2017	5411449	8315359	13617740	27068640	59771970
2018	5937278	8434324	14029890	27531560	61199700
2019	6283128	8578095	14534630	29135720	64420690
2020	6470247	8717259	14963830	30999530	65745700
	X71	X72	X73	X74	X75
2014	98009140	14669950	60805320	17151540	47673040
2015	1.04E+08	15995670	67413110	19149380	48748210
2016	1.08E+08	17585750	74560320	20945430	49569380
2017	1.1E+08	18495260	78710520	21993060	50362000
2018	1.09E+08	19066810	81822590	22939780	51158540
2019	1.09E+08	19453750	84540960	23793790	51963030
2020	1.1E+08	19976270	87617290	24785360	52777720
	X76	X77	X78	X79	X80
2014	24960640	49281650	7473400	21564730	2565102
2015	25262470	50108330	6568264	25728660	2754883
2016	25472600	51020550	8237278	29601510	2944261
2017	25689670	51571490	8461019	32081470	3057374
2018	25963470	51953330	9358610	31718140	3174933
2019	26260560	52610550	9681727	32176000	3279164
2020	26559710	53327580	11074260	34853440	3376961

(*Continued*)

Table A6.7. (*Continued*)

	X81	X82
2014	4942645	1.14E+09
2015	5404619	1.24E+09
2016	5804462	1.34E+09
2017	5975585	1.39E+09
2018	6119679	1.43E+09
2019	6242149	1.47E+09
2020	6367051	1.51E+09

Note: Sector classification, see Table A6.1.

Table A6.8. Sectoral wage and salaried employees (LW) in Abenomics scenario 2, FY2014–2020.

	LW01	LW02	LW03	LW04	LW05
2014	112.6666	50.2247	11.51187	0.430497	23.86306
2015	108.9739	51.81456	12.79577	0.45125	21.51647
2016	96.89979	52.05512	14.4425	0.476611	17.90184
2017	85.87538	52.48828	15.40533	0.493348	13.39075
2018	76.32497	52.53714	15.33516	0.504263	9.301755
2019	69.11479	51.74294	14.43921	0.508039	6.089458
2020	63.52368	50.79538	12.67763	0.506525	3.867766
	LW06	**LW07**	**LW08**	**LW09**	**LW10**
2014	44.22356	35.6861	1.174133	1.91973	10.11822
2015	44.47694	34.30556	1.088546	1.930621	10.00808
2016	45.82889	33.6135	1.060773	1.868684	9.364378
2017	50.34849	33.52398	1.169	1.892443	8.516431
2018	53.77151	34.17751	1.378246	2.070957	7.596096
2019	55.18678	35.45885	1.427994	2.241388	6.610358
2020	54.85222	36.47712	1.526173	2.128268	5.746383
	LW11	**LW12**	**LW13**	**LW14**	**LW15**
2014	8.50234	0.157609	40.4871	163.5493	168.844
2015	10.06913	0.1534	43.51035	167.8524	173.9454
2016	12.03571	0.150023	48.10965	171.3717	182.7557
2017	11.44544	0.160117	51.0175	173.6879	194.3267
2018	9.720222	0.174814	52.92739	173.8023	205.598
2019	9.40559	0.1613	55.89679	172.6086	213.0107
2020	9.830366	0.144342	60.65661	171.04	215.8386

(*Continued*)

Table A6.8. (*Continued*)

	LW16	LW17	LW18	LW19	LW20
2014	21.66375	1002.299	237.5382	19.15598	21.12126
2015	21.67741	1004.245	244.084	20.60414	21.49983
2016	21.64528	1019.984	237.225	20.99704	20.99605
2017	21.57778	1045.557	221.6	20.33373	19.42665
2018	21.4933	1068.972	200.8941	19.36512	17.08486
2019	21.4244	1088.913	179.7163	18.27685	14.6644
2020	21.36845	1103.853	162.4923	16.82285	12.25097
	LW21	LW22	LW23	LW24	LW25
2014	33.93645	36.84886	457.3121	56.14424	139.0741
2015	34.04621	30.04575	460.5505	55.47184	156.0084
2016	34.11289	23.56887	466.4013	54.23779	175.0722
2017	34.11167	18.14701	475.669	52.55135	194.8919
2018	34.07208	15.975	485.436	50.66346	214.2035
2019	34.06706	15.74714	494.6431	48.55425	231.2698
2020	34.09086	14.91982	500.2823	46.19365	244.038
	LW26	LW27	LW28	LW29	LW30
2014	202.6807	380.2163	530.8357	9.606881	41.09356
2015	216.1232	395.1483	526.2624	9.044476	42.12532
2016	229.0492	411.482	520.2109	8.402035	42.77627
2017	237.2658	424.8671	512.2374	7.864934	40.54221
2018	242.4494	436.2001	501.8772	7.429322	37.75312
2019	244.6278	443.9585	489.757	7.104696	36.85375
2020	243.7632	447.2703	475.7544	6.866259	36.81277
	LW31	LW32	LW33	LW34	LW35
2014	124.8842	880.1543	55.72721	603.5521	200.0581
2015	124.5114	905.4334	49.64287	623.4061	207.1592
2016	124.8333	933.5744	43.56191	645.5678	214.6203
2017	124.2279	964.2793	37.53904	663.6858	218.5311
2018	121.641	1003.362	31.61915	679.3496	220.2393
2019	118.1828	1042.777	26.50222	692.7233	219.9556
2020	114.5542	1080.043	22.28019	704.2749	218.4133
	LW36	LW37	LW38	LW39	LW40
2014	273.9256	93.38612	232.913	25.78436	203.7994
2015	290.5864	109.4617	245.0679	25.53118	210.1421
2016	307.2042	124.3554	259.6406	25.17689	220.0038
2017	311.7726	134.2812	274.0142	24.89591	229.7069
2018	309.5062	142.3611	290.3161	24.20478	239.0751

(*Continued*)

Table A6.8. (*Continued*)

2019	303.7762	148.1523	308.5306	24.23531	247.6861
2020	297.6005	155.3322	328.4217	24.52943	254.3813
	LW41	LW42	LW43	LW44	LW45
2014	1236.879	41.39028	1389.277	2668.386	297.2529
2015	1351.068	41.6122	1445.056	2759.936	281.5714
2016	1471.55	45.51241	1444.416	2891.893	266.2988
2017	1531.347	53.40574	1371.148	3044.339	252.8459
2018	1562.733	66.22804	1307.523	3219.711	241.4148
2019	1581.457	84.10782	1266.932	3402.919	235.6166
2020	1589.473	107.1538	1244.806	3587.967	230.7392
	LW46	LW47	LW48	LW49	LW50
2014	287.0351	785.4025	27.3432	135.2878	93.33037
2015	302.2969	802.3361	27.25553	154.9487	98.67794
2016	308.7129	847.2543	27.21814	178.6523	104.2093
2017	296.7673	844.9242	27.1606	200.7381	109.6322
2018	289.1452	859.7791	27.04608	223.9202	114.8187
2019	290.718	866.3752	26.86815	249.8629	119.9173
2020	292.2566	878.13	26.7232	279.3448	125.0051
	LW51	LW52	LW53	LW54	LW55
2014	47.4069	262.7216	976.5434	1282.96	1316.53
2015	47.88166	263.3031	1086.288	1259.334	1368.359
2016	48.26933	262.8195	1202.707	1227.612	1443.59
2017	48.51188	261.449	1348.15	1188.997	1516.399
2018	48.71082	259.4525	1510.526	1144.726	1553.911
2019	48.90751	256.4581	1680.608	1095.448	1547.497
2020	49.03231	252.8907	1836.675	1041.917	1535.206
	LW56	LW57	LW58	LW59	LW60
2014	720.2244	320.9698	58.93613	68.83919	298.6877
2015	741.032	345.4371	59.7195	65.04376	302.9692
2016	778.7107	374.2828	60.5528	60.59384	306.0569
2017	817.8268	402.7572	61.48367	55.70089	307.0206
2018	855.3512	432.3007	62.40456	50.56588	306.0354
2019	888.1146	463.888	63.28655	45.31745	303.9483
2020	908.8328	497.8597	64.01796	40.0734	301.5112
	LW61	LW62	LW63	LW64	LW65
2014	11287.98	269.5033	5210.1	385.9015	2637.144
2015	11496.38	277.0589	5416.474	402.3858	2662.228
2016	11727.93	293.6424	5573.605	425.3797	2686.811
2017	11868.62	325.5506	5685.261	455.9675	2709.426

(*Continued*)

Table A6.8. (*Continued*)

2018	11874.71	401.5544	5747.238	493.3132	2728.11
2019	11776.89	408.4809	5742.324	539.0738	2744.306
2020	11627.38	369.9287	5679.841	594.5868	2759.515
	LW66	LW67	LW68	LW69	LW70
2014	120.7775	70.81817	887.8505	558.7561	2309.797
2015	118.4426	72.21537	965.3557	563.472	2345.415
2016	117.8022	73.59229	1045.365	565.545	2346.334
2017	118.2228	74.92941	1103.912	564.9598	2286.372
2018	95.59337	76.18266	1056.025	561.3328	2227.355
2019	76.86042	77.33593	926.1584	555.8354	2185.909
2020	70.23742	78.40885	777.2677	549.4138	2103.069
	LW71	LW72	LW73	LW74	LW75
2014	1434.4	968.258	3179.299	946.7475	2684.667
2015	1535.675	1038.043	3265.452	913.3681	2657.814
2016	1616.425	1121.772	3327.86	844.5672	2590.659
2017	1656.867	1168.012	3390.869	780.9076	2498.668
2018	1652.529	1198.209	3439.726	730.2416	2393.172
2019	1639.81	1218.847	3420.856	662.897	2283.839
2020	1614.916	1244.077	3351.009	580.8853	2180.537
	LW76	LW77	LW78	LW79	LW80
2014	3491.155	10374.07	1951.964	2749.347	0
2015	3375.635	11373.89	1972.285	2734.15	0
2016	3118.532	12492.28	1811.235	2761.485	0
2017	2778.398	13750.77	1668.909	2814.178	0
2018	2429.955	15164.8	1481.192	2853.553	0
2019	2116.887	16757.73	1295.881	2881.299	0
2020	1865.856	18562.05	1108.444	2920.519	0
	LW81	LW82			
2014	0	70388.19			
2015	0	72695.37			
2016	0	74776.22			
2017	0	76465.76			
2018	0	77875.06			
2019	0	79038.34			
2020	0	80204.3			

Note: Sector classification, see Table A6.1.

Table A6.9. Sectoral output (X) in Abenomics scenario 3, FY2014–2020.

	X01	X02	X03	X04	X05
2014	7771727	1112544	3324629	117571.8	744340.5
2015	7482228	1143451	3346746	132253.5	732452.5
2016	8142157	1179600	3236222	149922.3	779375
2017	8673472	1200053	3132570	135779.7	811854.7
2018	8553285	1161571	2980082	124209.4	796899.7
2019	8151998	1127857	2832068	115978.6	768563.6
2020	7700311	1092793	2678381	115996.1	734950.9
	X06	X07	X08	X09	X10
2014	945465	1336942	20202.13	13172.61	97029.95
2015	982593.2	1481617	19656.39	12290.86	98258.94
2016	1082430	1510400	19571.49	11967.76	99578.29
2017	1146144	1479186	20661.37	13579.31	102179.8
2018	1160650	1447998	22210.09	15168.52	105706.4
2019	1145339	1411673	22496.31	14217.96	109177.9
2020	1112260	1311538	23301.96	13736.79	114184.9
	X11	X12	X13	X14	X15
2014	60.61374	12170.41	1259507	5884778	3467933
2015	60.66448	11400.43	1507956	5840711	3798516
2016	62.407	10726.2	1708752	5376240	4048910
2017	61.12394	12379.49	1717907	5006370	4294480
2018	60.49288	13971.74	1753240	4770499	4228857
2019	64.23149	11839.03	1768152	4607750	3792939
2020	67.19973	10038.98	1790076	4423086	3232466
	X16	X17	X18	X19	X20
2014	2417998	13429840	10939790	1439257	3128736
2015	2395166	13447420	10909710	1432039	3088822
2016	2915594	14128430	10922290	1326016	3036334
2017	3266803	14795100	11116910	1214717	3051884
2018	3409942	15018530	11154740	1146763	3080807
2019	3095136	15070700	10999170	1105911	3017218
2020	2686450	14691840	10675810	1070437	2911166
	X21	X22	X23	X24	X25
2014	828668.8	2050476	2969583	797187.3	2940121
2015	847071.7	2571789	3479409	780481.3	3652443
2016	834168.6	2890467	4101070	761506.7	3943615
2017	828947.8	3033876	4705023	777999.4	4100030
2018	833642.5	2601114	4866005	818534.4	4135258
2019	866928.8	2044822	4692872	827520.7	4119134
2020	902129.2	1901964	4335450	798353	4071445

(*Continued*)

Table A6.9. (*Continued*)

	X26	X27	X28	X29	X30
2014	2825993	10529960	14026290	1235885	10933400
2015	3272225	10923530	14575090	1404842	10880520
2016	3674923	11250330	15386970	1575132	11213130
2017	3877887	11278800	15570020	1584132	11603300
2018	3866721	11190340	15492310	1588518	11844350
2019	3731171	11082810	15214090	1596841	11969250
2020	3637663	11083130	15129030	1627108	11985790
	X31	X32	X33	X34	X35
2014	11895380	23217990	3757766	13156480	4151676
2015	12315370	23806420	4146409	14400560	4620350
2016	12139660	24542020	4387050	15642330	4964842
2017	11717770	24880150	4360859	16205820	4964137
2018	11593580	24940960	4229031	16247640	5055051
2019	11789360	25024420	4101274	16103730	5064930
2020	12219230	25204520	4084695	16202600	5044192
	X36	X37	X38	X39	X40
2014	5288683	5184009	14105380	1984522	5469668
2015	5689373	5538347	15266080	2120169	5721535
2016	5980171	5709589	16007540	2270932	6145270
2017	6035707	5586859	15782970	2334920	6255971
2018	6044668	5382746	15181630	2390234	6307842
2019	6052249	5219747	14659470	2384482	6321648
2020	6102717	5185177	14581340	2353242	6363043
	X41	X42	X43	X44	X45
2014	13421060	2505263	29966460	60234150	7567960
2015	15598630	2635693	32294750	68431480	7027171
2016	17626800	2788077	35209710	77302410	6859256
2017	18908190	2798995	36353580	81668610	6724561
2018	19500660	2729979	36775930	85119210	6231085
2019	19170480	2583130	36233070	87083210	5961467
2020	18853910	2530961	36565970	90515690	5804957
	X46	X47	X48	X49	X50
2014	4723563	52532090	932389.8	3417953	5515689
2015	4958937	61960940	969418.9	3906001	5678264
2016	4623591	68211780	1055937	4016461	5927144
2017	4147517	68472530	1145689	3348528	5939980
2018	3709740	64717200	1251290	2526814	5781817
2019	3623881	62369080	1269676	1954559	5711794
2020	3697522	63318120	1276408	1778042	5797688

(*Continued*)

Table A6.9. (*Continued*)

	X51	X52	X53	X54	X55
2014	1876397	4831389	16458140	21468580	16485290
2015	2095598	5273796	23852250	23615050	22657770
2016	2159181	5625865	25792640	26282170	29704010
2017	1971903	5627738	29449400	27168000	31089220
2018	1663808	5458685	31446580	27296260	32531230
2019	1456486	5277522	32134790	26738150	34031660
2020	1393312	5169786	31735440	26689190	35614460

	X56	X57	X58	X59	X60
2014	11192150	21622380	3361411	4016203	5813181
2015	12778920	22327170	3429963	4149742	6163528
2016	15077560	23185280	3540124	4278690	6522173
2017	16074260	23191680	3620364	4301052	6639304
2018	16405060	23380010	3619927	4233139	6596508
2019	15999140	23472120	3571233	4150349	6541731
2020	15966090	23654960	3531051	4113910	6555191

	X61	X62	X63	X64	X65
2014	1.11E+08	14590050	46649000	8114675	18341890
2015	1.15E+08	15166220	47459680	8224363	18890810
2016	1.21E+08	16340550	48329790	8422652	19561180
2017	1.25E+08	16243340	48429260	8340101	19795470
2018	1.26E+08	14950150	47363680	8306648	19788830
2019	1.25E+08	12729250	46165990	8219331	19620260
2020	1.25E+08	12130240	45524590	8222082	19588500

	X66	X67	X68	X69	X70
2014	5180418	7527423	11646080	22002770	50365450
2015	5387370	7779160	11920700	23188160	50663150
2016	5277270	8013107	12377420	23929960	54588300
2017	4423736	8115911	12456930	25075680	53633730
2018	4270112	8128737	12317350	24440090	52783470
2019	4600998	8171641	12311510	24445690	52501290
2020	5031642	8249263	12409940	24824830	52930670

	X71	X72	X73	X74	X75
2014	96797270	14370050	59400010	16953230	47658580
2015	99111010	15265180	63997790	18668660	48708640
2016	99350390	16663410	70342700	20307180	49510820
2017	97622390	17301670	72894960	20942730	50262440
2018	95066330	17258540	73155030	21148410	51001130
2019	93382490	16717950	72046580	21240320	51753330
2020	92413700	16507100	72373060	21749590	52539220

(*Continued*)

Table A6.9. (*Continued*)

	X76	X77	X78	X79	X80
2014	24956020	48881060	6612521	20554540	2529213
2015	25253100	49429360	5003349	23304680	2660159
2016	25417510	50320790	6440549	25843300	2800604
2017	25548810	50735460	5986608	25643610	2830855
2018	25723760	50861870	6090192	20173450	2834500
2019	25909010	51237720	5800696	14009850	2813546
2020	26091150	51818720	6548437	10624700	2822860

	X81	X82
2014	4858895	1.12E+09
2015	5174704	1.19E+09
2016	5464622	1.27E+09
2017	5396996	1.29E+09
2018	5204613	1.28E+09
2019	5022333	1.27E+09
2020	4979093	1.27E+09

Note: Sector classification, see Table A6.1.

Table A6.10. Sectoral wage and salaried employees (LW) in Abenomics scenario 3, FY2014–2020.

	LW01	LW02	LW03	LW04	LW05
2014	112.2129	50.2244	11.40624	0.427128	24.42624
2015	109.3325	51.81417	12.0863	0.441621	22.99547
2016	98.86557	52.04238	12.45075	0.461203	19.9983
2017	88.46889	52.46906	11.44761	0.469716	15.50714
2018	78.86905	52.47417	9.011373	0.470205	11.1469
2019	71.39477	51.88952	6.237846	0.463502	7.724034
2020	65.81397	51.54642	3.912833	0.506525	3.867766

	LW06	LW07	LW08	LW09	LW10
2014	44.22323	35.42913	1.166101	1.919911	10.15315
2015	44.50006	33.30723	1.05261	1.93211	10.34501
2016	45.56081	31.57587	0.960078	1.811048	10.0748
2017	48.87428	30.19936	0.983849	1.753019	9.502742
2018	51.14285	29.35151	1.076148	1.948001	8.852039
2019	50.92761	29.12778	1.039159	2.151339	8.295898
2020	54.85222	28.80664	1.084684	2.032619	8.174511

	LW11	LW12	LW13	LW14	LW15
2014	8.335342	0.157495	40.01294	162.9343	168.683
2015	9.268947	0.146905	42.27578	165.6287	171.9759

(*Continued*)

Table A6.10. (*Continued*)

2016	10.49754	0.132779	45.79439	167.0386	176.9264
2017	9.313196	0.138536	46.09327	165.998	182.9348
2018	6.694934	0.151091	44.31483	161.3374	186.8744
2019	5.215969	0.13371	43.57743	154.8369	185.5971
2020	4.522271	0.109182	46.19833	148.7112	178.4946
	LW16	LW17	LW18	LW19	LW20
2014	21.65801	1000.26	234.1364	19.0048	21.1429
2015	21.66172	997.4597	236.7618	19.84537	21.8836
2016	21.62766	1007.152	229.131	19.20434	22.06646
2017	21.55504	1021.858	212.5453	17.11287	21.25427
2018	21.45984	1031.586	189.3435	14.55392	19.67731
2019	21.39299	1035.892	167.5517	12.16501	18.16392
2020	21.37508	1032.219	154.3377	10.07048	16.90107
	LW21	LW22	LW23	LW24	LW25
2014	33.89892	36.49324	456.65	56.27062	137.3406
2015	33.9536	29.22544	459.1904	55.98463	148.8168
2016	33.98104	22.45634	466.3183	55.43663	162.3895
2017	33.88471	16.63701	476.6082	54.56764	175.7549
2018	33.67854	13.78484	487.8115	53.58035	187.1216
2019	33.48118	12.86759	499.5694	52.72609	196.0253
2020	33.36411	11.96714	508.6012	52.09961	202.2858
	LW26	LW27	LW28	LW29	LW30
2014	201.1905	378.6005	532.199	9.634782	41.0785
2015	210.9822	389.9258	529.1686	9.104411	42.06167
2016	221.3325	402.0414	524.5052	8.451948	42.20459
2017	227.0123	408.2345	517.1913	7.898257	38.74512
2018	228.9321	408.6807	506.8581	7.435325	34.50083
2019	229.8751	404.0391	495.1032	7.042612	32.05761
2020	231.0298	396.9867	482.3123	6.731652	31.01667
	LW31	LW32	LW33	LW34	LW35
2014	124.9302	877.2136	55.40538	601.7647	199.6991
2015	124.8088	897.2385	49.19883	617.9439	205.5891
2016	125.4535	914.7684	43.38203	636.3611	211.9297
2017	124.9521	926.3504	37.6045	647.5736	213.7496
2018	121.914	938.6487	32.08464	651.3075	212.6267
2019	117.1552	944.7492	27.65612	649.8179	209.7327
2020	111.9049	946.4266	24.48285	647.8179	206.9701
	LW36	LW37	LW38	LW39	LW40
2014	271.9751	92.33404	232.2467	25.48317	203.8868
2015	283.5108	105.3928	242.1528	24.95613	210.0908

(*Continued*)

Table A6.10. (*Continued*)

2016	290.8872	115.5875	252.1572	24.78652	218.4026
2017	279.565	114.3532	256.3409	24.76905	224.5142
2018	255.3685	105.9621	255.4255	23.83006	228.625
2019	229.5246	95.47378	251.3185	23.45737	231.4696
2020	211.6077	90.10964	246.945	23.41922	233.4934
	LW41	LW42	LW43	LW44	LW45
2014	1227.877	40.91354	1385.496	2662.645	296.5238
2015	1312.987	39.9126	1426.407	2746.178	283.5807
2016	1389.882	41.8696	1384.888	2869.188	275.5802
2017	1380.661	46.03639	1221.44	2996.703	268.6368
2018	1310.922	51.15753	1047.61	3122.34	262.6838
2019	1233.708	54.44831	920.1303	3233.838	261.6251
2020	1181.216	53.79611	853.407	3339.416	259.997
	LW46	LW47	LW48	LW49	LW50
2014	286.0152	780.2515	27.33604	135.2473	93.31938
2015	296.7187	790.5013	27.23249	154.0981	98.63997
2016	297.3311	830.7915	27.19487	173.5895	104.1053
2017	276.9691	808.0488	27.13671	178.0527	109.3427
2018	251.5372	781.3682	27.01038	162.1633	114.1389
2019	236.0382	749.664	26.78202	134.9704	118.6533
2020	232.4645	736.9284	26.57113	111.1104	123.059
	LW51	LW52	LW53	LW54	LW55
2014	47.40616	262.5166	955.5478	1283.435	1314.156
2015	47.87075	262.8362	1014.231	1262.485	1366.824
2016	48.19908	262.3196	1082.989	1235.939	1448.269
2017	48.13904	261.0441	1173.773	1204.12	1524.109
2018	47.68022	259.6355	1270.721	1169.541	1561.343
2019	47.06859	258.0165	1369.023	1133.655	1557.997
2020	46.53261	256.6604	1456.025	1097.707	1560.731
	LW56	LW57	LW58	LW59	LW60
2014	719.1391	320.7992	58.93611	68.9878	298.1357
2015	737.4047	344.8248	59.64791	65.57648	301.6299
2016	772.9845	372.6266	60.31352	61.65909	304.195
2017	810.0787	397.6721	61.05159	57.45284	304.2831
2018	843.334	419.5612	61.77392	53.19661	301.8921
2019	867.6498	439.341	62.4686	49.00942	298.4658
2020	888.8183	458.8149	62.95708	44.9234	295.6521
	LW61	LW62	LW63	LW64	LW65
2014	11242.78	269.4511	5198.178	385.7597	2638.133
2015	11371.66	278.9667	5386.336	400.1798	2664.632

(*Continued*)

Table A6.10. (*Continued*)

2016	11531.7	299.4779	5531.673	418.5172	2691.261
2017	11595.5	336.8101	5627.289	441.2642	2716.669
2018	11507.37	455.9245	5687.126	465.2574	2737.683
2019	11298.67	493.0102	5710.852	491.069	2756.574
2020	11078.42	400.7276	5709.1	518.3441	2775.674
	LW66	LW67	LW68	LW69	LW70
2014	119.465	70.7905	872.4239	558.404	2328.191
2015	116.8226	72.12542	934.8666	562.7259	2366.805
2016	121.378	73.43355	1055.611	564.8351	2372.103
2017	135.7291	74.68493	1254.922	564.1106	2311.049
2018	114.0883	75.82255	1416.896	559.9965	2247.176
2019	79.30565	76.8148	1477.788	554.1295	2173.175
2020	61.73133	77.67634	1456.93	548.3993	2060.954
	LW71	LW72	LW73	LW74	LW75
2014	1446.385	952.2405	3159.796	951.4842	2689.088
2015	1513.668	999.152	3208.971	932.4723	2676.369
2016	1529.858	1072.822	3252.558	888.0738	2629.773
2017	1496.112	1105.518	3311.77	857.0431	2560.537
2018	1436.133	1104.61	3390.968	856.5813	2482.781
2019	1385.022	1078.6	3433.862	854.3008	2412.543
2020	1340.245	1068.19	3439.238	833.4358	2362.324
	LW76	LW77	LW78	LW79	LW80
2014	3485.867	10382.69	1938.437	2735.648	0
2015	3390.937	11403.08	1955.326	2696.096	0
2016	3185.869	12554.81	1862.18	2696.375	0
2017	2873.22	13868.52	1871.263	2707.237	0
2018	2541.643	15370.59	1897.481	2652.424	0
2019	2274.253	17094.52	1928.127	2501.367	0
2020	2118.293	19083.41	1943.984	2299.991	0
	LW81	LW82			
2014	0	70226.15			
2015	0	72215.32			
2016	0	74122.49			
2017	0	75629.67			
2018	0	76829.65			
2019	0	77743.63			
2020	0	78792.79			

Note: Sector classification, see Table A6.1.

Chapter 7

Concluding Remarks

7.1. Summary and Policy Recommendation

With respect to the conclusion of this book, there are many research implications based on our study of DEMIOS in the past and hence we focus on the major issues discussed in each chapter. As discussed earlier, the major objectives of this book are to present the model structure of DEMIOS and to discuss the policy implications through some policy scenario simulations, especially, focusing on the policies how the Japanese economy could overcome the current long-term economic deflation. Therefore, this chapter concludes each chapters' discussion.

Chapter 2 discusses general feature of DEMIOS, focusing on the basic structure of the model, DEMIOS, and sectoral classification and database development. Unlike a conventional macroeconomic model, DEMIOS has three model blocks such as the Input–Output (I–O) model, the macroeconomic model block and the demographic model block. Therefore, the size of DEMIOS in terms of the number of variables is large with more than 3,500 variables, but, the chapter emphasizes the strong advantages of the model which could find appropriate structures of equations including behavioral equations and their adequate parameters as a deep parameter. In addition, the VRAS algorism could play an important role to introduce dynamic changes in input coefficients together with changes in prices, factor costs and technical progress in the model system.

Chapter 3 analyzes the framework of the conventional Leontief I–O model which is one of the core blocks in DEMIOS as a Keynes–Leontief-type Model (KLM). Therefore, Chapter 3 elucidates the production and factor demands sub-block, the prices and factor costs sub-block, the I–O sub-block with the VRAS algorism and the final demand sub-block.

In the production and factor demands sub-block, the supply-side sectoral variables theoretical model specifications are introduced, in which sectoral business investment, which is one of the key variables in the I–O block, sectoral labor demand function and sectoral imports are discussed, and their regression results are also introduced. Particularly, in the sectoral business investment equations, government investment plays a very important role to induce the business investment in some machinery related sectors.

In the prices and factor costs sub-block, the theoretical framework of the conventional I–O technique related to prices and factor costs is introduced, and theoretical model and the regression results of some major sectoral prices and factor costs are discussed. In the regression results, it is noteworthy that sectoral nominal wage rates are heavily dependent on the relative sectoral labor productivity and national level nominal wage rates.

In the I–O and VRAS algorism sub-block, the VRAS algorism is mainly discussed and the dynamic input coefficients derived through a rectangular matrix resulted in the dynamic relations among technical progress, substitution parameters and prices. Therefore, it is worth noting that technical progress in a specific sector would result in changing substitution parameters positively and declining the related prices directly and indirectly and finally improving whole economies.

In the final demand sub-block, the analyses are focusing on how the sectoral final demands are derived in the model system. As discussed, there are eight final demand components such as household consumption, consumption of non-profit organization, residential investment, business investment, government sector consumption, government investment, inventory changes and exports. This section mainly focuses on the sectoral household consumption disaggregation by employing the modified Rotterdam School Model from aggregated household consumption to 12 category base household consumption. According to the regression results based on the Rotterdam School Model, most of the household consumptions have strong performance and more disaggregation is also implemented fairly well.

In Chapter 4, the macroeconomic model block is discussed for analyzing the structure of the eight sub-blocks, including real expenditure sub-block, the nominal expenditure sub-block, the prices and wage rate sub-block, the production and labor force sub-block, the money and finance sub-block, the government finance sub-block, the income distribution sub-block and the external and balance of payment (BOP) sub-block. In addition, this section discusses how the model system mains feedback chains in between the macroeconomic model and I–O model. Nominal wage rates are one of the important variable for the feedback relations between both the models, in which nominal wage rates derived by labor demand–supply, productivity and so on influences not only macroeconomic variables but also sectoral variables by way of sectoral wage rates.

In addition, this section introduces the macro capacity GDP based on a Cobb–Douglas function. According to the capacity GDP estimated in this study, there are still large deflationary gap and it is assumed at −8.92% in 2000, at −6.58% in 2005 and −11.07% in 2010, respectively.

In Chapter 5, the cohort-type demographic and labor force block is introduced, focusing on the simplified demographic sub-model. However, DEMIOS is able to forecast the Japanese economy up to 2030 at this moment and hence DEMIOS will employ the cohort-type demographic and labor force model for the long-term projections. Furthermore, the cohort-type demographic and labor force model has 18 groups by age group and gender for population and seven groups by age group and gender for labor force. Accordingly, the cohort-type demographic model is very useful for some policy simulation related to the issues of a fewer children and aging society in Japan.

In Chapter 6, three scenario projections such as (1) the national resilience plan (2) the growth alternatives in Abenomics and (3) the analysis of huge earthquake damages of East Japan are examined for forecasting some growth alternatives of the Japanese economy up to the year 2020. For the national resilience plan, the result of the two projections such as the baseline projection and the national resilience plan scenario projection, could depict the lager Keynes multiplier even in the present Japanese economy. Although many economist and policy makers doubt the effectiveness of the Keynesian policy, the simulation results could clarify large multiplier effects on the economy. Therefore, it is worth noting that the central government should understand the true Keynes multiplier of Japan for planning the policy mixture to overcome the long-term deflationary economy.

In addition, for the growth alternatives of Abenomics, three policy simulations such as the growth scenario, the growth scenario plus leisure expansion scenario and the growth scenario plus consumption tax hikes scenario are examined. As a result of these three scenario projections in Abenomics, the third scenario projection is very likely to predict the present Japanese economy, in which the positive effects of the policy package with fiscal and monetary policy are canceled by consumption tax hikes.

In the case of the scenario simulation of the analysis of reconstruction from huge earthquake damages of East Japan, the baseline projection and the reconstruction scenario projection are examined by DEMIOS and eight regional models, including Hokkaido, Tohoku, Kanto, Chubu, Kinki, Chugoku, Shikoku and Kyushu. According to the scenario simulations, it can be seen that vital reconstruction policy could improve not only the Japanese economy but also regional economies despite of the different effects on the regional economies.

Based on the results of these scenario projections discussed above, we can summarize the feature of DEMIOS, as follows.

(1) In comparison with the other models, the labor supply is rather flexible, because demographic factors such as active population, net migrants and so on, are endogenized, which allows for milder wage rates adjustment and price reaction in the economy.
(2) Both business investment and residential investment are more sensitive to the changes of aggregate demand side and supply side, especially to government investment. It can be seen that business investments by some of manufacturing industry sectors such as automobile sector are stimulated by highway network expansion, which would be disregarded in the short-term macroeconometric models. In addition, similarly, business investment in communication and IT sectors are also sensitive to the government investment for infrastructure of IT network.
(3) The response of the demand components of GDP is relatively slow in all scenario simulations as a multiplier effect. However, the multiplier effects on the demand-side components, especially household consumption expenditure, gradually keep growing. It seems that these phenomena are dependent on mainly the time-lag structure between dependent variable and independent variables in each behavioral equation, including sectoral final demand components.
(4) Demographic factors are especially noticeable in the case of government sector consumption for medical care and welfare expenditures. While the demand components' responses are still delaying in the first half decade in simulation period, but in the latter half of the simulation period, the multiplier effects are getting large owing to the increase in population.

(5) As for the fiscal issues, the scenario simulations could reveal that though the multiplier effects are still small in the first period of the simulation, the effects on nominal GDP are getting larger than the government expenditures and finally tax revenues are also larger than the government expenditures. Therefore, it is noteworthy that the government expenditure increase will induce the larger outcomes based on cost–benefit relations. As a result, government outstanding debt ratio to nominal GDP will probably decline from 89.6% in FY2014 to 27.0% in FY2020 through an automatic tax revenue increase even in the growth scenario of Abenomics Scenario 1.

(6) With the strong and aggressive fiscal and monetary policy measures as the accommodated fiscal policy with the Bank of Japan plus leisure expansion, the Japanese economy will be able to achieve the strong growth alternatives. The economy will probably achieve 742.5 trillion yen in terms of real GDP and the annual average growth rates of real GDP will be 4.45% in FY2015–2020, whereas inflation rates will be fairly limited at 3.5% in terms of GDP deflator in FY2015–2020 because of the strong production capacity with vital private sector's investment behaviors. In comparison with the current economic performance in Abenomics at around 1% growth, the 4.5% growth on average will be able to improve various macro imbalances of the Japanese economy, especially fiscal balance and IS balance and hence the economic deflation. Therefore, the government should introduce more effective economic policy measures to vitalize the Japanese economy as demonstrated in several scenario simulations by DEMIOS in this book.

7.2. Further Study in the Future

DEMIOS project started in the mid-1980s, but several papers were published since 1991. It means that it took around five years to develop database, regression analysis and database correction, model justification for scenario simulations and so on.

Since then, we could compile a lot of knowledge, skills, new theories and experiences, attending some international conferences for paper presentation and submitting our papers to journals. Now, we could concentrate on DEMIOS based on the VRAS algorism. The new version of DEMIOS with 81 sectors has been started since 2007 and it takes more than 10 years because expansion of the number of sectors from 64 to 81 needed enormous efforts and time. Still many unknowns remain in modeling and forecasting. However, we believe that DEMIOS is one of the answers to various criticisms raised by many economists and practitioners who handle economic policy analyses. In addition, we could find 'deep parameters' through expanding the number of sectors and hence endogenous variables in the model and taking account of time-lag structure between dependent and independent variables in regression analysis, which would cope with structural changes in any economy.

In the mid-1980s, Klein, deeply described that modeling and forecasting with structural multi-equation models are still one of the strongest tools for policy analyses when some economists criticized a large scale econometric model, as the model could not anticipate oil crises and their impacts on the world economy. The authors participated in Project LINK meetings which were mainly established and organized by Klein and felt deeply Klein's intention to strengthen the structural multi-equation models. Accordingly, we have continued the DEMIOS project and improve DEMIOS by solving various problems in the model.

Bibliography

Barten, A. P. (1964) "Consumer Demand Functions under Conditions of Almost Additive Preference," *Econometrica*, 32, 1–38.

Engle, R. F. and C. W. J. Granger (1987) "Co-integration and Error Correction: Representation, Estimation, and Testing," *Econometrica*, 55(2), 251–276.

Honda, Y. and M. Tachibana (2011) "Financial Crisis and Japanese Quantitative Easing," in Iwai, K. and Y Seko (eds.) *Financial Crisis and Macro Economy*, Chapter 3, pp. 51–74, University of Tokyo, Press.

Ichimura, S. and L. R. Klein (eds.) (2011) *Macro-econometric Modeling of Japan*, World Scientific.

Lam, W. R. (2011) "Bank of Japan's Monetary Easing Measures: Are They Powerful and Comprehensive?" IMF Working Paper, No. 11/264.

Nakamura, O. (2013) *Income Distribution and Economic Growth of Japan under the Deflationary Economy: Theory and Evidence based on an Econometric Analysis*, World Scientific.

Nakamura, O. (2014) "The Effectiveness of Non-traditional Monetary Policy with an Inflation Target: The Case of Japan in Comparison with the US," Working Paper Series, IRI, International University of Japan, No. 2014-08.

Nakamura, O. and S. Shishido (1990) "Demographic and Labor Supply Block in Revision of the Japanese Long-Term Multi-Sectoral Model," in Adams, F. G. and S. Shishido (eds.) (1990) *Structure of Trade and Industry in the US–Japan Economy: Phase II, Integration with Project LINK and Simulation Application*, NIRA Research Output, 3(1), NIRA.

Oda, N. and K. Ueda (2007) "The Effects of the Bank of Japan's Zero Interest Commitment and Quantitative Monetary Easing on the Yield Curve: A Macro-Finance Approach," *Japanese Economic Review*, 58(3), 303–328.

Peterson, W. (ed.) (1991) *Advances in Input–Output Analysis: Technology, Development, and Planning*, Oxford University Press.

Shinohara, M. (1947) "The Multiplier and the Marginal Propensity to Import," *American Economic Review*, 147, 608–624.

Shishido, S., A. Kawakami and K. Tamashiro (2011) "Policy Alternatives for Japan Toward 2020," in Ichimura, S. and L. R. Klein (eds.) (2011) *Macro-econometric Modeling of Japan*, World Scientific.

Shishido, S. and O. Nakamura (1992a) "Induced Technical Progress and Structural Adjustment: A Multi-Sectoral Model Approach to Japan's Growth Alternatives," *Journal of Applied Input–Output Analysis*, 1(1), 1–23.

Shishido, S. and O. Nakamura (1992b) "Commercial Policy and Restructuring the International Economy," *The Journal of Asian Economics*, 17(3), 64–81.

Shishido, S., K. Hamada and Y. Matsumura (1991) "Technical Progress in an Input–Output Framework with Special Reference to Japan's High Technology Industries," in Peterson, W. (ed.), *Advances in Input-Output Analysis: Technology, Development, and Planning*, Oxford University Press.

Theil, H. (1965) "The Information Approach to Demand Analysis," *Econometrica*, 33, 67–87.

Ueda, K. (2011) "The Effectiveness of Non-traditional Monetary Policy Measures: The Case of the Bank of Japan," *Japanese Economic Review*, 63(1), 1–22.

Ugai, H. (2007) "Effects of Quantitative Easing Policy: Survey of Empirical Analysis," *Monetary and Economic Studies*, 25(1), 1–47.

Vogel, E. F. (1979) *Japan as Number One: Lessons for America*, Harvard University Press.

Index

A

Abenomics, 5, 113–114, 121, 145, 149, 152, 155, 159, 162, 169–171
Adams, F. G., v–vi
Akira Kawakami, xi
asset bubble, 2

B

backward linkage, 30, 108
Bank of Japan (BOJ), 4, 12, 113, 129, 171
Barten, A. P., 31
base money, 86
baseline projection, 108, 115–116, 131, 135, 169–170

C

capacity GDP, 79, 169
capacity output, 22
capital share, 81
capital stock, 12, 21–23, 77–80
Cobb–Douglas, 77
Cobb–Douglas function, 169
cointegrating relationships, 12
convergent criteria, 12
Cowles Commission, 12

D

database development, 4, 10
deep parameter, 167, 172
deflation, 2
deflationary gap, 81, 109, 169
DEMIOS, v–vii, xi, 3–4, 7, 10, 12, 22, 24–25, 29–30, 34, 67–68, 77, 80–81, 84–85, 89, 91, 93, 107, 109, 113–114, 121–122, 125, 130, 167, 169–172
DEMIS, 29
disposable income, 30, 69–70, 81, 83
dummy variable, 76–77, 86
dynamic econometric model, v

E

econometric model, 113–114, 172
econometric modeling and forecasting, 15
economic deflation, 109, 113, 116, 121, 171
economic dynamics, 3
economic dynamism, 2
Economic Planning Agency, 1
efficiency parameter, 27–29
endogenous, 7, 22
endogenous variables, 69, 74, 86, 108, 172
Engle, R. F., 12
ERINA (Economic Research Institute of North-East Asia), 3
exogenous variable, 7, 85–86
ex post historical simulation, 4

F

FDI, 88
final demand, 8, 15, 21, 26, 29–30, 33–35, 168
final test, 15
fiscal debts, 4

fiscal policy, 113–114, 125, 171
forward linkage, 30

G

Gauss–Seidel method, 12
GDP capacity, 77, 79
global economy, 4
Goldberger tests, 15
Granger, C. W. J., 12
growth alternatives, 113–114, 116, 130, 169, 171

H

Hamada, K., 121
Hayato Ikeda, 1
Honda, 114
hyperinflation, 1

I

Ichimura, Shinichi, vii, xi
Ikeda Cabinet, 1
income distribution, 8, 23, 68, 81, 84, 169
income distribution sub, 81
income doubling plan, 1, 114
income effect, 22, 69–70
input coefficient, 21, 29–30, 67, 168
input–output (I–O) model, 15, 77–78, 130, 167
input–output (I–O) tables, 10, 12, 15, 27, 30, 122
input–output system, v
interest rate parity, 76–77
intermediate demand, 21, 29
intermediate input, 21, 25
international university of Japan, 12
IT revolution, vi

J

Jorgenson, 23

K

Keynes multiplier, 109, 113, 169
Keynes–Leontief model (KLM), v, 3–4, 93, 113, 167
Keynesian macroeconometric model, v
Keynesian policy, 169
Keynesian-type macroeconometric model, 7
Kiyoshi Tamashiro, xi
Klein's econometric series, xi
Klein, L. R., v–vi, 1, 3, 172
KLM-type model, 67
Kumasaka, Y., vi

L

labor share, 81
Lam, W. R., 114
Leontief cross, 122
Leontief economics, 30
Leontief input–output (I–O), 21
Leontief's input–output (I–O) system, v
Leontief-type input–output (I–O) model, 7, 167

M

macro model, 4
macroeconometric models, 170
macroeconomic model, 5, 24
Mandell–Fleming Model, 34
measurement error, 12
modeling and forecasting, 12
Motohiro Kurokawa, xi
multi-sectoral econometric model, 7
multiplier, 4
multiplier effects, 170–171
Mundell–Fleming model, 22

N

Nakamura Osamu, vi, 29, 77, 89, 93, 114
National Accounts Statistics (SNA), 3, 10
NIRA-LINK Project, 7
Niwa, 77

O

Oda, N., 114
omitted variables, 12

P

partial test, 15
Plaza Accord, 2, 76, 77
policy scenarios, 129, 130
policy simulation, 4, 169
policy variable(s), 35, 86
price effect, 22, 30, 70
principle of three equivalence of national income, 81
Project LINK, 7, 172
public finance, 8
purchasing parity, 77
purchasing power parity, 76–77

Q

QE policy, 114
quantity-easing, 121

R

RAS, 12, 27
Reaganomics, 121
recursive-type method, 12
Rotterdam School Model, 31–32, 168
R&D, 1

S

Saburo Okita, 1
Sato, 77
scenario projections, 12, 108–109, 114–116, 121, 129, 169–170
scenario simulations, 85, 91, 107–108, 114–115, 167, 170–171
Shinohara, M., 109
Shinozaki, A., vi
Shishido, S., 1, v–vi, 3, 29, 77, 93
SIMNEW, 7
simultaneity, 12
simultaneously determined structural equation models, 12
social infrastructures, 107, 113
spurious estimators, 12
stagflation, 1
Stone, R., 27
structural changes, 1, 3
structural multi-equation models, 172
substitution parameter, 27–29, 168
superconsistency, 12
supply side, 1
supply-side variables, 7

T

Tachibana, M., 114
technical progress, 1, 67
technological progress, 1
Theil, H., 31
total factor productivity (TFP), 21, 29
total test, 15
trade imbalance, 1
transaction and pre-cautionary motives, 86

U

Ueda, K., 114
Ugai, H., 114
unit root tests, 12
university of Tsukuba, 12

V

Vogel, E. F., 1
VRAS algorism, 5, 27–29, 167, 168, 171

W

world financial crisis, 2
world scientific, xi

www.ingramcontent.com/pod-product-compliance
Ingram Content Group UK Ltd.
Pitfield, Milton Keynes, MK11 3LW, UK
UKHW022103170926
8624IPUK00024B/37

9 789813 278219